Books are to be returned on or before
the last date below.

LIBREX–

Street Gangs, Migration and Ethnicity

Edited by

Frank van Gemert, Dana Peterson and Inger-Lise Lien

WILLAN
PUBLISHING

Published by

Willan Publishing
Culmcott House
Mill Street, Uffculme
Cullompton, Devon
EX15 3AT, UK
Tel: +44(0)1884 840337
Fax: +44(0)1884 840251
e-mail: info@willanpublishing.co.uk
website: www.willanpublishing.co.uk

Published simultaneously in the USA and Canada by

Willan Publishing
c/o ISBS, 920 NE 58th Ave, Suite 300,
Portland, Oregon 97213-3786, USA
Tel: +001(0)503 287 3093
Fax: +001(0)503 280 8832
e-mail: info@isbs.com
website: www.isbs.com

First published 2008

ISBN   978-1-84392-396-1 paperback
         978-1-84392-397-8 hardback

British Library Cataloguing-in-Publication Data

A catalogue record for this book is available from the British Library

Project managed by Deer Park Productions, Tavistock, Devon
Typeset by GCS, Leighton Buzzard, Bedfordshire
Printed and bound by T.J. International, Padstow, Cornwall

Contents

Acknowledgements

A number of thanks are due, not just to the contributors for sharing their research and for their timeliness and patience, but also to others who furthered this project. We are appreciative to Juanjo Medina who organized the May 2005 Eurogang meeting at which many of these papers were first presented and to the Eurogang network of researchers who remain committed to our goal of cross-national comparative research. Thanks are due as well to Scott Decker and Frank Weerman, who graciously donated a portion of the proceeds from the second Eurogang book for this manuscript's preparation. We thank our two anonymous peer reviewers for their time, expertise, and insight which have certainly improved this work. The editors wish to express much appreciation to University at Albany doctoral students Nicole Schmidt, who read and edited most of the chapters, and Vanessa Panfil, for historical research; and to Wasja Rijs from VU university in Amsterdam, for bibliographic editing of all of the chapters. We also appreciate all the support we received from Brian Willan and his excellent staff and affiliates at Willan Publishing. Finally, we wish to thank all of those who take a chance to discuss and research sensitive issues such as gangs, migration, and ethnicity; we hope our work adds positively to the discussion.

Foreword

Malcolm W. Klein

This third book emanating from the Eurogang Programme presents a significant line of progress over the first two (Decker and Weerman 2005; Klein *et al.* 2001). It moves the programme from its initial phase of technical development over some seven years to an expanded concern for the contextual underpinnings of comparative, international street gang research. My excitement over the publishing of this new volume stems only partially from my proprietary interest as a founder of the programme. It also reflects my appreciation for a number of insights offered by the various authors in the volume. My comments will, rather briefly, cover three topics: programme rationale, programme history, and the nexus between street gangs and marginal populations as highlighted in some of the ensuing chapters.

Programme rationale

Most street gang research has been carried out in the USA over a period of about 80 years. Although there has been a publication crescendo, what progress has been achieved in understanding gangs has been more by post hoc synthesis than by planning. American gang studies have been largely uncoordinated exercises in different locations, using different research methods, and driven by different perspectives among researchers and their funders. Our first hope for the Eurogang Programme was therefore that it could develop coordination of methods and perspectives across sites.

A second problem with the American experience has been the well-documented failure to settle upon a common definition, or at least common components of a definition, that would permit replicable data collection. If there is such a thing as a street gang, we should be able to define it both conceptually and operationally. Our second hope for the Eurogang Programme, then, was a resolution of the definitional problem.

A third problem in the USA has been that most street gang programmes and policies have been unrelated to available data, especially as truly relevant, policy-related data have become readily available over the past 50 or so years (see the recent data and programme summaries in Klein and Maxson 2006). Our third hope for the Eurogang Programme – not yet realised at all – has been that data-based gang policy can indeed be developed.

The European setting with its rapidly emerging gang problems has been, for the American participants in the programme, a way to start over, to get in before the door is again closed. For the European participants, it has been a way for mostly unconnected gang researchers to come together across national lines to share a set of relatively new experiences – a search for synergy.

History

The Eurogang Programme started at an informal gathering in Leuven, Belgium, in 1997, where a few American and European researchers traded notes on what seemed to be an accelerated emergence of street gangs in Europe. The impressions were mostly anecdotal but consistent. Further discussions led to a series of increasingly focused workshops in Belgium, The Netherlands, Norway, and Germany, in which gang research papers were delivered and discussed. At the same time, a working group was established to obtain agreement upon both conceptual and operational approaches to defining street gangs. Five additional working groups undertook the task of developing, pretesting, revising and settling upon five research instruments that could be used (with translations) across many nations to yield common and comparable data on street gangs. By 2005, seven workshops had led to the culmination of these processes, as well as the identification of 50 gang-involved cities in Europe and over 100 American and European researchers interested in participating in what became known as the Eurogang Programme. This period between 1997 and 2005 constituted the first phase of that programme.

The second phase, concentrating on the conceptual contexts of street gangs, evolved in two further workshops, one in the USA and one in Spain. By then, over 60 gang-involved cities had been recognised (the number continues to grow, still) and over 200 participants signed on. This second phase is represented by many of the chapters in this book, and some expansion beyond Europe is also evident. Phase three is yet to evolve but the ultimate goal will see the implementation of a series of prospective, multi-method, cross-national, comparative studies of street gangs *as defined in the Eurogang Programme and using the five Eurogang research instruments*. I cannot overstate my belief that reaching that third phase is of paramount importance. This current volume is a critical step in that direction, as it helps us focus on both specific and general patterns of street gang phenomena, especially those formed by patterns of migration and ethnicity.

Street gangs and marginal populations

The phase two chapters in this volume portray a more complex picture than the rather stable relationships generally described in the USA between street gangs and minority status (i.e. primarily blacks and Hispanics). Europe provides us with more varied categories of marginalised populations. Some are racial, some ethnic, and some national. Some gang-producing populations are immigrants and some are refugees. Their growth has paralleled the emergence and increased recognition of street gang problems. And unlike the minor differences to be found between the 50 states of the USA, major differences exist among the many nations of Europe in their policies toward crime generally and gangs in particular.

In what follows, I have selected a few instances in which this volume's authors have piqued my particular interest. These are not necessarily the 'best' chapters, or the most important ones (although I note that all of them have been independently peer-reviewed twice). They are merely the ones that caused me special thought; I claim the foreword writer's privilege.

The chapter by Decker and van Gemert (Chapter 2), especially for non-European readers, provides a very instructive primer on migration patterns. It sets the conceptual context for much of the volume. Lien's exposition on the cultural context of immigrant gangs brings the Decker and van Gemert piece into nice focus in a particular setting.

The Aldridge *et al.* chapter (Chapter 3) appeals to me in particular because of its concern for moral panics and denials as continuing problems for gang research. The issue was highlighted in the very first volume to be produced by the Eurogang Programme (Klein *et al.* 2001) reflecting discussions in the first workshop.

I have a similarly personal interest in Björk's description (Chapter 15) of the situation he observed in Gothenburg, in which he plays out the tie between ethnicity and group process. In much of my own research in the USA, I have relied heavily on the explication of group processes in the gang arena. My view has been that group process trumps ethnicity. Björk's treatment is one of the very few to treat the combination of group process and ethnicity.

White's chapter (Chapter 9), although not from the European area, is useful to me because of its emphasis on the functions of violence in the gang world. The rhetoric (if not the amount) of violence is one of the significant unifying factors in gang cohesiveness, yet analysis of violence among European gangs suggests it is less prevalent than in the USA, and less evident in the form of intergang rivalries. This is an area of research that demands more of our attention, especially as it relates to differences in ethnicity and national origin.

Finally, I am intrigued by the Debarbieux and Blaya chapter's (Chapter 12) depiction of how French teachers manoeuvre around state restrictions on identifying the ethnic status of students. Research on our ethnically related gang issues has to be sensitive to such issues, both to build knowledge and to make programmes sensitive to cultural differences. The Fiori-Khayat chapter (Chapter 10), also from France, emphasises the point by noting that a researcher there who records ethnicity is committing a felony and could end up in jail!

The phase three comparative research that is my eventual goal could be seriously damaged if, in the search for cross-national patterns, it did not simultaneously account for the subtleties of differences accompanying race, ethnicity, and national origin. It must in addition be sensitive to differences in migration patterns over both space and time. It is a large order, but perhaps the foreword to the phase three book could comment on how well this is all articulated. Certainly, this current volume edited by van Gemert, Peterson, and Lien sets the stage well.

References

Decker, S.H. and Weerman, F.M. (eds) (2005) *European Street Gangs and Troublesome Youth Groups.* New York: AltaMira Press.

Klein, M.W., Kerner, H.-J., Maxson, C.M. and Weitekamp, E.G.M. (eds) (2001) *The Eurogang Paradox: Street Gangs and Youth Groups in the U.S. and Europe.* Dordrecht: Kluwer Academic Press.

Klein, M.W. and Maxson, C.M. (2006) *Street Gang Patterns and Policies.* Oxford: Oxford University Press.

About the editors

Frank van Gemert is Assistant Professor at VU University in Amsterdam. He studied cultural anthropology and conducted research in various fields, such as street level drug dealers, illegal gambling, and juvenile delinquency. His current research is on street gangs, especially on the element of conflict. Furthermore, he is involved in the emergence of cultural criminology in the Netherlands. He is part of the Eurogang Steering Committee and member of the Eurogang Ethnography Working Group. Among his publications is one chapter in *The Eurogang Paradox* (M.W. Klein, H.-J. Kerner, C.L. Maxson and E.G.M. Weitekamp, eds) and two chapters in *European Street Gangs and Troublesome Youth Groups: Findings from the Eurogang Research Program* (S.H. Decker and F. Weerman, eds). Forthcoming is an article in the *Journal of International Migration and Integration* (with S.H. Decker).

Dana Peterson is an Assistant Professor in the School of Criminal Justice at the University at Albany (New York) who teaches and conducts research in the areas of youth violence, youth gangs and gang prevention, delinquency treatment, and sex/gender issues in delinquency and gang involvement. She currently is an Investigator on the 'Process and Outcome Evaluation of G.R.E.A.T.', a multi-site longitudinal evaluation of a school-based gang prevention program recently funded by the National Institute of Justice and directed by Professor Finn Esbensen of the University of Missouri – St. Louis. She is active in the Eurogang Program and is a member of its Youth/ Community Survey and Prevention/Intervention workgroups. Her co-authored articles about gangs and gang prevention have been published in such journals as *Criminology, Criminology and Public Policy, Evaluation Review, Journal of Interpersonal Violence,* and *Justice Quarterly,* and co-authored chapters appear in *The Eurogang Paradox* (M.W. Klein, H.-J. Kerner, C.L. Maxson and E.G.M. Weitekamp, eds); *Gangs in America* (3rd ed.) (C.R. Huff, ed.); *Responding to Gangs: Evaluation and research* (W.L. Reed and S.H. Decker, eds); and *American Youth Gangs at the Millennium* (F-A. Esbensen, L.K. Gaines, and S.G. Tibbetts, eds.).

Inger-Lise Lien is a senior researcher at the Norwegian Center for Studies on Violence and Traumatic Stress (NKVTS). She is currently working on a project comparing criminal careers of inmates with different ethnic backgrounds in Norwegian prisons. She is a member of the Eurogang Program, and was previously a member of the steering committee. She has administered the 'Gangs in four cities' project financed by the Norwegian Council of Research and written both nationally and internationally on migration from Pakistan, integration, ethnicity and gender, the honour code and immigrant gangs in Norway. Recent publications include two chapters in *European Street Gangs and Troublesome Youth Groups: Findings from the Eurogang Research Program* (S.H. Decker and F. Weerman, eds); a chapter on honour in *Tournaments of Power – Honour and revenge in the contemporary world* (T. Aase, eds); a chapter on gangs in Oslo in *The Eurogang Paradox* (M.W. Klein, H.-J. Kerner, C.L. Maxson and E.G.M. Weitekamp, eds). She wrote her Ph.D. on Islam and the caste system in Pakistan: *Morality and emotion in Pakistani Punjab.* She is a member of the UNESCO liaison committee within the Most Programme.

Part I

Introduction and methods

Chapter 1

Introduction

Frank van Gemert, Inger-Lise Lien and Dana Peterson

It is not because the boys of the middle and wealthier classes are native white that they do not form gangs but because their lives are organized and stabilized for them by American traditions, customs, and institutions to which the children of immigrants do not have adequate access. The gang, on the other hand, is simply one symptom of a type of disorganization that goes along with the breaking up of the immigrant's traditional social system without adequate assimilation to the new. [...] The extensive demoralization which exists in the Polish-American community is a good example of the cultural frontier which provides fertile soil for the development of the gang. Intense pride of nationality, which has sometimes been described and explained as an 'oppression psychosis', has often led the Poles in America to concentrate their energies on the development of Polish spirit and patriotism at the sacrifice of adjustment to American society. There is a high degree of disorganization in Chicago among the poor Polish populations. (Thrasher 1927: 217–18)

Afternoon, school has ended. At that moment the boys from Rosenborg School go into the schoolyard at Singsaker School. They hang around here every evening, dressed as if they are gang members of the Crips in the USA. 'I got the idea from the gang in the USA. We have been Crips in Trondheim for almost two years now. We are around 20 boys,' says Odin Knutsen, or

'Smoke', as all have their own nicknames. The boys are 12–16 years of age, and most of them attend Rosenborg School. They have no leader, no specific requirements for membership. They are just friends that meet every day, to 'chill out', to take it cool, to talk shit and to play basketball, says Niklas 'Top Dog' Helgesen. Rap and friendship. Trondheim does not have gangs like Oslo, but Crips exist everywhere in the world. They are inspired by the famous Crips gang in Los Angeles. But the boys at Singsaker are not famous, 'No, we don't do anything wrong. We have just copied the blue scarfs and the signs of the Crips because we like the same music, Tupac and Ice Cube,' the boys assure us. Everybody writes rap texts, and most of them are with a band. They skate and play basketball. They do not mind that their role models are hard-core criminals. 'They are just cowards that use violence,' says Jo Erlend Hillestad, or 'T Gun'. He is in the Crips for friendship. 'It is good to know that whatever happens, the boys in the Crips are there for me. I find them here in the schoolyard every afternoon,' says Jo Erlend. (www.adressa.no/nyheter/trondheim/article351522.ece) [translation by the editors]

These are two accounts of gangs from 1927 and 2004, almost 80 years apart, stemming from Chicago and from Trondheim in Norway. Apart from time and place, there are obvious differences between the two. The Chicago gangs from the first citation are comprised of second-generation Polish youth marginalised in and maladapted to American mainstream culture, while the Crips in Trondheim have adopted stereotypical traits from American West Coast gangs. They are interested in basketball and rap music, and use nicknames as if they were African-American homies from Compton, Los Angeles, but probably they have blond hair and blue eyes. Still, these Polish and Norwegian accounts also have resemblances, as both portray groups that are referred to as gangs. Furthermore, in both cases there is an international component of their group identity. The Polish gangs developed an ethnic identity; the Scandinavians, on the other hand, are inspired by the global youth culture. These resemblances, thin as they may seem, touch upon the central elements of this book that explores the relation between street gangs, migration and ethnicity. These two examples can be seen as extremes on both sides of a continuum that is the scope of this book.

Street gangs

One is inclined to agree with Thrasher that the Polish youth could form gangs. These Norwegians, by contrast, even though they use all kinds of gang symbols, would not be considered a gang by most scholars. Since gangs are generally associated with crime, the first reason to refuse the gang label is the fact that the Scandinavian Crips do not seem to engage in criminal activities. Refusing the gang label is also related to context. The fact that most American cities have gangs is common knowledge now, as Klein and Maxson (2006) have shown. In Europe, however, the existence of gangs is a vexed matter. In discussions, the word 'gang' easily triggers the remark: 'That's America, we don't have that.' Yet, because of the popularity of gang elements in youth culture, confusion is near at hand.

In the literature, the word has been used to refer to various kinds of groups, including cliques of corner boys, transnational organisations, urban tribes, or even formal youth associations. However, when it comes to gangs, the authors of the chapters in this volume all share the notion of street gangs as physical groups of young people with illegal activities found in public space. In this sense, this book is quite strict, and to determine whether a group is a street gang, the Eurogang definition is applied:

> a street gang (or problematic youth group) is any durable, street-oriented youth group whose involvement in illegal activity is part of their group identity.[1]

Migration

Since the early twentieth century, sociologists and criminologists have pointed to the culture conflict, social disorganisation, and strain that immigrants experience when they fail to live up to the American Dream as root causes of crime and deviance. It has become a general finding in criminology that second-generation immigrants are often more involved in criminal behaviour than both the actual migrants of the first generation, and the third generation. These concepts, in different ways, have also linked migration to the emergence of gangs, albeit often implicitly. The socio-economic position of newcomers, social control within their communities, and loosening of their family ties – all of these phenomena offer interesting avenues for studying the formation of gangs in immigrant populations.

In more recent years, a new specific variety of the gang–migration link has been documented in the USA and in Central America. Gang members who had been incarcerated in American prisons were repatriated to their native soil. Thus, MS-13 gang members were sent to El Salvador and Honduras, aggravating the national problems with gangs and violence. Conversely, in Central American countries, street youth nowadays are being socialised into gang life well before a number of them migrate to the USA (Bibler Coutin 2007; McGuire 2007).

However, in the emergence of Crips in Norway, other elements come into play. No gang members have moved from Los Angeles to this Arctic part of Europe. Here, not newcomers, but new media play a decisive role. Television, films, rap music, and the Internet probably all need to be included in the explanation, because, nowadays, in Norway just as elsewhere, global youth culture influences the lifestyle of youngsters.

In the chapters to follow, migration is a crucial factor. All authors address gang formation or gang behaviour in relation to the presence of immigrant groups. A central framing question is, *in what ways does migration contribute to gang formation?* This means that the focus is on people who are on the move, but not only that. The 'migration' of gang symbols and 'gangsta' lifestyle as a part of global youth culture is also a recurring theme. Even though the above MS-13 gang example points to the migration of individual gang members, in Europe, there is little or no evidence for the existence of this variety. So far, this also seems to apply to the Latin gangs in Spain and Italy that have been portrayed as transnational organisations (Brotherton 2007; see Feixa *et al.* (Chapter 5) in this volume). Indeed, Howell (2007) calls the idea that local gangs came from elsewhere to set up an organisation in a new location one of the key myths about gangs. This variety is not central to this book.

Ethnicity

In his famous book on ethnicity, Barth (1969) defines ethnic groups on the basis of their boundaries and not so much on cultural content. An ethnic group can be maintained by a limited set of cultural features, but these can change through time. Ethnicity pinpoints an origin or background with which the person can identify. This identity is imperative, implying that it may be as important to the individual as gender, as it establishes belonging in an abstract way. But this identity can also be played out. It is communicated, over-communicated or under-communicated, depending on the situation. It can be forgotten and taken for granted, or it can be visible and made relevant for certain groups and be ascribed by others.

In many cities, the gang issue has become an ethnic phenomenon, as ethnic criteria often are used to designate the group. Groups have often been given or have taken names that identify them with a foreign background. The Moroccan gangs in Amsterdam, Mexican gangs in Los Angeles, Pakistani gangs in Oslo and Latin gangs in Barcelona that will be portrayed in this book, are all identified by their ethnic characteristics. Gang members may use ethnicity as a relevant criterion to separate themselves from others in order to establish enemies and allies. So, ethnicity can work to see either how gangs are perceived or how the gang members see themselves and others.

Concerning ethnicity, two framing questions of this book are, *how does ethnicity relate to gang characteristics and gang behaviour?* and *is ethnicity relevant for understanding gangs?* Questions such as these may lead to research going in different directions. First, there can be a focus on identity. Gangs have membership and as a rule they are involved in conflicts. Because of this, belonging to a certain gang defines who are friends and who are enemies. Second, cultural elements can come into play. Cultural content is not central to the ethnicity concept used by Barth, and some gang scholars argue that group processes have a more or less uniform outcome no matter what ethnicity is involved. Still, diversity is hard to understand without paying attention to cultural differences. For example, the relevance of a code of honour has been reported in earlier research on Mexicans, but this code also seems to be a key element for understanding how Pakistani gangs in Norway operate (see Chapter 14). Third, on a national level, ethnicity can be dealt with in specific ways. In France, the law prohibits any distinction between 'French persons of French origins' and 'French persons of foreign origins'. Creating ethnically based files is a felony. In The Netherlands, quite differently, in popular and political, as well as scientific, discussions, there is some emphasis on ethnic background of offenders, not least gang members.

Stigma

Gangs draw attention. Police have a natural interest in gangs because of their criminal activities. Adolescent gang members often use colours, signs, language, tattoos, etc., to stress their identity, and because of these symbols, gangs are often easily noticed. Their orientation to the public space of the streets makes gangs visible in most neighbourhoods. So gangs stand out, and that contributes to the fact that they often get blamed for things that happen in their vicinity.

Global changes result in massive migration movements. Migrants may be political dissidents or war refugees, or they may leave poor regions in Africa, Asia, or Central America for economic reasons and seek new opportunities, mostly in the West. Because exotic appearance and new cultural aspects catch the eye, the involvement of migrants adds to the fact that gangs stand out. This may take the social reaction to gangs one step further and lead to gangs becoming scapegoats.

The relation between gangs, migration and ethnicity is a subject fraught with controversy, because it deals with newcomers and delinquency. Inevitably, this touches upon stigmatisation or even discrimination. When popular media report on gangs, as a rule crime and violence are underscored. In addition, if gang members turn out to be migrant youth, this fuels negative sentiments and feelings of unsafeness by the settled population. Newcomers can meet with xenophobia or even aggression. Several if not all European nations have extremist groups, mostly known as neo-Nazis or skinheads. These groups may or may not be linked to political organisations. In some countries juvenile gangs exist that merely use extremist symbols to add to their identity, while in other places youth groups seem to have become part of extremist right-wing political parties.

In the blender of public debate, gangs, crime, violence, and migrants have become intertwined. Policymakers in most European countries are aware of this, and in official accounts the word 'gang' is avoided, or used only with reluctance. By the same token, European scholars are hesitant to use the gang label. Research can be used for political ends, and research on gangs especially runs the risk of leading to repression of marginalised youth or to blaming the victim. Because of this, the aim of this book to explore the relation between street gangs, migration, and ethnicity is controversial and difficult.

The chapters of this book come from various continents, mostly

Europe (Germany, England, France, Russia, Spain, The Netherlands, Norway and Sweden), but also North America (United States and Canada) and Australia. Each country has a specific socio-political context in which gangs have emerged and were studied. All of the authors are aware of the burden of this book, and some make an explicit statement. They have not formulated any political suggestions to stop, continue, or increase migration to the different countries even though the connection between gang formation and migration is clearly demonstrated. The ambition is rather to provide evidence of what is going on and give insights into the real dilemmas with which nations are faced when it comes to gang problems. The authors have decided to present their research that is based on empirical data. They do so in order to understand the gang phenomenon. The results may carry some alarming facts, but they also work to refute opportunistic popular interpretations based on stereotypes. Practitioners and politicians can find scientific bases for their decision making.

Part I: Introduction and methods

Gang literature offers many examples of the relation between gangs and migration. Especially American sociological publications from the first half of the twentieth century provide these, but also gang literature from the last decades bears these accounts. European literature on gangs is relatively sparse, as the gang phenomenon seems to have surfaced or been recognised only recently. The fact that large-scale migration to the USA is from an earlier date than migration to Europe is related to historical facts of politics and economy on a national and international level. Van Gemert and Decker examine these differences in Chapter 2, which gives an overview of existing American literature and contrasts it with recent European research findings.

Gangs should be researched, according to Aldridge, Medina and Ralphs, but they note academic and political resistance to the 'gang' label in Britain. They mention the different sociological traditions for the study of youth formations in Europe and empathise with the concerns raised by those who point to the risk of stigmatisation of gang research. In Chapter 3, they discuss the ethical problems and practical obstacles they encountered while doing research in an English city. They describe their strategy for anonymising research locations.

Part II: Migration and youth gangs

Repeatedly, the literature has shown that upon migration, it is the second generation that becomes involved in delinquency and gang activities. Nowadays, American scholars speak about the 'new second generation' when they point to the constant stream of migrants and their recurrent socialisation in gangs. Perhaps best documented is the case of the Mexicans who gravitate to Los Angeles. In Chapter 4, Vigil draws upon his own extensive research when he examines why gangs became a problem in this process of adaptation. Central questions in this assessment are how and why changes materialise in one time period and not others, and where and when these changes emerge.

A murder case in 2003 brought the phenomenon of Latin street gangs to the Spanish media and started a moral panic. Feixa, Canelles, Porzio, Recio and Giliberti present the first results of research about Latin American young people in Barcelona (in Chapter 5) and look at what is going on behind the commotion in the forefront. They point to the ignored presence of thousands of boys and girls of Latin American origin who have arrived in Barcelona since the late 1990s. The authors confront the idea of traditional gangs with new forms of youth sociability that cross geographical and time borders to reconstruct global identities.

In Chapter 6, Thrasher's concept of gangs as groups in conflict is applied to youth groups in The Netherlands. Van Gemert and Stuifbergen present a typology based on various reports, as well as ethnographic material, and discuss its distribution. They describe Lonsdale groups of white Dutch with sympathy for the extreme Right that seek confrontation with groups of migrant youth. Basically, this is a conflict between the settled and newcomers. A second 'conflict within the hood' is about corner groups that get into conflicts with residents, shopkeepers, and the police, resist their authority, and claim the street. Here, the authors point to over-representation of second-generation Moroccan boys.

A Russian contribution comes from Shashkin. He examines (in Chapter 7) the emergence of racist skinhead gangs in the 1980s and early 1990s in Moscow that became the focus of public fears, media attention, and policy concerns. By using interviews with experts and practitioners, the author examines what structural, cultural, and political conditions influenced the choice of young people to become racist and involved in racist gangs.

Part III: Ethnicity and youth gangs

At a given time and place, specific ethnic groups are found to participate more in gangs than others. This fact may relate to a minority status or represent the opportunity structure for that ethnic group. Youth may also indulge in gang behaviour, including violence, because they feel it fits their identity. In short, there is a complex relation between gang activity and ethnicity, and in this section contributions show various forms of this relation.

Chapter 8 presents quantitative research by Esbensen, Brick, Melde, Tusinski and Taylor on an American school-based sample. This research employs the Eurogang definition and measurement of youth gangs. The goal was to examine the distribution of gang membership, its prevalence and its demographic characteristics. Specifically, the authors present the epidemiology of individual offending by gang membership and race or ethnicity, and describe gang characteristics by the race or ethnicity of gang members.

The dynamics and complexities of ethnicity in relation to youth gangs are explored in Chapter 9 by White. The author argues that in Sydney, Australia, ethnicity is the linchpin upon which social relationships are forged and social identity bestowed. He describes how young people get caught up in events and processes that transform visible social difference into social deviance in the public eye. By quoting lively interviews, White demonstrates how group membership is socially constructed. This affects the nature of group violence, and how gang fighting varies depending upon ethnic background and social circumstances.

Partly because of its recent history of rioting gangs, France is an interesting locale for gang research. Fiori-Khayat has interviewed street youth, and in Chapter 10 she emphasises the role of ethnicity in explaining the existence, but also the apparent stability of juvenile street gangs. Gang members may use ethnicity to construct an identity and to justify offences. Street gangs are seldom politicised, but ethnicity is used by juvenile gang members as a justification for their reactions to discrimination. This is especially relevant in regard to riots and the destruction of goods, but also as a way of keeping distance from gangs of other minorities.

Kerner, Reich, Coester and Weitekamp present a quantitative study in Germany in Chapter 11. The authors use data from a small but multiethnic sample of relatively high-risk youths, collected in a youth survey that included the core criteria of the Eurogang school survey. They focus on involvement in troublesome youth groups in a selected quarter of Stuttgart. These data allow for aptly dividing the total sample into three subgroups based upon migration status, showing different levels of engagement in socially problematic activities. Relationships to several issues, including socio-demographic and socio-economic factors, gang affiliation, family attachment, and school commitment, are analysed. The general criminological finding that second-generation immigrants often are involved in criminal behaviour is upheld in these findings.

Why do young people become involved in gangs? This is the key question in Chapter 12 by Wortley and Tanner. Age, gender, poverty, ethnicity, family background, and educational performance are strong predictors of gang membership. But why are some racial or ethnic groups more involved in gang activity than others? The 2005 Toronto Youth Gang Pilot Project directly asked known criminal gang members about their first involvement in a gang and their reasons for staying with the gang lifestyle. The results show numerous utilitarian justifications, but in addition many ethnic minority youth link their involvement in gangs to social alienation and exclusion. These youth construct their own gang involvement as an act of pride and defiance brought on by discrimination, social injustice, and inequality. The authors discuss the theoretical and policy implications of these results.

Part IV: Issues and challenges of migration and ethnicity in dealing with youth gangs

In the last part of the book, we turn to questions about how to deal with gangs, be it prevention or repression. The similarity between the two last chapters may be a coincidence. They both stem from Scandinavia, and both discuss cultural phenomena of immigrant groups with a Muslim background. While the Swedish and Norwegian authors focus on police work, the second French contribution of this book turns to a different institution.

Chapter 13 by Debarbieux and Blaya, focuses on the school system and its relation to the emergence of gangs. In France, it is widely believed that small 'cores' that hold power in certain neighbourhoods and schools organise extortion and violence in liaison with people outside the schools. The authors challenge this representation, both in quantitative terms and in terms of its social construction, by looking in particular at the role of schools in this construction process. Rather than gangs as external factors that have an impact on schools, the schools themselves spawn this kind of group through an 'anti-school', identity-building process.

In Chapter 14, the success of the Nemesis programme of the Norwegian police is described by Lien. She demonstrates the importance of the gendered honour code in the Pakistani community in Oslo and in the gangs. The honour code may externalise the law, leading to the state losing control and gangs filling the vacuum thereby created. Because of this code, 'following the money' tactics by the police were effective. This breaks down the moral spheres separating the sexes within the community. In exposing the shame of women and men publicly, it also breaks down the wall between the Pakistani community and the mainstream society.

Björk writes on the tactics and strategy in policing of criminal gangs in Gothenburg, Sweden (Chapter 15). The main problem for the police is not criminality per se, but the unwillingness of the population to testify and report crime, as many inhabitants (i.e. non-gang members) are engaged in black-market activities. He argues that criminal gang activities take place in a Muslim-migration context, where avoiding interaction with the police is a wise practice. This fits culturally marked religious representations of free men that obstruct common law and avoid taxations. Silence then becomes a matter of group solidarity, making gang prevention and policing extremely complex.

In the final chapter (Chapter 16), the editors reflect on the previous contributions, and once again address the framing questions for the different sections.

This book is the outcome of a process that started in May 2005. At that date, an international Eurogang meeting, organised by Juanjo Medina, was hosted in Spain by the University of Oñati. This seventh Eurogang meeting had the title: 'The Social Contexts of Gangs and Troublesome Youth Groups in Multi-ethnic Europe'. The preceding meetings had mostly reflected the Eurogang goal to establish international comparative research on gangs, and focused on general issues such as definitions and instruments. The Spanish meeting was the first to have a thematic approach. The papers that were presented showed a wide variety, coming from a number of nations, inside and outside Europe. At the end of this meeting, we, the editors, agreed to gather the existing papers and look for supplements to produce a volume on street gangs, migration, and ethnicity.

Note

1 'Durability' means several months or more and refers to the group, which continues despite turnover of members.

'Street-oriented' means spending a lot of group time outside home, work, and school, and often on the streets, in malls, parks, cars, and so on.

'Youth' refers to average ages in adolescence or early twenties or so.

'Illegal activity' generally means delinquent or criminal behaviour, not just bothersome activity.

'Identity' refers to the group, not individual self-image.

References

Barth, F. (1969) *Ethnic Groups and Boundaries: The Social Organization of Culture Difference.* Long Grove, IL: Waveland Press.

Bibler Coutin, S. (2007) *Nations of Emigrants: Shifting Boundaries of Citizenship in El Salvador and the United States.* Ithaca, NY: Cornell University Press.

Howell, J.C. (2007) 'Menacing or mimicking?: realities of youth gangs', *Juvenile and Family Court Journal*, 58(2): 39–50.

Klein, M.W. and Maxson, C.L. (2006) *Street Gang Patterns and Policies.* New York: Oxford University Press.

McGuire, C.M. (2007) *Working Paper on Central American Youth Gangs in the Washington, D.C. Area.* [online] Washington Office on Latin America (WOLA). Available from: http://www.wola.org/index.php?option=com_content&task=viewp&id=272&Itemid=2 [accessed 5 February 2008].

Thrasher, F.M. (1927) *The Gang: A Study of 1,313 Gangs in Chicago.* Chicago: University of Chicago Press.

Chapter 2

Migrant groups and gang activity: a contrast between Europe and the USA

Frank van Gemert and Scott Decker

Introduction

Immigrant groups and ethnic identification have been crucial in understanding the formation and proliferation of gangs from the earliest studies (Thrasher 1927) to the present (Martinez and Lee 2000). The earlier studies underscored the role of European immigrants in the formation and expansion of gangs in Chicago. Just as in the USA, migration to and within Europe is of importance for the emergence of gangs. Obviously, there are similarities, but the context of the two continents is different. These differences reflect divergent political, economic, and migratory patterns. Because of the political and economic transformations, migration patterns to and within the USA evolved earlier than those in Europe. Consequently, the gang phenomenon in the USA is older, while in most European countries gang formation – or at least that owing to immigration – seems to be relatively new.

A consistent finding from studies of immigration has been that gangs often form among new immigrant groups. Martinez and Lee observe that 'much of the recent work on migration and crime has focused on gangs' (2000: 499). This finding extends as far back as the early twentieth century (Puffer 1912; Thomas and Znaniecki 1920; Thrasher 1927). Curry and Decker (2002) identified four periods of gang growth in America, the 1890s, 1920s, 1960s, and 1990s. In each of these periods, the growth in gangs was fuelled in part by an increased presence of immigrants. Covey's (2003) analysis also supports this conclusion, noting that the movement of immigrant groups to the USA led to the growth in gangs in the early part of the twentieth century as well as at the end of the twentieth century. Weerman and Decker (2005) argue that a similar process of migration and its impact on gang formation has occurred in Western European countries over the past two decades.

But, what is the relation between gangs and migration? When it comes to the American situation, a wide range of publications shed light on these matters (see review articles by Bankston 1998; Coughlin and Venkatesh 2003; Spergel 1990). In Europe, however, gang research does not have a long tradition, and not as much literature exists[1]. It certainly did not result in clear cut conclusions on the relation between gangs and migration.

This chapter examines the relation between migration and the formation of gangs in Europe. We use the USA as a starting point when we discuss migration patterns and explore the relation between gangs and migration. We focus on the central themes of ethnicity, marginalisation, and neighbourhoods that derive from literature and offer explanations. Next, we draw upon European research to give more detailed descriptions. Finally, we point to characteristics of the relation between migration and gangs in Europe.

It is important to note that there is a difference between migration *within* countries and the immigration of new residents *to* countries. Migration within countries (e.g. African-Americans from the South to the North and to the West) is a very different process from the immigration of outsiders. In the first case, within-migrants share culture and country with the individuals with whom they will live in close proximity. In the second case, the new arrivals bring less of the comfortable cultural or institutional baggage; they are outsiders. And these new residents are outsiders in a variety of important ways; significantly, in language, cultural, religion, ethnicity, and associational patterns.

Migration patterns

Migration may play a central role in the emergence of gangs, but the nature of that role is by no means a simple one. It is hard to talk about migration as a definitive term, because it is a variable in itself. Migration concerns people with different backgrounds, who move for different reasons, and whose reception in the host country can be diverse. This can be reflected in gang formation.

In 1965, the Immigration and Nationality Act put an end to the quota system that restricted the number of immigrants who could enter the USA. Before that date, mostly European migrants had entered the USA. In addition, the within-US migration by African-Americans from the rural South to the urban-industrial North and West was a significant force in understanding the formation of gangs in the 1960s. This illustrates the salience of population movement in understanding the difficulties faced by new groups. After 1965, new non-European groups were allowed to enter the USA. Large numbers of immigrants from Central and South America entered the country. Even though regulations had changed, a large number of these immigrants could not get a permit. Still, they entered America illegally and gravitated toward urban areas such as Los Angeles. From Asia, different groups from former war zones (Vietnam, Laos, and Cambodia) entered the USA as refugees after a period of American military involvement that ended in 1975. Recent gang studies have focused on these newer Latino and Asian groups that, once again, produce gangs (e.g. Chin 1990; Du Phuoc Long 1996; Vigil 1988, 2002).

Migration patterns to and within Europe are different. The imperialism of many Western European countries resulted in colonial territories in Asia, Africa, North America, and South America. Because of their special relation with their European conquerors, these non-Europeans were allowed to travel between the ex-colony and its former colonizer in Europe. A number of European nations now have large immigrant populations with roots in former colonies, including the UK (from India, Pakistan, and the West Indies), France (from Algeria, Morocco, and Senegal), Portugal (from Brazil, Mozambique, and Angola), and The Netherlands (from Indonesia and Surinam). Some of these migrant groups, especially those in the UK, may be third or fourth generation, while most of the others, because of relatively recent changes, are first or second generation.

During periods of economic expansion, beginning in the 1960s, several countries in northern Europe recruited 'guest workers' from Mediterranean countries to fill the demand for mainly manual labour in factories. Even though both parties saw these arrangements as temporary solutions to a demand for labour, many immigrants did not leave when they lost their jobs as the economy declined in the 1980s. This led to situations where the new immigrants were marginalised in two ways, economically because of lost jobs and culturally because of their difference from the dominant host culture. After years of successfully participating in the northern factories, Spanish, Portuguese, Italian, and Greek guest workers mostly returned to their native southern European soil. Considering the options, others chose differently. Immigrants were entitled to access the social welfare system, which meant a low but stable income even while being unemployed. For some, it seemed better to reunite families in the northern European nations than to return to a poor living standard in their homelands. Moroccans and Turks, among others, decided to stay where they were in Western Europe (Engbersen *et al.* 2007).

The aftermath of the Second World War and the fall of the Iron Curtain brought a new social order in Europe. For some groups, this led to a reunion. The *Aussiedler*, people of German descent, had been cut off from their German homeland, and were forced to live in Russia for decades. Since the reunification of Germany, these people have been provided with German passports. The resulting process of migration back to Germany, however, has been fraught with complications (see below). Asylum seekers were another group of migrants that came to Europe, mainly from African countries, the Middle East, and China. One category sought refuge from violence, war, or political persecution, while another migrated for economic reasons that are generally not sufficient for legal entrance to countries of Western Europe. Therefore, many find themselves living the life of an illegal immigrant, unable to gain legitimate work status. The opening of internal European borders, a process that started in the early 1990s, has made it easier for citizens of the European Union (EU) to apply for employment in other member states. Once inside the EU, the open borders also make travel easier for migrants without legal documents.

Gangs and migration

Recently, deportation of thousands of immigrants with criminal records, including a large number of gang members, has been identified as a factor in the problem of gangs. Upon their deportation, individuals who had been imprisoned in US jails and prisons and exposed to US gangs spread gang culture to other countries. Members of MS13 and another well-known gang, called Eighteenth Street, from Los Angeles, were returned to El Salvador or Honduras, introducing a severe gang problem to these countries (Cruz 2007). Members of these groups are said to have returned to the USA, bringing the gang migration full circle (Papachristos 2005). There is scant support for these conclusions, however, despite their widespread popularity in the media, and there is controversy over the degree to which migration within countries contributes to the spread of gang problems (Maxson 1998).

The predominant reason for migration is economic. Most immigrants – whether within or between countries – expect to find better employment in their new country, but often they have to take jobs at the bottom of the economic ladder, even if they have skills or degrees from their former country. Because of their focus on employment, the first generation of immigrants typically works hard for a better living; often it is their offspring, the second generation, that have difficulty in school or engage in criminal activities. This social mechanism was first described in detail in the famous study *The Polish Peasant in Europe and America* (Thomas and Znaniecki 1920), and it is played out in much of the migration literature. American scholars researching migration after 1965 speak about the 'new second generation' (Bankston 1998; see also Chapter 4, this volume).

Classical American gang research has produced theoretical trends that can be distinguished in more recent gang studies. Neighbourhoods, marginalisation, and ethnicity are key themes that, each in different ways, explain the link between migration and gangs. The social disorganisation approach is originally linked to the Chicago school of sociology. Scholars studied young immigrants who were gang members, emphasizing the nature of social organisation of the neighbourhoods where gangs were found (Thrasher 1927; Whyte 1943). These studies identified the role of ethnicity among new immigrants in defining territory and affiliation patterns. Where the 'edges' of ethnic neighbourhoods bordered, there were often conflicts, and such conflicts played a role in sharpening ethnic identification. Rapid social change after migration resulted in a breakdown of social control within immigrant groups, and gangs provided an alternative social order that compensated for the loss of traditional ties.

The opportunity structure approach stresses the structure of American society, and mainly focuses on access to sources of economic opportunity and the socio-economic position of new groups. Using Merton (1938) for theoretical inspiration, subcultural studies (e.g. Cloward and Ohlin 1960; Cohen 1955) point to social processes that produce strain, either in the form of status frustration or blocked social opportunities that lead youths to form gangs and engage in illegal activities. These studies focus on class, rather than on culture, to account for deviance, crime, and gang activity by migrant groups.

But class cannot fully account for differences in the success or failure to assimilate, and subsequent gang formation or involvement in crime. Some migrant groups with similar class characteristics show evidence of higher crime rates than others, and gang participation is not equally distributed among immigrant groups. This observation has validity in the USA (Curry *et al.* 1994: 9), but it also applies to European contexts. For example, Moroccans and Turks in The Netherlands are similar when it comes to migration history, size of population, and socio-economic position. However, in Amsterdam, over 60 per cent of the gang membership is accounted for by Moroccan boys, while Turkish boys are almost absent as gang members (van Gemert 2005: 163). Opportunity structure has an ethnic dimension that can help to explain these differences. In general, migrants are found in economic niches that are easy to penetrate. For example, in many big cities, taxi driver is a job typically for newcomers. But ethnic groups differ in the way they can access formal institutions; in the past this was because of language. They also vary in the ability to participate in specific illegal job markets or criminal networks. For example, Chinese gangs have developed ties with existing Chinese organised crime groups (Chin and Fagan 1994). So, for many reasons, specific ethnic groups cannot enter particular settings, while they may have easy access to others (Engbersen *et al.* 2007). Moreover, it is not only what people have access to but also their preferences (or aversions) that help to explain why certain opportunities are taken by a particular ethnic group while others are not (van Gemert 1998: 26).

Cultural approaches emphasise the beliefs, norms, and values of group members. The development of gangs is traced back to the culture of a particular ethnic group, or to a specific social situation in which the members are involved. Again, the relation is not a direct one in the sense that culture dictates gang participation. Gangs are not produced by culture, but in specific situations interaction with cultural norms can lead to the formation of gangs. Youth of different ethnicity, after migration, may find themselves confronted with other groups in the street. To establish a position, or just to protect themselves, they form groups that learn to use violence and become gangs. This process has been documented for Chinese (Chin 1990), for Mexican (Vigil 1988), and Salvadoran youths (McGuire 2007). This has led to the formation of ethnic gangs that may use ethnic elements to stress their identity (names, tattoos, religious symbols, etc.).

In the USA, an urban tradition of gangs has put forward focal concerns (Miller 1958) related to street life under difficult conditions. One can argue that some of these concerns fit particular ethnic groups. For example, masculinity and honour are said to be elements of Mexican culture (machismo), but many non-Hispanic gang members would say that they are also key issues for them. So, for some ethnic groups that claim a chance at popular street life, the stereotypical gang repertoire may be more familiar than for others.

Currently, groups draw upon existing gang codes and symbols that have become part of a global youth culture. Modern media, particularly through the music genre of 'gangsta rap', have distributed cultural traits, mostly from stereotypical African-American gangs, to remote places all over the world. Crips and Bloods may have started out as gangs in particular neighbourhoods in Los Angeles, but nowadays gangs with the same names are found in The Netherlands (van Gemert 2001), while Latin Kings are present in Italy and Spain (see Chapter 5, this volume). This is not so much the result of migrating gang members that start new sets in different places, but rather the outcome of a process of adaptation and imitation of popular youth culture (Nilan and Feixa 2006). This suggests the importance of the cultural transmission of gang symbols, including names, clothing, language, posturing, reputation, and affectations. These aspects of gang life can be lived, reproduced, and transmitted through a variety of means, including movies, videos, the Internet, and other forms by which popular culture spreads.

We believe that to understand fully the impact of migration on gang formation and behaviour, it is important to meld both cultural transmission theory and neighbourhood marginalisation theory. We have sketched out the key components of cultural transmission theory above. We now turn to the role that social marginalisation plays in gang formation, particularly in light of the pressures of migration. Social marginalisation theory is particularly appropriate for understanding the role of migration and immigration in gang formation (Vigil 2002), as it identifies the role of differences of language, ethnicity, religion, and other institutional affiliations in the isolation of individuals from the dominant society. Social marginalisation theory hypothesises that individuals who face multiple marginalising factors are less likely to be integrated into mainstream cultural values. As a consequence, these individuals and groups cannot integrate into the dominant practices and belief systems of the society and culture within which they reside. We use this dual framework – cultural transmission and social marginalisation – as the key theoretical elements with which we frame our work.

The following sections of this chapter examine the European migration situation. The use of the term 'gang' is based on the Eurogang definition. We begin with a discussion of the role of ethnicity in the formation of new immigrant gangs. We then focus on the concept of marginalisation, one that has been used with considerable utility in American gang research. Finally, we discuss the role of neighbourhoods for European gangs, particularly as it bears on the formation and activities of immigrant gang groups.

Ethnicity

Gangs can be comprised of members of a single ethnic group or can include members of a variety of ethnic groups. In the case of multiethnic gangs, one specific ethnic group is often dominant. Gang rivalries often emerge along ethnic lines both within gangs and between gangs, but does ethnicity have the same influence in European gangs as in the American context?

Weitekamp *et al.* (2005) assess the role of ethnicity in the formation and activities of German gangs. Their study focuses on the *Aussiedler*, repatriated Russians of German descent who migrated to Russia during the post-World War II separation of Germany into East and West. This repatriation is burdened with irony, as the former German citizens had lost most of their language, customs, and relationship with Germany after they had moved to Russia. Over time they had become more Russian than German, and the challenge of their transition back to Germany has been similar to those faced by many immigrant groups new to a country or culture. These repatriated Germans engage in a large number of fights with other Germans and other ethnic groups. Their ethnic origins have important implications for forming gangs, as most members of this group share a common country of origin. These affiliation patterns are compounded by the social, economic, and cultural deprivation faced when the *Aussiedler* returned to Germany.

There is diversity in the ways that ethnicity correlates with gang formation. On the one hand, ethnic newcomers can find it hard to connect to their new cultural context and retreat to ethnic gangs. On the other hand, members of street gangs can also be alienated from their own ethnic roots, as the experience of Moroccan boys from Windmill Square in West Amsterdam illustrates. In the 1980s, Moroccan families were recruited to fill labour shortages. The gang boys that van Gemert and Fleisher (2005) report on are the children of the first generation of immigrants. Their parents were raised in Morocco according to Moroccan norms and values. However, this generation of Moroccan youths grew up in the context of Dutch culture, in this respect similar to what was described by Thrasher (1927) for Chicago and Vigil (1988, 2002) for Los Angeles. The majority of gangs in Amsterdam form along ethnic lines, with Moroccan boys dominating these gangs (van Gemert 2005).

The Oslo gangs studied by Lien (2005) are primarily Pakistani in ethnicity, a factor that plays an important role in understanding their integration into – and exclusion from – Norwegian society. In

Pakistan, kinship relations are quite important, and these remain so for Pakistani youth in Oslo. Kin networks promote fighting and conflict between individuals, as members of the same kinship group will fight to defend other kinsmen, producing an accepted pattern of affiliation and conflict. Lien (2005) notes the extent to which these practices can blur the lines between gang conflicts and family conflicts. This is an important element, particularly for understanding second-generation immigrant youth already marginalised by economic and cultural factors. Lien reports that this marginalisation stems from the youths' attempts to straddle both Pakistani and Norwegian cultural and behavioural categories, producing 'part-time conformists'.

Ethnicity also plays a role in the Italian gangs described by Gatti and colleagues (2005). Ethnicity has implications for both the formation and activities of Italian gangs. Italy has migrants from different regions of Italy, as well as from several non-EU nations in North Africa and western Asia. These new immigrants are often met with distrust and viewed as outsiders, increasing ethnic isolation and strengthening intraethnic ties among youths. Family honour and culture are important aspects of the gangs that Gatti and his colleagues study, and these traditions are tied to ethnicity.

There is another element of protest in European street gangs that has not been documented in their American counterparts. Recently, in several countries such as Norway (Bjørgo 2005), France (Petrova 2006), The Netherlands (Chapter 6), and Russia (Chapter 5), groups have surfaced that have political sympathy for the extreme Right. They are outspoken about their nationalist, anti-immigrant ideas. Often these are racist groups that advocate white supremacy, meaning a strong link to ethnicity. Violent confrontations with migrant groups seem to be a key activity. Some have connections with political organisations, but others do not. To what extent these groups can be considered gangs that fit the Eurogang definition is not always clear.

Marginalisation

A key component in the study of gangs is the focus on their ties to institutions such as family, school, and work. It is in these links that marginalisation appears. The Moroccan boys of the Windmill Square group in Amsterdam generally come from big families with low incomes, often with family disruption. These contribute in part to their lack of success in the workplace and at school, as the boys often lack discipline. Most members of the group also have police contact for a variety of offences. These youths are often described by adults as 'ill prepared for a role in society'. Thus, they find themselves excluded from mainstream institutions in Dutch society.

Similarly, the members of the Pakistani gangs in Oslo described by Lien (2005) also have impressive numbers of charges brought against them. Interestingly, however, these youths do not have the problematic family background found among members of the Windmill Square group. On the contrary, the Pakistani members have broad family networks and belong to tightly knit families, and this, in turn, is a risk factor because of the group cohesion that such characteristics present. Lien means that Pakistani youths must put on the appearance of conformity to traditional religious attendance and observations, but they combine such conformity with Western influences, including nightclubs, drinking, and involvement in crime when they are among their friends. In this way, these Pakistani immigrants resemble the Mexican-American gang members of Los Angeles barrios described by Vigil (1988). Both groups are marginalised by the majority community, but marginalised by their own ethnic community as well.

Gatti *et al.* (2005) describe the members of an 'old-fashioned Genoa gang' who come from a heavily marginalised group of poor southern Italian migrants. The gang youths have shared the experiences of failure at school, family breakdown, and lawbreaking, and began their involvement in crime early in their lives. In most cases, they have experienced family disintegration and disruption. Some members have been institutionalised in group homes and even been imprisoned.

The *Aussiedler* described by Weitekamp *et al.* (2005) are not integrated into the social fabric of German society. They remain an isolated ethnic group, much as they were in Russia. These individuals were marginalised as Germans in Russia, and are marginalised as Russians in Germany. The descriptions of these Germans portray gang members in marginalised positions who grew up in adverserial social circumstances. In a small number of cases, major problems are reported in the areas of family, education, and work, and all of the gang members are criminally active. These experiences are consistent with the pattern of multiple marginalisation identified by Vigil (1988) for Mexican-Americans in southern California. The *Aussiedler* are neither fully German nor Russian, and as such find cultural and economic integration into mainstream German society to be quite difficult, a close parallel to the experiences of ethnic groups in America (Vigil 2002) who form gangs as a response to their marginalisation.

Neighbourhoods

The neighbourhood context has been one of the enduring variables in the study of gangs across the last century and across continents. Upon migration, newcomers often find themselves in less favourable settings – more explicitly, in bad neighbourhoods. One example is Mexicans who live in the poor areas of Los Angeles (Vigil 1988). Gangs are described as springing from ghettos, whether isolated because of ethnic or economic reasons, where marginalisation and lack of social capital dominate social relations. A corollary of the importance of neighbourhoods is the role of 'turf', a place where members meet and that they consider their own. American street gangs are classically depicted as very territorial groups that engage in conflicts to protect their turf.

The role of neighbourhoods and turf for European gangs shares some common features with the American gang scene. However, as is the case in the USA, diversity exists across gangs, cities, and countries. The Moroccan members of the Windmill Square gang (van Gemert and Fleisher 2005) live in a neighbourhood that has a relatively high percentage of ethnic minorities, but is still heterogeneous, particularly compared to the American scene. The neighbourhood is not deteriorated, there are many public services, and, generally, it is clean with some open green spaces. By no means could it be described as a ghetto. Gang members hang out on the street or in the shopping area. Their activities are not confined to their own neighbourhood, as they cause trouble in the city centre and in other locales near Amsterdam. There is no evidence that the gang has conflicts with other gangs over their territory, and they do not initiate fights with other groups over turf. There are conflicts with shopkeepers, but these have more to do with inhibiting commerce than protecting turf.

The Pakistani A and B gangs described by Lien (2005) are clearly not territorial. In fact, these gangs do not restrict their activity to a particular neighbourhood at all, as gang members often meet in restaurants or clubs outside their own neighbourhoods. The members from the B gang come from various suburbs, and are highly mobile, using cars to travel. Although the A and B gangs are not territorial, they are rivals and do engage in a considerable number of fights.

The gang studied by Gatti *et al.* (2005) hang out on the street or in a bar in Genoa. They do not have a specific place they identify as their own, and thus cannot be described as territorial. Despite this, they do tend to congregate in the neighbourhood where they live. This is a socially and economically deprived area. Neighbourhood residents feel intimidated by the gang, as was the case for the Windmill Square group in Amsterdam. There are also groups of younger children in these neighbourhoods that cause nuisances, particularly vandalism. The culture of the gang is described as the result of 'a spatial and cultural isolation and a tendency to remain within the confines of the neighbourhood' (Gatti *et al.* 2005: 75). The *Aussiedler* also live in neighbourhoods that are characterised by economic and social decline. They are often housed in dreadful conditions, occupying temporary units that are very crowded. Youths often hang out in hallways or outside the buildings, because in their homes they have no place of their own.

As is the case in the USA, neighbourhood conditions matter in understanding the activities and allegiances of European gangs. However, neighbourhoods in Europe do not have the same meaning as for American groups. This reflects differences in neighbourhoods as much as it does differences in gangs. The Italian gang and the *Aussiedler* live in poor and deprived neighbourhoods with unfavourable housing conditions. The neighbourhood clearly played a role in bringing youths with the same background together in these groups and in confining them to their own area and culture. The low tendency for gangs and groups to see the neighbourhood as a place with which to identify clearly departs from the classical picture of American street gangs. A study from The Netherlands (van Gemert and Fleisher 2005) shows that the emergence of gangs and troublesome youth groups is not especially tied to deteriorated areas in the city. Furthermore, none of these studies report fights over turf. Gangs may be rivals without having a territory (like the A and B gangs in Oslo), or they may be bound to a particular area without having to defend a territory (like the gang of southern Italians in Genoa).

Conclusion

In Europe, migration has specific political, economic, and cultural backgrounds. There have been a number of significant changes in Europe. These include the need for a workforce in the expanding Western European economies (and subsequent family formation and reunion), a substantial influx of refugees and asylum seekers in many European countries due to global instability, and population changes after the fall of the Berlin Wall. There have been waves of change in Europe that followed these titanic changes, including the impact on family formation, the mixing of religious and cultural groups, and the attempt to absorb new groups into the economies. As a result, European countries have many young inhabitants who are second-generation ethnic minorities, and big cities have become more multicultural. Population change and the availability of gang culture through modern media have created a breeding ground for gangs. This is an example of the role that cultural transmission has played in the spread of gangs.

It is important to note that, just as in the USA, street gangs and troublesome youth groups in Europe are not a monolith. European gangs are not all alike, nor are the gangs of a particular nation such as Norwegian, Dutch, or Italian gangs. However, it is possible to draw several conclusions about the relationship between migration and gangs in Europe, about the characteristics of this relationship, and about the impact migration has on gangs. One of the most important conclusions is the role that social marginalisation theory plays in understanding the role of migration in gang formation in Europe. The evidence, even though it is only suggestive at this point, shows that isolation from mainstream institutions and behaviour leads to gang formation, and consequently to negative behaviour.

This review raises several important questions about the relationship between gangs and immigration in Europe. Are new immigrant gangs simply the result of migrant families moving into neighbourhoods where gangs would exist anyway? Such a proposition suggests that social conditions in certain neighbourhoods are conducive to gang formation. To what extent does migration bring together ethnic groups and create competition that produces gangs? New ethnic groups often live in the same neighbourhoods and experience social isolation from the mainstream culture. Does migration lead to a breakdown of traditional social structures that allows gangs to become alternative forms of social order? This is especially true of young people who find challenges to their old culture on the street, in school, and in youth culture. As migrants move to a new land, their old customs and traditions become more difficult to maintain, and those customs lose their ability to control behaviour.

Just as in the USA, because of its strong history of migration, gangs in Europe show considerable participation of ethnic minorities. Specific ethnic groups and cultural elements vary from country to country, because of different migration histories. The gangs inhabit poor neighbourhoods, and gang members often find themselves in a marginal position. In most cases, not surprisingly, the presence of gangs is linked to deprivation. Gang rivalry, subsequently, seems to be the outcome of competition over scarce goods among the poor. Recently, changes have occurred because migrants with a Muslim background find themselves in a somewhat different position. Since 11 September 2001, these migrants have been looked upon differently and cultural differences seem to be more salient and important. It will be interesting to see the effect of this on gangs.

Note

1 Perhaps the UK can count as an exception, but British criminologists, especially those of the Birmingham school, have focused on youth subcultures instead of gangs (see Campbell *et al.* 1982; Campbell and Muncer 1989).

References

Bankston, C.L. (1998) 'Youth gangs and the new second generation: a review essay', *Aggression and Violent Behavior*, 3(1): 35–45.

Bjørgo, T. (2005) 'Conflict processes between youth groups in a Norwegian city: polarization and revenge', *European Journal of Crime, Criminal Law and Criminal Justice*, 13(1): 44–74.

Campbell, A., Muncer, S. and Galen, J. (1982) 'American gangs and British subcultures: a comparison', *International Journal of Offender Therapy and Comparative Criminology*, 26(1): 76–89.

Campbell, A. and Muncer, S. (1989) 'Them and us: a comparison of the cultural context of American gangs and British subcultures', *Deviant Behavior*, 10(3): 271–88.

Chin, K. (1990) 'Chinese gangs and extortion', in C.R. Huff (ed.), *Gangs in America*. Newbury Park, CA: Sage, 7–21.

Chin, K. and Fagan, J.A. (1994) 'Social order and gang formation in Chinatown', in F. Adler and W. Laufer (eds), *Advances in Criminal Theory* (vol. 6). New Brunswick, NJ: Transaction Press, 216–51.

Cloward, R.A. and Ohlin, L.E. (1960) *Delinquency and Opportunity. A Theory of Delinquent Gangs*. New York: The Free Press.

Cohen, A.K. (1955) *Delinquent Boys*. New York: The Free Press.

Coughlin, B.C. and Venkatesh, S.A. (2003) 'The urban street gang after 1970', *Annual Review of Sociology*, 29: 41–64.

Covey, H.C. (2003) *Street Gangs Throughout the World*. Springfield, IL: Charles C. Thomas Press.

Cruz, J.M. (2007) *Street Gangs in Central America*. El Salvador: UCA Publishers.

Curry, G.D., Ball, R.A and Fox, R.J. (1994) 'Gang crime and law enforcement recordkeeping', in *National Institute of Justice, Research in Brief.* Washington, DC: United, National Institute of Justice.

Curry, G.D. and Decker, S.H. (2002) *Confronting Gangs: Crime and Community.* Los Angeles: Roxbury.

Du Phuoc Long, P. (1996) *The Dream Shattered: Vietnamese Gangs in America.* Boston: Northeastern University Press.

Engbersen, G., Leun, J. van der and Boom, J. de (2007) 'The fragmentation of migration and crime in the Netherlands', in M. Tonry and C. Bijleveld (eds), *Crime and Justice in the Netherlands* (vol. 35). Chicago: University of Chicago Press, pp. 389–452.

Gatti, U., Angelini, F., Marengo, G., Melchoirre, N. and Sasso, M. (2005) 'An old-fashioned youth gang in Genoa', in S.H. Decker and F.M. Weerman (eds), *European Street Gangs and Troublesome Youth Groups.* Lanham, MD: AltaMira Press, pp. 51–80.

Gemert, F. van (1998) *Ieder voor zich; kansen, cultuur en criminaliteit van Marokkaanse jongens.* Amsterdam: Het Spinhuis.

Gemert, F. van (2001) 'Crips in orange: gangs and groups in the Netherlands', in M.W. Klein, H.J. Kerner, C.L. Maxson and E.G.M. Weitekamp (eds), *The Eurogang Paradox: Street Gangs and Youth Groups in the U.S. and Europe.* Dordrecht: Kluwer Academic, pp. 145–52.

Gemert, F. van (2005) 'Youth groups and gangs in Amsterdam: an inventory based on the Eurogang expert survey', in S.H. Decker and F.M. Weerman (eds), *European Street Gangs and Troublesome Youth Groups.* Lanham, MD: AltaMira Press, pp. 147–68.

Gemert, F. van and Fleisher, M. (2005) 'In the grip of the group: ethnography of a Moroccan street gang in the Netherlands', in S.H. Decker and F.M. Weerman (eds), *European Street Gangs and Troublesome Youth Groups.* Lanham, MD: AltaMira Press, 11–30.

Lien, I.L. (2005) 'Criminal gangs and their connections: metaphors, definitions and structures', in S.H. Decker and F.M. Weerman (eds), *European Street Gangs and Troublesome Youth Groups.* Lanham, MD: AltaMira Press, 31–50.

Martinez, R. and Lee, M.T. (2000) 'On immigration and crime', *Criminal Justice,* 1: 485–524.

Maxson, C.L. (1998) *Gang Members on the Move.* Washington, DC: US Department of Justice, Office of Juvenile Justice and Delinquency Prevention.

McGuire, C. (2007) *Working Paper on Central American Youth Gangs in the Washington, D.C. Area.* Washington, DC: Washington Office on Latin America.

Merton, R.K. (1938) 'Social structure and anomie', *American Sociological Review,* 3: 672–82.

Miller, W.B. (1958) 'Lower class culture as a generating milieu of gang delinquency', *Journal of Social Issues,* 14(3): 5–19.

Nilan, P. and C. Feixa (eds) (2006) *Global Youth, Hybrid Identities, Plural Worlds.* London: Routledge.

Papachristos, A.V. (2005) 'Gang world', *Foreign Policy*, 147 (March/April): 49–55.

Petrova, Y. (2006) 'Global? Local? Multi-level identifications among contemporary skinheads in France', in P. Nilan and C. Feixa (eds), *Global Youth, Hybrid Identities, Plural Worlds*. London: Routledge, pp. 186–205.

Puffer, J.A. (1912) *The Boy and His Gang*. New York: Houghton-Mifflin.

Spergel, I.A. (1990) 'Youth gangs: continuity and change', in M. Tonry and N. Morris (eds), *Crime and Justice: A Review of Research* (vol. 12). Chicago: University of Chicago Press, pp. 171–275.

Thomas, W. and Znaniecki, F. (1920) *The Polish Peasant in Europe and America*. Chicago: University of Illinois Press.

Thrasher, F.M. (1927) *The Gang: A Study of 1,313 Gangs in Chicago*. Chicago: University of Chicago Press.

Vigil, D. (1988) *Barrio Gangs*. Austin, TX: University of Texas Press.

Vigil, D. (2002) *A Rainbow of Gangs*. Austin, TX: University of Texas Press.

Weerman, F.M. and Decker, S.H. (2005) 'European street gangs and troublesome youth groups, findings from the Eurogang research program', in S.H. Decker and F.M. Weerman (eds), *European Street Gangs and Troublesome Youth Groups*. Lanham, MD: AltaMira Press, pp. 287–310.

Weitekamp, E., Kerner, H.J. and Reich, K. (2005) 'Why do young male Russians of German descent tend to join or form violent gangs?', in S.H. Decker and F.M. Weerman (eds), *European Street Gangs and Troublesome Youth Groups*. Lanham, MD: AltaMira Press, 81–104.

Whyte, W.F. (1943) *Street Corner Society. The Social Structure of an Italian Slum*. Chicago: University of Chicago Press.

Chapter 3

Dangers and problems of doing 'gang' research in the UK

Judith Aldridge, Juanjo Medina and Robert Ralphs

Introduction

Researchers and commentators have raised moral, political and scientific objections to conducting research that is explicitly 'gang' research. We begin by discussing the dangers of carrying out gang research; in particular, we focus on the risk of stereotyping communities, ethnic groups, and young people more generally. We sympathise with the concerns raised, but proceed with carrying out research that is explicitly 'gang' research in our ethnographic study, 'Youth Gangs in an English City' (YOGEC), funded by the UK Economic and Social Research Council (ESRC). We do so for a number of reasons that we discuss in this chapter, but in particular to remedy the predominant focus within research, police, and journalistic accounts on ethnic minority youth and their gang involvement. Our second aim is to discuss the strategies we employ in our research design that explicitly address the concerns with which we contend. In other words, we designed our research with the intention that it does not stigmatise individuals and communities, that it paints a nuanced picture of the individuals and communities in which we conduct our research, and that it be attuned to complex subjectivities. At the time of writing, we have just completed our data collection, and therefore are in a position to reflect upon the experience of implementing the strategies we employ.

Objections to 'gang' research

'Might not the launching of coordinated gang research in Europe serve inadvertently to create or strengthen the existence of street gangs?' (Klein *et al.* 2001: 335). This question was posed in the concluding chapter of the first Eurogang-edited collection in 2001. No other issue at the first meeting of the Eurogang Network in 1998 raised as much controversy. Some researchers were concerned that engaging in this type of research might contribute to the development of moral panics about gangs. It was argued that gang research (1) may stigmatise individuals, communities, or ethnic groups (the last particularly relevant in the context of this book); (2) can reify, and therefore strengthen, gangs and the perception that ethnic minority youth dominate them; and (3) may contribute to unintended punitive policy outcomes. In contrast, others were worried that by denying the problem and neglecting research, uninformed public policy and public opinion could develop (Klein *et al.* 2001). Almost a decade later, these moral dilemmas and controversies remain, as was made evident in some of the debate during the eighth Eurogang meeting (Oñati, Spain 2005). Need for this kind of discussion remains, particularly in a time when there is growing political debate on immigration and ethnic minority youth throughout Europe.

Resistance to the use of the 'gang' label in academic discourse runs strong in Britain (e.g. Campbell and Muncer 1989; Sanders 2002, 2005; Bullock and Tilley 2008), where there has been a longer critical tradition within criminology than in the USA and where different sociological traditions for the study of youth and their experiences have prevailed. While much 'gang' research with its origin in the USA has delinquent *groups/networks* of young people as its object of study, British research since the 1960s has focused instead on youth *subcultures*, differentiated by class, gender, and race, where delinquency may or may not play a key or defining role. British researchers have studied subcultural groups ranging from teddy boys (e.g. Cohen 1972), skinheads (e.g. Taylor and Wall 1976), and punks (e.g. Hebdidge 1979) to the more hybrid 'rave' drug, dance and music cultures (e.g. Moore 2003; Thornton 1995). There is an apprehension about gang research among British social constructionists, who argue that such a paradigm further alienates inner-city youth belonging to ethnic minorities and simplifies their experiences (Alexander 2000). The extent to which this 'foreign' paradigm is even necessary in the UK has therefore been questioned. Even across the Atlantic, however, where gang research has long been established, some have argued that the gang concept obscures rather than clarifies the complexities of youth crime and violence (e.g. Sullivan 2006).

In addition, there is a perception among some that many of the most negative aspects of policymaking in criminal justice have resulted from the transfer of ideas from the USA (Newburn 2002; Wacquant 2004). This may lead some to believe that the import of the American 'gang' label may result in policy outcomes likely to criminalise and further marginalise youth from poor communities (e.g. Hallsworth and Young 2004). In a media and policy context characterised by an undue emphasis on the portrayal of youth as antisocial – ethnic minority youth in particular – this type of reaction to the Eurogang project is not surprising. The 'crusade' against youthful antisocial behaviour promoted by New Labour politicians (in government in Britain since 1997) has reached the point that the Chairman of the Youth Justice Board expressed his concern about the risk of demonisation of large numbers of youth (*The Independent*, 23 April 2006) and then resigned in January 2007. This concern is shared by the European Commissioner for Human Rights (Office of the Commissioner for Human Rights 2005).

There is no question that the issue of gangs is a contentious one in research, and that the concept is conceptually and methodologically slippery, even problematic. Nevertheless, we think that there are a number of good reasons to carry out gang research in Europe. We contend that it is important to marry the best of the American tradition of gang research with the long-standing tradition of particularly British and other European social research on youth groups and subcultures.

Despite the concern of some who state that researchers are creating a moral panic about the gang phenomenon by imposing the term in the British context, the reality is that the term has long had popular currency – and long before British criminologists began carrying out gang research. In cities like Manchester and Glasgow, for example, groups refer to themselves as 'gangs', as do police and other community members, and the term has existed in these cities for at least 25 years and probably longer (Mares 2001; Patrick 1973). Social historians, in fact, have documented street gangs in the UK going back to the nineteenth century (Davies 1998, 2006; Macilwee 2006).

An important reason for carrying on with the term is to provide balance in the form of academic study that goes beyond the journalistic accounts of gangs that are anyway being produced. Recent accounts include John Davison's *Gangsta* (1997), Andy Hailwood's *Gun Law* (2004), McLagan's *Guns and Gangs* (2006), Tony Thompson's *Gangland*

Britain (1995) and *Gangs* (2004), and Peter Walsh's *Gang Wars* (2003). These accounts should be considered problematic for a number of reasons, not least the sour community responses to their publication, which we discuss specifically in relation to Walsh's *Gang Wars* below. Such accounts, it can be argued, provide a distorted view of gangs, gang members, and their communities through their sensationalised, skewed, and superficial emphasis on crime and violence. Moreover, some of these publications over-emphasise the relevance of ethnicity or immigration status as factors that 'explain' or define gangs.

Objections to gang research also reflect the long-standing view that troublesome British youth groups do not meet the definition of gangs and are instead unstructured, loose-knit and, therefore, different from American gangs (Campbell and Muncer 1989; Downes 1964; Parker 1974). However, American gangs, too, are different from the stereotypical perception of them; instead they are generally 'unstructured' and 'loose-knit' (e.g. Fleisher 2002). Klein (2001: 7) calls this the 'Eurogang paradox'. Our view is that if delinquent youth groups or 'gangs' in Britain and the USA are different, this can best be established through empirical observation that provides the benchmark for comparison. While this type of empirical observation has been lacking in the British context, more recently, a number of research studies have investigated gangs directly, such as the 12 studies identified by Marshall *et al.* (2005) and Pitts (2008). Moreover, large- scale government data collection initiatives have included questions assessing the prevalence and role of gangs (e.g. NEW-ADAM [Bennett and Holloway 2004] and the Offending Crime and Justice Survey [Sharp *et al.* 2006]).

As mentioned above, an objection to gang research is that it may contribute to punitive policy outcomes (Hallsworth and Young 2004). This assumes that the only policy outcome that can be associated with explicitly 'gang' research is punitive. Punitive policy approaches to youth behaviour, however, have long preceded gang research and are currently developing particularly in the British context – for example, around the use of public space. It is not only possible to do 'gang' research in such a way as to be critical of punitive policy directed towards youth, it is, arguably, almost inevitable. In fact, American gang researchers have been keen to show how punitive social, economic, and immigration policies can contribute to making gang problems worse by further marginalising ethnic minorities and young people and legitimizing 'gangs' as a source of identity (Fleisher 2002; Hagedorn 1998; Klein and Maxson 2006; Vigil 2002). We aspire to do research that provides a rounded understanding of the youth who are being targeted by these policies in assessing the impact that these policies are having.

Our research: problems and our solutions

At the University of Manchester, we are carrying out a portfolio of 'gang' research, including the ESRC-funded ethnographic study *Youth Gangs in an English City* (YOGEC). Here we outline our attempts to design research that contends with the concerns we outlined above, particularly with reference to this three year ethnographic study. The multiple case-study design based in a northern city (referred to as 'Research City') incorporated data collection over from October 2005 to December 2007 including: 107 formal interviews with 'gang members', their associates and families, and other key informants; and nine group interviews with non-gang involved youths, parents, and representatives of community groups and local agencies. Our aim was to address the following: gang characteristics; the roles of ethnicity and gender; the role of violence, illegal activities and drug economies; relationships between gangs and community; and the process of leaving the gang.

Representations of ethnic minorities and immigrant groups

Media accounts (e.g. Davison 1997) and police accounts of British gangs emphasise the ethnic dimension of gangs (Marshall *et al.* 2005). This emphasis has been heavily criticised by sociologists who argue that doing so simplifies the issue and contributes to the stereotyping of ethnic minorities (e.g. Alexander 2000). It is true that ethnographic research documents that gangs often emerge in areas populated by ethnic minorities and immigrant groups (e.g. Moore 1991; Vigil 2002). Certainly, the marginalisation of ethnic minorities and conditions in the communities that receive immigrant groups play a role in the understanding of gangs (Vigil 2002). However, some criminologists have criticised the ethnographic tradition of 'sampling' primarily or exclusively ethnic minority gangs because doing so may reinforce the notion that gangs are solely an ethnic minority problem (Martinez and Lee 2000).

Indeed, gang research more generally suggests that the relationship between ethnicity and gang membership is complex. The ethnic composition of gangs tends to reflect the ethnic composition of the neighbourhoods where they appear (Fagan 1996). Moreover, self-report surveys employing more representative samples do not find ethnicity to be such a strong predictor as these ethnographic studies might be interpreted to imply (Esbensen and Winfree 1998). Ethnicity may also not be such a strong predictor of gang membership in England and Wales, a less segregated context than the USA (Peach 1996), where most gang research has taken place. Indeed, research on gangs in Britain provides evidence for this view: South Manchester gangs are ethnically mixed when the neighbourhood is ethnically mixed (Tilley and Bullock 2002), whereas in the more ethnically homogeneous Edinburgh, gangs tend to be mostly white (Bradshaw 2005).

In 2004, the Home Office, in collaboration with researchers at the University of Manchester, conducted the first representative survey of England and Wales incorporating gang membership questions (Offending Crime and Justice Survey). Results showed that only a tiny minority of youth gangs in England and Wales were exclusively from ethnic minority groups. Among those delinquent youth group members who stated their group was ethnically homogeneous, 60 per cent of groups were white only, 3 per cent were black only, and 5 per cent were Asian only. Just under one-third of respondents in youth gangs (31 per cent) said their group included a mix of different ethnic groups. The ethnic composition of gangs is not widely divergent from the ethnic composition of other youth groups in England and Wales (Sharp et al. 2006).

In our research, we were determined not to fall into what we perceived to be the 'trap' of directing our gaze only towards gangs dominated by ethnic minority youth, and in particular, towards specific areas of Research City that had already suffered considerable stigmatisation. In other words, while there is a demonstrated empirical link between ethnicity and gangs, we take the view that it is important to examine the limitations of this link at every turn. Our decision to focus on a number of different sites within Research City follows from this determination. We used a template laid out by other researchers (e.g. Sullivan 1989) designed to allow us to capture and represent ethnic and other diversity and to develop a better understanding of how diversity plays a role in gang dynamics. Putting this strategy into place, however, was surprisingly difficult (see as well our discussion on community issues).

In Research City, criminal justice professionals generally have a fairly specific idea of what a 'gang' is. Prior to carrying out our research, our administration of the Eurogang 'expert survey' (which involved us additionally probing agency respondents for their definitions of a 'gang') (Medina and Aldridge 2004) demonstrated clearly that, for practitioners, gangs *were* groups that formed in ethnic minority neighbourhoods, since they are the ones that, ostensibly in Research City, carry firearms. For local agencies, it would seem therefore, firearm possession is a defining element of the gang. Using our purposefully very broad working definition of gangs, we took great pains to make clear to our professional respondents that our desire was to focus on youth gangs *wherever* they exist in Research City, and not only on gangs involved in firearm use, in contrast to local agency definitions. Even still, we were constantly 'guided' by these community professionals toward these ethnic minority groups. In fact, not only did we find white youth gangs in predominantly white areas, but also found that some of these groups carried and used firearms. It may be fair to ask the question as to whether local police were either inadequately applying their own definition, or unconsciously using ethnicity in their very definition of gangs.

It was not only police and community professionals whom we discovered to have entrenched notions of the importance particularly of black British ethnicity in understanding gangs; grass-roots community organisations did also. We observed a community meeting aimed at dealing with the problem of gun crime and attended by police, statutory community agencies, and grass-roots community groups. While a number of views were expressed about causes of and solutions to the problem of guns and gangs, the problem was clearly seen by some community groups to be located particularly within black ethnic minority culture; this view was held in spite of the fact that gun crime and gang activity in Research City are not the preserve of ethnic minorities.

Community concerns

Communication and engagement with relevant voluntary and statutory organisations commenced two years before the research began; in particular, as we began to make access arrangements during the process of preparing our research proposal in 2003. In the months before the project, we attended local events, such as community-based anti-gun and anti-gang workshops, as well as various conferences and meetings, including those with local politicians and community groups. The response to our research was different throughout the locations in the city in which we conducted our research. The site with the largest black British communities ('Inner West') had been extensively researched and had received considerable publicity due to its 'gang problem', and therefore was 'research weary' and sceptical.

A second site was exclusively white ('South City') and undergoing a process of heavy investment for urban redevelopment. Statutory and voluntary agencies in this site could be thought of as 'research wary' because of concern that their participation might result in negative publicity as a result of the identification of their area as one with a 'gang problem'. This wariness continued in spite of our assurances of confidentiality and anonymity, and it eventually resulted in our abandoning data collection in this site in the greater depth we had planned. The almost exclusively white area that we relocated to ('Far West') was, by contrast, 'research craving'. Its communities recognised the growing gang problem and thought that our research could help raise the profile of the issue and result in more official attention, thereby allowing them to deal more effectively with what they perceived to be their own gang problem. Crucially, it is these latter two predominantly white areas that have, up to now, received little official attention to their gang problems, by researchers, the police, other local agencies, and the media.

In 'Inner West', we were often faced with questions such as, 'What will your research do for us?', 'What's in it for us?', and 'What will it change?' People were quick to understand that their cooperation would result in our work being completed and published, and that, in turn, would benefit our academic careers. What reasons could we provide for these stakeholders to risk their reputations and personal safety by endorsing our research and introducing us to gang members? There was an onus placed upon us to prove we cared, had a genuine desire to make a difference, and were not just 'another' research team only trying to advance our careers. This sceptical and suspicious reaction often resulted in our backgrounds and motives being questioned. In this respect, employing local researchers helped to provide common ground with community members.

Residents in 'Inner West' believed that two decades of media and research attention focused on their neighbourhoods had resulted in little change. We have witnessed similar community reactions in Manchester, where our university is located. Peter Walsh's *Gang Wars: The Inside Story of the Manchester Gangs* was published in 2003. This journalistic account provided locations of specific, often notorious incidents, along with photographs and names of individuals purported to be involved. People we spoke to accused Walsh of exploiting the community by making the author a substantial amount of money off the back of other peoples' suffering, yet putting back little, if anything, into the communities he had exposed and further stigmatised. The book was viewed by many as inciting fresh gang rivalry by providing a new generation with 'war stories' of old incidents and by publishing details of murders and their perpetrators. Community members also believed that Walsh's book contributed to the stigmatisation of certain areas of the city and of ethnic minority groups, particularly those of Afro-Caribbean descent. The legacy of *Gang Wars*, which became something of a regional best-seller, was felt even in Research City; community members did not distinguish between an academic approach to research and the journalistic approach of Walsh, in which he 'named names' and included pictures. Therefore, it was not surprising that we had considerable work to do in order to allay fears among community members that our research would result in a similar kind of publication.

Local residents and community leaders in Research City also provided many specific examples of (primarily journalistic) research that failed to inform those who had taken part of the findings or even how the data were going to be used. One horror story occurred when both current and ex-gang members agreed to be interviewed on camera but were then dismayed to discover that their interviews had been edited into a film shown in local schools. One ex-gang member recalled walking through his estate when a group of young children starting shouting: *'Hey you're famous! You're the guy who was on TV in our school the other day. You're a gangster, aren't you?'* [Fieldworker notes]. This ex-gang member told us that he was never informed that his interview was going to be used for this purpose and had no idea it had been. In such instances, we responded by highlighting the distinction between academic research and non-academic investigations, particularly and especially popular media reporting. In addition, we were asked for reassurances and promises that we would keep people informed of publications and outcomes. We also determined that any profits that might result from our publications would be given to local charities.

Community members, particularly those in the steering group for our research, not only voiced fears that our research could harm them, but also demanded that we clarify how we could help them. This presented us with perhaps an even greater challenge: can we as researchers ever guarantee to have a genuinely positive impact on the communities we research and the lives of the individuals in them? We are not naive enough to believe that our research is going to change the lives of individuals and communities in Research City, and we were honest about this with the people who asked us. All we could do was to provide assurances that we care about their plight, and that, unlike previous researchers, we were not going to 'disappear' from the community once this project was completed. We actively engaged community stakeholders in deliberations about directions of the research by including them on our research steering group, we provided respondents with the opportunity to comment on our emerging explanations and understandings, and we promised to follow a strategy of dissemination that would reach policymakers and local practitioners alike. In other words, we know that our behaviour as researchers has effects – what we have sought to do is reduce, as far as possible, the negative effects of our presence, and increase the possibilities of positive benefits.

As discussed above, some community members initially identified researchers they had encountered over the years as 'outsiders': white, middle-class academics carrying out research *on* them – part of the 'gang industry' that includes professionals working in the police, the probation service, and the media, who make a living from the troubles of those in Research City. In spite of this, our research team was not identified within the communities in which we conducted our research in this way; we think this was for a number of reasons. First, although four of us are white, one is mixed-race, and this fieldworker was able to discuss shared experiences with mixed race informants. Most importantly, two members of the research team were 'from' the research sites, which resulted in at least some shared backgrounds, acquaintances, and understanding between 'researchers' and 'researched'. We did face criticism in not involving the community 'from the start' by allowing them (exclusively) to define our research objectives, and by not employing all who may have wanted employment to carry out the data collection. We were praised, however, for using the experienced and professional researchers we did, especially the two who were indigenous to the communities we researched, and also for providing training and employment to local community people for additional data collection later in the project. Interestingly, many of the gatekeepers we encountered were trained as local youth and community workers and had taken on board principles of community 'action research', in which community members are involved in the design and implementation of research projects. While we did not hand over control of the project and its aims and objectives to these community members, they saw from a very early stage that we were willing to compromise. The paradox, perhaps, is that this 'research weary' community does want research, and even research involving collaboration with outsiders, but research in which they hold a greater degree of control from inception to implementation, analysis and dissemination.

Attending community events and meetings and seeing the same faces that at first were suspicious of our motives enabled others to see the commitment and community relationships we had built. The same people who were at first wary became the ones who introduced our fieldworkers as 'sound' and 'from the street'. Even so, the generally negative view of researchers/academics remained evident, as they described us as 'not like your typical academic'. This type of validation from key individuals made subsequent relationships of trust much easier and facilitated further links with gang members. Obtaining such levels of trust and acceptance takes time and commitment. Our research team engaged in voluntary work at youth clubs and community centres and worked alongside community groups who directly addressed gun crime and gangs. We also helped with funding applications for them to continue their work and with designing and evaluating local research projects.

Avoiding stigmatisation

The primary strategy we adopted to reduce possible stigmatisation was our plan not to disclose publicly the city in which we conducted the research. It is important to point out that we positively and voluntarily adopted this strategy; it was not designed to satisfy the requirements of an ethics committee. The city is known instead as 'Research City' in all our public references to it. A similar strategy has been successfully adopted and carried out by other researchers in the UK (Hobbs *et al.* 2003; Measham *et al.* 2001). We know, therefore, that maintaining location, site or setting anonymity in research is possible; we did not know how feasible it would be with our particular project in Research City. There are two aspects to maintaining location, site or setting anonymity: in publications that emanate from the research, and in the communications made during fieldwork itself. Anonymity in dissemination is by far the easiest, although even here there are variations among researchers in terms of approaches to doing so. At the simplest level, the researcher can simply use pseudonyms to replace actual names of people and places. In addition, it is possible to change identifying details in relation to them (where doing so is not important to the context), effectively to mislead readers who might otherwise be able to make identifications based on published descriptions.

Our plan not to divulge the location of Research City has been met with surprise, and not a little scorn, by colleagues at conferences, who spoke to both the impossibility of such a task and its undesirability.

We were warned of the likelihood that most people in our various audiences, from readers of academic journal articles and books, to community practitioners and even gang members themselves, would nevertheless recognise the locations. We accept that some locals or insiders may make educated guesses, but we will falsify identifying details, as other researchers have done, in order to work against a definite identification.

The undesirability of maintaining location anonymity referred to by colleagues is clear, because what we give up is not trivial. We will be unable to provide accurate maps of the city. Maintaining location anonymity also raises challenges in terms of how we talk about the local history of the areas within the city and make reference to the work of others who have, or in allowing other researchers specifically interested in accounts of Research City to use our work to infer local knowledge. Even providing descriptive demographic and socio-economic statistics becomes tricky. In other words, it becomes more challenging – but not impossible – to situate our research findings within literature and data that provide historical, geographical, and socio-economic context. But what we gain is far more important. This strategy has already been key in garnering support and collaboration from key community stakeholders who did not want more publications that further stigmatised their communities and glorified particular gangs as 'brand names'.

Maintaining location and site anonymity in communications made during the fieldwork itself is perhaps trickier. The reality is that our research has involved talking to many individuals all over Research City: asking questions, checking stories, and verifying our developing understanding. There was no way to do this without, at least to some extent, identifying communities and areas within the city in conversations with others also working and living in Research City. Our approach has been to limit this kind of 'identifying talk' as much as possible, and with a view to remembering that long after our actual time spent in the field, the only thing that will remain is our written accounts of it; over these, we have much more control.

A clear advantage of anonymising research location is that we are much less likely to fall into the trap of glamorising or strengthening gangs through explicit attention, a problem that has been demonstrated by other researchers. Klein (1971), for example, in his evaluation of a programme that attached street workers to particular gangs, found that the programme contributed to increasing the cohesiveness of the groups themselves, perhaps reifying those structures. There is anecdotal evidence that in Manchester the book *Gang Wars* (Walsh

2003), through its identification of people and places and historical criminal events (including murders), may have functioned to increase the reputation of certain gangs as brand names, creating renewed rivalry between younger generations. It may not be only through publication that named gangs are strengthened by research. Perhaps simply receiving attention from professionals keen to listen and understand without judging is what strengthens gangs. In other words, we may not be able to avoid glamorising or strengthening gangs if it is just the *fact* of our carrying out research, rather than the manner in which we do it, that creates it.

Conclusions

We concur with those commentators who have pointed out that studying gangs might be 'dangerous'; for us, it is important to take the point seriously when designing research on any youth behaviour that involves delinquency. We acknowledge the risk of reification (Sullivan 2006), and the duty to take steps to reduce its risk when conducting this sort of research. In the ten years of the Eurogang Network's existence, considerable energy has been devoted to developing research instruments and protocols for studying gangs and youth delinquent behaviour; however, ethical issues in relation to these have not received enough explicit attention. A (re)opening of ethical debates might help to build bridges with critics who remain sceptical about the Eurogang enterprise, as well as with researchers in Britain coming from different intellectual traditions that have historically eschewed the 'gang' label when studying youth behaviour.

Certainly, one of the dangers of gang research is that it might, if not conducted and disseminated properly, contribute to the stereotyping of ethnic minorities and their communities. Here, then, the issues of ethnicity and ethics go hand-in-hand. This is particularly pertinent in Europe within the context of demographic changes, the growing movement of immigrants, the politicisation and representation of immigrant groups, and changing sentiments about foreign nationals (Semyonov *et al.* 2006). We have developed a research protocol that has 'worked' without (so far) alienating the communities in which we conducted our research, and that works to engage directly and productively with those critical of conducting research that is explicitly and self-consciously 'gang' research. Our experiences thus far in the communities we are researching leads us to conclude that it is possible to conduct research that is explicitly 'gang' research even in research-weary communities with savvy and sceptical community members who have wholeheartedly rejected the efforts of previous journalistic and other research approaches.

Acknowledgement

The research for this chapter was funded by the ESRC (RES-000-23-0615), and entitled 'Youth Gangs in an English City'.

References

Alexander, C.E. (2000) *The Asian Gang: Ethnicity, Identity, Masculinity.* Oxford: Berg.

Bennett, T. and Holloway, K. (2004) 'Gang membership, drugs and crime in the UK', *British Journal of Criminology,* 44(3): 305–23.

Bradshaw, P. (2005) 'Terrors and young teams: youth gangs and delinquency in Edinburgh', in S.H. Decker and F.M. Weerman (eds), *European Street Gangs and Troublesome Youth Groups.* Lanham, MD: AltaMira Press, pp. 193–218.

Bullock, K. and Tilley, N. (2008) 'Understanding and tackling gang violence', *Crime Prevention and Community Safety,* 10: 36–47.

Campbell, A. and Muncer, S. (1989) 'Them and us: a comparison of the cultural context of American gangs and British subcultures', *Deviant Behaviour,* 10(3): 271–88.

Cohen, P. (1972) *Subcultural Conflict and Working Class Community: Working Papers in Cultural Studies, No. 2.* Birmingham: Birmingham Centre for Contemporary Cultural Studies, University of Birmingham.

Davies, A. (1998) 'Youth gangs, masculinity and violence in late Victorian Manchester and Salford', *Journal of Social History,* 32(2): 349–69.

Davies, A. (2006) *Street Gangs and Violence in Glasgow in the 1920s and 1930s.* Edinburgh: Edinburgh University Press.

Davison, J. (1997) *Gangsta: The Sinister Spread of Yardie Gun Culture.* London: Vision Paperbacks.

Downes, D. (1964) *The Delinquent Solution.* London: Routledge & Kegan Paul.

Esbensen, F. and Winfree, L.T. (1998) 'Race and gender differences between gang and non-gang youth: results from a multi-site survey', *Justice Quarterly,* 15(3): 505–25.

Fagan, J.A. (1996) 'Gangs, drugs and neighborhood change', in C.R. Huff (ed.), *Gangs in America II.* Thousand Oaks, CA: Sage, pp. 39–74.

Fleisher, M.S. (2002) 'Doing field research on diverse gangs: interpreting youth gangs as social networks', in C.R. Huff (ed.) *Gangs in America III.* Thousand Oaks: Sage, pp. 199–218.

Hagedorn, J. (1998) *People and Folks: Gangs, Crime and the Underclass in a Rustbelt City*. Chicago: Lakeview Press.

Hailwood, A. (2004) *Gun Law*. Weigh Green, Lancashire: Milo Books.

Hallsworth, S. and Young, T. (2004) 'Getting real about gangs', *Criminal Justice Matters*, 55: 12–13.

Hebdidge, D. (1979) *Subculture: The Meaning of Style*. London: Methuen.

Hobbs, D., Hadfield, P., Lister, S. and Winlow, S. (2003) *Bouncers: Violence and Governance in the Night-Time Economy*. Oxford: Oxford University Press.

The Independent (2006) 'The ASBO kids: how Blair's "respect" agenda is turning society against our children', 23 April.

Klein, M. (1971) *Street Gangs and Street Workers*. Englewood Cliffs, NJ: Prentice-Hall.

Klein, M. (2001) 'Resolving the Eurogang paradox', in M. Klein, C. Malcolm, H.-J. Kerner, C. Maxson, and E. Weitekamp (eds), *The Eurogang Paradox. Street gangs and youth groups in the US and Europe*. Dordrecht: Kluwer Academic, pp. 7–20.

Klein, M., Kerner, H-J., Maxson, C. and Weitekamp, E. (2001) 'Bridging the American/European contexts: interventions, communities, youth groups, and moral panics', in M. Klein, C. Malcolm, H.-J. Kerner, C. Maxson, and E. Weitekamp (eds), *The Eurogang Paradox. Street Gangs and Youth Groups in the US and Europe*. Dordrecht: Kluwer Academic, pp. 325–38.

Klein, M. and Maxson, C. (2006) *Street Gang Patterns and Policies*. Oxford: Oxford University Press.

Macilwee, M. (2006) *The Gangs of Liverpool: From the Cornermen to the High Rip: Street Gangs in Victorian Liverpool*. Weigh Green, Lancashire: Milo Books.

Mares, D. (2001) 'Gangstas or lager louts? Working class street gangs in Manchester', in M. Klein, C. Malcolm, H-J. Kerner, C. Maxson and E. Weitekamp (eds), *The Eurogang Paradox. Street Gangs and Youth Groups in the US and Europe*. Dordrecht: Kluwer Academic, pp. 153–64.

Marshall, B., Webb, B. and Tilley, N. (2005) *Rationalisation of Current Research on Guns, Gangs and Other Weapons: Phase 1*. London: UCL Jill Dando Institute of Crime Science.

Martinez, R., Jr. and Lee, M.T. (2000) 'Immigration and crime', in G. LaFree, R.J. Bursik, Jr., J.F. Short, Jr. and R.B. Taylor (eds), *National Institute of Justice Criminal Justice 2000: The Nature of Crime: Continuity and Change* (vol. 1). Washington, DC: National Institute of Justice, pp. 485–524.

McLagan, G. (2006) *Guns and Gangs: The Inside Story of the War on Our Street*. London: Allison and Busby.

Measham, F., Aldridge, J. and Parker, H. (2001) *Dancing on Drugs: Risk, Health and Hedonism in the British Club Scene*. London: Free Association Books.

Medina, J. and Aldridge, J. (2004) 'Identifying Gangs in a Large English City: Measurement Criteria and Conflicting Accounts', Paper presented at the European Society of Criminology Conference, August (Amsterdam).

Moore, J. (1991) *Going Down to the Barrio. Homeboys and Homegirls in Change*. Philadelphia: Temple University Press.

Moore, K. (2003) 'E-heads vs. beer monsters: researching young people's drug consumption in dance club settings', in A. Bennett, S. Miles and M. Cielslik (eds), *Researching Youth*. London: Palgrave.

Newburn, T. (2002) 'Atlantic crossings: "policy transfer" and crime control in the USA and Britain', *Punishment and Society*, 4(2): 165–94.

Office of the Commissioner for Human Rights (2005) *Report by Mr. Alvaro Gil-Robles, Commissioner for Human Rights*, on his visit to the UK 4–12 November 2004. Brussels: Council of Europe.

Parker, H. (1974) *View from the Boys*. London: David and Charles.

Patrick, J. (1973) *A Glasgow Gang Observed*. London: Eyre Methuen.

Peach, C. (1996) 'Does Britain have ghettos?', *Transactions of the Institute of British Geographers*, 21(1): 216–35.

Pitts, J. (2008) 'Describing and defining youth gangs', *Community Safety Journal*, 7: 26.

Sanders, W. (2002) 'Breadren: exploring the group context of young offenders in an inner city English borough', *International Journal of Comparative and Applied Criminal Justice*, 26(1): 101–13.

Sanders, W. (2005) *Youth Crime and Youth Culture in the Inner City*. London: Routledge.

Semyonov, M., Raijman, R. and Gorodzeisky, A. (2006) 'The rise of anti-foreigner sentiment in European societies, 1988–2000', *American Sociological Review*, 71(3): 426–49.

Sharp, C., Aldridge, J. and Medina, J. (2006) *Delinquent Youth Groups in England and Wales*, Online Report 14/06. London: Home Office.

Sullivan, M. (1989) *Getting Paid: Youth Crime and Work in the Inner City*. Ithaca, NY: Cornell University Press.

Sullivan, M. (2006) 'Are "gang" studies dangerous? Youth violence, local context and the problem of reification', in J.F. Short and L.A. Hughes (eds), *Studying Youth Gangs*. Oxford: AltaMira Press, pp. 15–36.

Taylor, I. and Wall, D. (1976) 'Beyond the skinheads: comments on the emergence and significance of the glam rock cult', in G. Mungham and G. Pearson (eds), *Working Class Youth Culture*. London: Routledge and Kegan Paul, pp. 105–23.

Thompson, T. (1995) *Gangland Britain*. London: Coronet Books.

Thompson, T. (2004) *Gangs*. London: Hodder.

Thornton, S. (1995) *Club Cultures: Music, Media and Subcultural Capital*. Cambridge: Polity.

Tilley, N. and Bullock, K. (2002) *Shootings, Gangs and Violent Incidents in Manchester: Developing a Crime Reduction Strategy*, Crime Reduction Research Series Paper 13. London: Home Office.

Vigil, D. (2002) *A Rainbow of Gangs: Street Cultures in the Mega-City*. Austin, TX: University of Texas Press.

Wacquant, L. (2004) 'Penal truth comes to Europe: think tanks and the "Washington consensus" on crime and punishment', in G. Gilligan and J. Pratt (eds), *Crime, Truth and Justice*. Cullompton: Willan, pp. 161–82.

Walsh, P. (2003) *Gang War: The Inside Story of the Manchester Gangs*. Chatham: Milo Books.

Part II

Migration and street gangs

Chapter 4

Mexican migrants in gangs: a second-generation history

James Diego Vigil

Gang researchers have long maintained that street gangs and groups emerge in the second generation of an immigrant population (Bogardus 1926, 1943; Vigil 1990, 2002b; Waters 1999). This chapter will address why this is the case, using Mexican-American gangs in Los Angeles as a prime example. An examination of the second generation in the Mexican-American, or any immigrant, population should include an historical dimension to examine why gangs became a problem in this phase of adaptation.

The central issue is the importance of time, place, and people in the assessment of what factors affect the second generation. While the immigrant parents adjust to a new place and source of livelihood, the children also are acculturating and, for many, theirs is an erring acculturation. Focusing on how and why changes materialise in one time period and not others, and where and when these changes emerge with the second generation for Mexican-Americans will allow for comparisons with other ethnic groups and other parts of the world. To make this assessment, the author has been observing and interviewing urban street youth for over three decades in various urban, rural, and suburban communities. In most instances, the studies have been longitudinal and provide insights over time in different places.

In each time period, place, and cultural milieu of an immigrant people, there are questions of access, exposure, and identity to the dominant culture that need to be addressed, such as the following. Do newcomers live near members of the dominant culture? Are public institutions the same in immigrant enclaves as they are in more upscale areas? What are the processes of identification with the new culture? The Mexican immigrants to southern California mostly settled in distinctive areas apart from members of the majority culture. But those who settled in rural enclaves were much more spatially separate and visually distinct. In contrast, those Mexicans who lived in urban enclaves had readier access to the dominant culture. Further, public institutions were much more accessible in the urban areas. Obviously, the processes of identification were markedly improved in the urban realm, for those able to avail themselves of the opportunity. Unfortunately, for many that was never the case.

Generally speaking, upon initial contact there are common problems that befall all immigrants during adaptation to a new country. First, the cultural transitional process is fraught with many potential pitfalls based on linguistic and cultural differences. Second, both adults and, especially, children undergo culture shock; the children more so since they must reconcile the culture of the dominant society (schools particularly) and that of their parents as they navigate their way through this new world. Finally, aside from the difficulties of cultural transition and culture shock, externally imposed barriers based on poverty forces and racism on their own can overwhelm immigrant parental stability. Some of the rural enclaves of early Mexican immigrants were so poor, the families barely survived, and the racism was so blatant that separate schools and limited social outlets seriously undermined acculturation opportunities.

In examining these adaptation features, we can better understand the integration or disintegration of immigrant groups as they adjust to a new society and culture. Most importantly in this regard, what is the association between adaptation difficulties and the rise of street gangs? Only a fraction of the youth population in these groups become street socialised and gang members, about 10–20 per cent (Morales 1982; Vigil 1988a, 1988b, 1996). In research starting in 1970, the author has been looking at immigrant adaptation, focusing on high-school students and youth in the greater east Los Angeles area. This investigation has been expanded to include other areas of southern California (Vigil 1997, 1999, 2004). Before and since the initiation of this study, there have been important changes in the status of Mexican immigrants and their children, and in the street gangs that have become a part of their lives.

First, there have been variations in the rate and direction of acculturation for the second generation since the 1920s, when the first critical mass of Mexicans began to arrive and settle in the USA. 'Americanisation' was then the predominant public policy for minority and immigrant populations, so a type of coerced assimilation was the path dictated to most immigrants during this period. There was a double bind to this policy, however. Newcomers were expected to drop all their ethnic baggage in becoming Americans, but, simultaneously, restrictions and barriers (social and residential segregation based on 'race', often hostile police, job discrimination, and so on) were placed in their way. The result was an intense marginalisation of the people, especially the youth, and the first stirrings of street-boy gangs surfaced (Bogardus 1926). After World War II, major changes were in store, as discriminatory barriers began to relax, particularly in urban areas. The 1950s brought the Chicano GI generation, who pushed for more change. With the civil rights movement and the War on Poverty of the 1960s, most of the government-imposed obstacles were challenged and removed. The gang problem was also considerably curtailed by prevention and intervention policies that addressed the needs of Chicano youth. Unfortunately, gangs subsequently became a more serious issue than even before when law enforcement suppression strategies began to supplant intervention efforts.

In the meantime, by the 1980s, other acculturation strategies were marked out for the children of newcomers. In contrast to earlier years, massive immigration in the contemporary period, combined with a more assertive Chicano ethnic identity inculcated by the events of the 1960s and 1970s, eventually became a torrent of 'Mexicanisation'. These changes increased the possibility and utility of a bilingual/bicultural identity for both Mexican immigrants and Mexican-Americans. At the same time, there were now many Anglicised Mexicans, third and fourth generation, and an entrenched street subculture became rooted in many areas of southern California. In this new context, the second generation still had to wade through and reconcile other problems, including those of poverty and lingering racism as well. Worse yet, the street gangs had by that time become a part of the immigrant youth's acculturation experience. After the 1980s, the street gang problem worsened.

Thus, the Mexican-American second generation and the gang phenomena associated with that generation reflect the dimensions of time, place, and people. Here, 'time' refers to the chronological developments in the social and economic conditions that are shaped by political forces and historical events. 'Place' denotes the regional variation in behavior and material circumstances, as well as how those factors differ in urban, suburban, and rural locales. Finally, 'people' refers to class, cultural, and racial differences. Each of these

51

dimensions applies to both the host and donor populations involved in the immigration phenomenon.

Time

Mexican immigration has ebbed and flowed since the 1920s. In certain time periods, American capital required cheap, expendable labour, and the rush was on for more Mexicans. However, in other time periods, racism and antiforeign hysteria reared its head again, with widespread efforts to keep Mexicans out. All government efforts and media campaigns to stem the tide of Mexican immigration have largely failed, however. At the end of the War on Poverty, right when more programs were needed and a culturally sensitive integration strategy was just starting, massive immigration overwhelmed the USA for several decades. Today, over one-half of the Mexican population of close to 40 million is first or second generation, a fact that, in large part, accounts for the critical mass and growth and expansion of gangs in this population. Further, high poverty rates and anti-immigrant hysteria continue to thwart acculturation efforts. Unlike other white ethnic groups in the nineteenth and twentieth centuries that also had gangs, a constant influx of Mexicans has ensured that there would always be plenty of second-generation children that become cultural marginals (those betwixt and between donor and host cultures) and find their way into gangs.

Critical avenues for access, exposure, and identification with the dominant culture were either blocked or considerably curtailed in the first decades of Mexican immigrant adaptation to the USA. Integration to the mainstream US culture through assimilation and the Americanisation learning programs in schools was the common strategy in vogue then. As noted, however, the dominant society's racist attitudes and practices prevented this integration process from occurring. Schools, restaurants, public facilities (e.g. swimming pools, movie houses), and, especially, neighbourhoods were segregated. Mexican settlements were clearly set apart from Anglo neighbourhoods and resources.

Mexicans initially came to the USA to labour in the fields, ranches, mines, railroads, and other light industries, and fashioned a settlement pattern that was common for newcomers in earlier immigration eras. As unskilled, low-paid workers, they settled close to the worksite in rural areas and established ethnic enclaves in undesirable locations in the city (Vigil 1988a). Worksite thus determined living site. Barrios

(Mexican neighbourhoods) sprung up all over the Southwest (territory that was part of Mexico before being taken away by the USA in mid-nineteenth-century wars). These barrios were small appendages to the mainstream-developed residential and commercial areas, with old, dilapidated homes, inferior amenities, and a sense of separation marking these enclaves.

Visually distinct in their dreary, worn-out appearance and spatially separate from a society into which they were supposed to be integrated, these barrios began to spawn street gangs. Key to the emergence of gangs was the racism and poverty noted above, but also the issue of cultural conflict. Mexican language and customs contrasted sharply with those of the Anglo, setting in place a clash of cultures that demeaned the newcomers' way of life while placing the dominant culture on a superior ledge. Although most immigrant men and women were able to abide the insulting assumptions of the 'gringo majorities' and make the best of their limited opportunities, typically they remained just a misstep away from social and economic crisis.

Separate schools for Anglo Americans and Mexicans were for decades blatantly unequal in facilities and resources, seriously undermining the educational, and thus, social mobility aspirations of the newcomers. The children of immigrants, the second generation, were especially affected. Since that time the educational status and trajectory of subsequent generations has been effectively slowed and undermined (Telles and Ortiz 2007). To reiterate, it is the second generation that suffers the most, given the transitional cultural phase it is in. Cultural transition processes often involve exchanging cultural values and practices, and if the conditions for this important phase are left unmet, there are voids and gaps that are replaced later by other socialisation experiences. During this time, home and school socialisation fell short, and street socialisation began to predominate.

Street socialisation has been a pivotal process historically. Beginning in the 1920s, a significant number of the parents had difficulty in adapting and struggled to gain and keep jobs. Often, both parents had to seek work, and when the Great Depression hit in the 1930s, matters worsened. There was a major repatriation effort to send Mexicans (including some US citizens) back to Mexico. Crowded housing conditions increased as families moved in together to make ends meet. Parenting habits from the old country were disrupted under these new US situations. As a result, the first families of the immigration waves were the ones initially to lose control of their children. Within the next two decades, the street socialisation process had taken its toll and begun to generate a permanent street group, the gang. Thus, the first gangs were boy gangs that were largely mischievous in nature, but with time, the gang took on a more ominous orientation. Today, as previously mentioned, it is a street fixture in certain neighbourhoods that all youth must confront, and to which they must adjust.

One interesting development was the cultural marginalisation of children who spoke Spanish at home, but were forced to, and punished if they did not, speak English in the schools. Thus, in addition to the social strains and economic stressors, cultural and linguistic difficulties added to the burden, which children particularly had to bear. An additional issue in this context is the mismatch between the aspirations of the children (made aware of America's opportunities by their school experiences and exposure to popular media) and their expectations, with the latter much lower as a result of the experience of exclusion and isolation suffered by the population (Buriel 1984).

Most children weathered this cultural morass in time, but a sizeable minority were caught betwixt and between cultures, and created a 'cholo' street culture (a blend of the two, buttressed by the street experiences). This cultural adjustment made for an alienated and antisocial second generation. When breakdowns in social control occurred in stressed families, and ineffective schooling and policing practices exacerbated the strains, the children of immigrants began to be raised on the streets. Street socialisation forged a new path, and for some individuals this newly minted subculture began to dominate their lives. In effect, the values and norms of the street under the aegis of a multiple-aged peer group took root.

Interestingly, with each wave of immigrant groups following one another on the shores of America, it was the second generation of each wave that was most likely to undergo the cultural alienation and street socialisation leading to a gang life, even in the contemporary era. Early studies of this adaptation experience detailed all the barriers and obstacles that the Mexican population faced, clearly showing how access was blocked, exposure minimised, and identity strivings thwarted in 'becoming American' in this hopelessly convoluted way (Bogardus 1926, 1934; Taylor 1934). 'Americanisation' was merely a meaningless slogan, and the resources and facilitators for this program were minimised, as, instead, obstacles and barriers kept the people distant and isolated. Because of such discriminatory segregation practices, one author outlined how the children fared as new Americans, in a classic academic article, 'Gangs of Mexican American Youth' (Bogardus 1943). What had started out as children of immigrants in the 1920s (Bogardus 1926) had now become, in the second generation, street gang youth, the dramatic culmination of which was the 'Zoot Suit Riots' of 1943 (Mazon 1985; McWilliams 1969). The latter Los Angeles affair placed the gang problem on the front pages for several days, as American servicemen and 'pachucos' (a street style of Chicano gang members) battled it out. In the aftermath, civic leaders and government officials stepped in to address the 'youth' problem by developing prevention and intervention programs, a strategy that lasted for a decade or more.

As the decades passed, and with the waning of youth programs, the gang problem grew and worsened, with steady immigration ensuring that there would always be a second generation from which the gang would recruit. Meanwhile, many of the earliest immigrants and their children moved out of the barrios and up the socioeconomic ladder, as discriminatory and segregation attitudes and practices softened and were eliminated. By the 1960s, the War on Poverty temporarily slowed these gang developments, but with its end a decade later, gangs again flourished. In Los Angeles, other ethnic groups also sprouted gangs, particularly the African-American population that over several decades had moved into the city. Coming mostly from rural areas in the South, they had experienced their own version of the second generation (Frazier 1939; Thomas 1997). With government programs to alleviate poverty and its effects sharply curtailed, there was an explosion of Crips and Blood gangs in the 1970s (Vigil 2002a).

Time is only one factor to consider, however, as we must turn to place and people to complete our analysis. For the Mexican people, additional developments have contributed to the proliferation of gangs.

Place

For most newcomers, both pre- and post-immigration, places influence their readiness for acculturation and help prepare them for a new setting and culture (Gamio 1969a, 1969b). Along the Mexican-US border, for instance, residents on both sides are familiar with the language and some cultural practices of the other side. This more expansive power of place connection would help explain ready access, exposure, and identification with the dominant culture before immigration. In fact, a bigger development based on place is the growth of Mexican sister cities from small pueblos to major urban sites in just 50 years.

Tijuana, Mexicali, and Juarez are such urban areas on the Mexican side and, through the process of diffusion, gang culture (that is, dress, language, signs, activities and other features of the cholo lifestyle) has spread from the USA and affected Mexican youth. This has been spurred in part by a constant flow of immigration where children come to the USA, stay for a time, and return home, having learned the gang culture (Valenzuela 1988). Moreover, immigrants from these border cities have already been marginalised in poverty-stricken enclaves in their home country. When they arrive in the USA, the process is exacerbated by the presence of street gangs in the barrios into which they move. Another factor is the circular cycle of immigration (people going to and from the USA). Gang culture has also diffused to the interior of Mexico, as far south as Chiapas and Oaxaca, regions from which many of today's immigrants come. One of the interesting results of this relationship is that many Mexican youth arrive in the USA already socialised in gangs. Known as the 1.5 generation (because, although born elsewhere, they came of age in the USA), they have added to the pattern initially established by the second generation.

During each immigration period, the immigrant group represented different places in Mexico, and recently they have migrated to different places in the USA. In early waves, these were mostly rural mestizos (mixed Indian and Spanish), and they came to settle in rural colonias (colonies) and urban barrios, largely in the southwest USA. Later waves were more mixed in region of origin and racial makeup, until the present, in which there is a large influx of indigenous peasants from southern Mexican states leaving their land for the USA. The latter have settled all over the USA, including large congregations in the Midwest, the East Coast, and the Southeast (Smith 2005). Thus, urban, rural, and regional variations in US settlement patterns are common for Mexicans today. Again, different acculturation routes and ways to access and identify with Anglo American lifestyles mark the experience. Even though gangs are rampant in many cities of these regions, cities have tended to be more conducive to integration than rural areas. Suburban locations are an even greater accelerator, when families in subsequent generations move from barrios and aspire to a better life in the USA and desire to assimilate faster. In short, these are place factors that can hinder or 'kick-start' acculturation opportunities. In other words, urban and suburban locales and settings in greater Los Angeles, as well as housing conditions and access to public amenities, are necessary correlates to cultural change processes.

Different time and place factors have resulted in considerable heterogeneity among immigrants, and the situations and conditions that aid or hinder adaptation. These variations are reflected in a number of ways, as in how they are integrated (or marginalised and disintegrated!) into a society. For the cultural marginals, the experience leads to street gangs in places such as public housing developments and different types of urban and rural enclaves. Persistent and concentrated poverty coupled with cultural breakdowns, rather than cultural resistance, is responsible for this marginalisation, especially in the second generation. These youths find themselves alienated and isolated from employment opportunities, and many public institutions – schools in particular – push and kick out such cultural marginals, adding even more to the critical mass of street children who join gangs.

Even with the diffusion of gangs to Mexico and the groundswell of immigration that created the 1.5 generation, it is still true that the second-generation phenomenon characterises the contemporary gang experience. In a recent study of a Mexican-American gang in a public housing project, this author identified all the gang members of a cohort (Vigil 2007). Foreign-born parents were very common, as 69 per cent of fathers and 92 per cent of mothers were first generation. Of 35 gang members who were surveyed, about 70 per cent were second generation. The most interesting fact is that those gang members who were born in a foreign country (Mexico or Vietnam) had arrived here as very young immigrants (4–8 years of age), and thus approximate a second-generation group, recognised as 1.5 generation immigrants. Thus, these findings seem to support the stance usually taken by researchers that gangs are generated most often in the second generation (Vigil 1988a, 1990; Waters 1999).

People

Strewn throughout the time and place discussions were allusions to the people, meaning the class status, cultural attributes, and racial makeup of each immigrant wave and settlement area. Although time and place are easier to document, ferreting out these status issues of people is a much more difficult task. In the early waves, most of the immigrants were mestizos (mixed Indian and Spanish racial heritage), characterised by the variation of white to very dark brown skin colour. For most of the first half of the twentieth century, this was the case. Since the 1970s, the increase of indigenous (meaning much more Indian in features and colour) immigrants has added 'colour' to the Mexican-American population. What this simply means is that, on several levels, Mexicans who appear more European have had an easier time of gaining access to, exposure to, and identification with Anglo American culture: (1) assimilation paths are open to them; (2) they are less likely to be stigmatised; (3) their self-confidence is increased; and so on. Conversely, the medium- and darker-hued Mexicans, as persons who obviously stand out in American society, experience the opposite effect. Detectable colour distinctions have always made a difference for Mexicans, including those who become gang members (Vigil and Lopez 2003).

Race and racism have thus made a difference, but also important are the class and cultural characteristics of a people. Throughout the span of immigration from Mexico, most of the people have come from humble stock, agricultural and service workers predominating. The few highly educated and trained ones came mostly during the period right after the Mexican Revolution of 1910, because they were political refugees rather than economic ones. Put another way, these people were strongly characterised as rural peasant or small town employees in Mexico and thus were unable to settle in upscale communities or seek better-paying jobs for the highly trained. This was particularly true at the beginning, when housing and educational segregation kept these 'people in their place'.

When cultural customs and traditions are factored into the equation, matters become more complex. Language background and usage is a good example to focus on for the moment, since it has already been mentioned as a problem source. Mexican language habits in the early decades were a mix of Spanish and one or another indigenous dialect, as the country was barely rectifying the acculturation strains left over from the colonial period. It was only after the 1910 Revolution that the Mexican government initiated a concerted Spanish language-learning program for most of the rural, peasant, indigenous or mixed mestizo population of villages and towns. Even today, in some highly indigenous areas of southern Mexico, one can find villages that have primarily maintained a Maya or Zapotec language base as they speak some form of Spanish.

What this means is that many immigrants of these early time periods were caught in a double acculturation bind. In the midst of reconciling the incomplete remains of culture contact and conflict (that is cultural transitional and culture shock experiences) from the Spanish and, later, Mexican governments, the immigrants to the USA had to undergo another level of acculturation. Such cultural transition and culture shock actions and episodes have been outlined already. Imagine what is going on in the minds of young children of the second generation, not yet familiar with the native country tongue and subjected to another language during a time when school authorities in the USA practiced a severe type of language and cultural suppression. Is this what Durkheim was talking about in another context when he used the word 'anomie' (normlessness)?

With the passage of time and with economic problems worsening in Mexico, the character and makeup of the people have changed. Today, there is, as noted, such a high rate of immigration, mostly undocumented, that it is well near impossible for US institutions (again, especially schools) to incorporate so many children, especially since settlement occurs in already highly affected neighbourhoods. Schools are overburdened and understaffed, and it is no wonder that the syndrome of 'pushing', 'kicking', and 'dropping' out of school has marked the lives of the second generation (suspension, expulsion, and leaving school completely are the technical terms for the range of disaffiliation with education). As recently as the 1970s, gang members in Los Angeles numbered about 50,000 individuals, including Mexican-American and other ethnic groups (Vigil 1988a). Today, there are at least 100,000 gang members in Los Angeles alone, not counting some of the other towns and cities in the greater megalopolis area (Vigil 2002a). Traditionally, a problem in the second generation, where it remains a problem, the new phenomenon of the 1.5 generation has now added to the argument that acculturation difficulties are at the root of the gang problem, perhaps even worthy of consideration at the international level. Waters (1999) has argued that immigrant children turn aggressive, and perhaps to the streets, when a demographic swell, such as we have here with the many millions of immigrants, considerably reduces the good jobs and power positions available, in turn, creating a different type of strain.

Conclusion

How can we apply the lessons of the Mexican experience of the second generation and the rise and perpetuation of street gangs during this adaptation phase? First, when do we establish the situations and conditions of immigration as a starting point in order to determine what transpired in the second and third generations? Second, what barriers and obstacles exist, especially culture conflict ones that prevent access to, exposure to, and identification with the dominant culture?

Finally, have gangs of street youth emerged in other contexts worldwide, especially Europe? The latter, like other parts of the world, has benefited from the labour and work of immigrants for decades, but as the second generation becomes more prominent, does this portend problems with youth generally, and specifically for those who are street socialised?

Research is beginning to show that such dynamics of immigration, integration, disintegration, marginality, and the rest reflect the situations and conditions in other parts of Europe, and, for that matter, the world (Davis 2006). Similarly, the rise of street gangs and street groups can be traced to such sources, highly represented by the second generation. In Amsterdam, we have the Moroccans; in Germany, the Turks and Palestinians; and, more recently, in Barcelona, Spain, the Latin Kings. In short, immigration, adaptation, integration (or disintegration), and marginality, among other macrofactors, have all affected whether there have been access to, exposure to, and identification with the dominant culture. We are still in the early phases of the European experience and have to wait until more research is completed to gauge the time, place, and people developments of each nation. In the meantime, policymakers and government officials can learn from the lessons and mistakes of others (Klein and Maxson 2006) and begin to fashion prevention and intervention strategies that can soften the effects of culture contact and conflict for the children of immigrants generally, and particularly for the second generation.

References

Bogardus, E. (1926) *The City Boy and His Problems*. Los Angeles: House of Ralston, Rotary Club of Los Angeles.

Bogardus, E. (1934) *The Mexican in the United States*. USC Social Science Series, No. 8. Los Angeles: University of Southern California Press.

Bogardus, E. (1943) 'Gangs of Mexican American youth', *Sociology and Social Research*, 28: 55–6.

Buriel, R. (1984) 'Integration with traditional Mexican American culture and sociocultural adjustment', in J.L. Martinez and R. Mendoza (eds), *Chicano Psychology*, 2nd edn. New York: Academic Press.

Davis, M. (2006) *Planet of Slums*. London: Verso.

Frazier, E.F. (1939) *The Negro Family in the United States*. Chicago: University of Chicago Press.

Gamio, M. (1969a) *Mexican Immigration to the United States*. New York: Arno Press.

Gamio, M. (1969b) *The Mexican Immigrant*. New York: Arno Press.

Klein, M. and Maxson, C. (2006) *Street Gangs Patterns and Policies*. Oxford: Oxford University Press.

Mazon, M. (1985) *The Zoot-Suit Riots: The Psychology of Symbolic Annihilation*. Austin, TX: University of Texas Press.

McWilliams, C. (1990 [1949]) *North From Mexico: The Spanish Speaking People of the United States*. New York: Praeger.

Morales, A. (1982) 'The Mexican American gang member: evaluation and treatment', in R. Becerra, M. Karno and J.I. Escobar (eds), *Mental Health and Hispanic Americans*. New York: Grune and Stratton, pp. 133–52.

Smith, R. (2005) *Mexican New York: Transnational Lives of New Immigrants*. Berkeley: University of California Press.

Taylor, P.S. (1934) *An American Mexican Frontier*. Chapel Hill, NC: University of North Carolina Press.

Telles, E. and Ortiz, V. (2007) *Racialized Ethnicity*. New York: Russell Sage.

Thomas, P. (1997) *Down These Mean Streets*. New York: Vintage.

Valenzuela, J.M. (1988) *A la Brava ese!: Cholos, Punks, Chavos Banda*. Tijuana: El Colegio de la Frontera Norte.

Vigil, J.D. (1988a) *Barrio Gangs: Street Life and Identity in Southern California*. Austin, TX: University Texas Press.

Vigil, J.D. (1988b) 'Group processes and street identity: adolescent Chicano gang members', *Ethos*, 16(4): 421–45.

Vigil, J.D. (1990) 'Cholos and Gangs: Culture Change and Street Youth in Los Angeles', in R. Huff (ed.), *Gangs in America: Diffusion, Diversity, and Public Policy*. Beverly Hills, CA: Sage, pp. 116–28.

Vigil, J.D. (1996) 'Street baptism: Chicano gang initiation', *Human Organization*, 55(2): 149–53.

Vigil, J.D. (1997) *Personas Mexicanas: Chicano High Schoolers in a Changing Los Angeles*. Belmont, CA: Wadsworth, Thomson Custom Publishing, 2002 (originally published: Fort Worth, TX: Harcourt Brace, 1997).

Vigil, J.D. (1999) 'Streets and schools: how educators can help Chicano marginalized gang youth', *Harvard Educational Review*, 69(3): 270–88.

Vigil, J.D. (2002a) *A Rainbow of Gangs: Street Cultures in the Mega-City*. Austin, TX: University of Texas Press.

Vigil, J.D. (2002b) 'Community dynamics and the rise of street gangs', in M.M. Suarez-Orozco and M.M. Paez (eds), *Latinos! Remaking America*. Berkeley, CA and Cambridge, MA: University of California Press and David Rockefeller Centre for Latin American Studies, Harvard University, pp. 97–109.

Vigil, J.D. (2004) 'Gangs and group membership: implications for schooling', in M. Gibson, P. Gandara and J. Koyama (eds) *Peers, Schools, and the Educational Achievement of U.S.-Mexican Youth*. New York: Columbia Teachers College Press, pp. 87–106.

Vigil, J.D. (2007) *The Projects: Gang and Non-Gang Families in East Los Angeles*. Austin, TX: University of Texas Press.

Vigil, J.D. and Lopez, F. (2004) 'Race and ethnic relations in Mexico', *Journal of Latinos and Latin America Studies*, 1(1): 49–74.

Waters, T. (1999) *Crime and Immigrant Youth*. Thousand Oaks, CA: Sage.

Chapter 5

Latin Kings in Barcelona

*Carles Feixa, Noemí Canelles, Laura Porzio,
Carolina Recio and Luca Giliberti*

The aim of this chapter is to present the first results of research about Latin American young people in Barcelona and their presence in the city's public life.[1] In recent years, there has been a surprising increase of the Latin American youth in the city, as in all Spain; at the same time, generally a negative social image has been constructed of Latin American youths. Since 2003, the 'discovery' of the 'Latin gangs' by the media and their configuration as criminal gangs has generated processes of moral panic and stigmatisation concerning all Latin American young people. The specificity of this process has been that, beyond the reality of Latin gangs, a distorted image of young immigrants of Latin American origin living in Barcelona has been produced. In this chapter, we will discuss the process of social construction of Latin gangs in Barcelona, underscoring the role played by the media. We will try to analyse the nature and the meanings of those groups, questioning their configuration as gangs and defining them as *gangs-in-process*. At the same time, we will outline some basic patterns of youth sociability to construct theoretical references to understand and explain Latin street organisations in Barcelona. We will present, too, the alternatives pointed out in the local institutions between their repression as (illegal) criminal organisations and their recognition as (legal) youth associations. In the meantime, we will produce general discourses about the situation of Latin American youngsters in Barcelona, their resettlement problems, and their processes of identity construction.

The research started at the beginning of 2005 and was initially focused on Latin American youth in general living in Barcelona. Gangs were not the only focus, but it was important to know their impact through the discourses of Latin American teenagers and of some other adults interacting with them (teachers, families, social educators, members of associations, journalists, policemen, etc.). This first phase of fieldwork was conducted in 2005–6 and included around 30 individual interviews with boys and girls of different Latin American countries, five focus groups at secondary schools (in which another 30 youngsters participated), 30 interviews with adults, media analysis, and participant observation in public spaces such as schools, parks and streets. The methodology, in this way, was constructed by a combination of techniques, including life histories of teenagers, in-depth interviews of adults, group discussions, participant observation, and document analysis. The research process allowed contacting the leaders of the local branches of Latin Kings and Nietas, which were going through important transformations at that time. The results here presented correspond to that first stage of the research.[2]

In Spain the information about Latin gangs is limited, as public institutions, such as schools and police departments, have not yet begun to gather data that would in any way aid our understanding of this relatively new phenomenon. Instead there is a flurry of print and television reportage that pretends to have uncovered the causes and effects of the youth street problem, labelling it a gang one. Our paper intends to refute the media stance on Latin youth, and what by now has become public opinion, by presenting a variety of qualitative data that suggest that the street youth who presently exist in Spain's cities comprise an incipient group-based entity and not yet gangs, the latter a criminal-oriented unit that is defined by the Eurogang research organisation (of which the senior author is a member). Labelling theory, in this case conceived as an extension of social constructionism (Berger and Luckmann 2005), drives our description and interpretation of the facts on street youth; we are speaking about hybrid identities that cannot be understood with a simplistic point of view, but only with a multiperspective vision (Brotherton and Barrios 2003; Cannarella et al. 2007; Feixa et al. 2006; Nilan and Feixa 2006; Queirolo Palmas and Torre 2005). The purpose is that our observations, interviews and analysis can begin to set the groundwork for an improved understanding of Latin groups and perhaps the generation of conscious policy strategies.

Gangs-in-process

> We're not a gang, but a nation of organised people.
>
> (Interview with a member of Latin Kings)

The Colombian teenager Ronny Tapias was murdered in Barcelona on 28 October 2003, when he was walking out of his high school and after he had been the victim of an act of aggression committed by a group of teenagers and young adults. According to the subsequent police investigation, the murder was an act of revenge by gang members (the Nietas), who had supposedly mistaken Ronny for a member of another gang (the Latin Kings), with whom they had had a fight some days before in a dance club. This case resulted in the 'discovery' by the news media of this phenomenon, from then on referred to as 'Latin gangs', and led to a wave of moral panic that has not yet ceased. Nine Ecuadorian and Dominican young people, three of whom were minors, were arrested after a month and charged for the crime. The minors were tried and convicted (the alleged principal of the crime was among them). The trial of the other six (over age 18) took place during the two first weeks of April 2005. It was a big media event with deep and widespread coverage. Gangs were a constant issue during the trial, both as real organisations and as media constructions that went beyond the facts of the case. Due to this event and others that followed in Madrid and Barcelona, together with the media overreaction, a criminalised image of Latin American youth was created; this image focused primarily on male masculinity, and it promoted the association of most immigrant teenagers with 'Latin gangs'.

In relation to the Eurogang definition,[3] we argue that most of the youth groups of migrant origin that we have been studying are only *gangs-in-process*. That is, there are group-like networks and behaviours at an incipient phase, even if the media tend to identify them with the criminal and durable organisations similar to the North American gang pattern. In this case, there are street-oriented youth groups, with names, symbols and long-established traditions, composed of youngsters of deprived social backgrounds. Some of their members have connections with illegal activities, even if those activities are not part of the core group identity. There is an ambiguity in the ordinary use of the Spanish world *'banda'* (gang) by the media and experts: it includes delinquent boys, informal street groups, music and fashion lifestyles, local formal networks, and transnational migrant organisations. The most interesting thing is that, nowadays, this concept tends to be related only to young people of Latin American origin, forgetting the long-established presence of youth gangs in Spanish urban history (Feixa 1998; Feixa *et al.* 2006).

In 2005, the Catalan police detected over 20 different groups in Barcelona and its metropolitan area that could be included in the 'Latin gang' classification, with around 2000 members. This represented not more than 5 per cent of the youth population of Latin American origin (even if the public perception was that 'all Latin youngsters are involved in gangs'). A minority of them had been in contact with penal institutions (sentenced or with other justice measures), but this seems to relate to individual or small-group criminal activities not related to the gang identity. Nevertheless, after Ronny Tapias' death, popular perception tended to identify these groups as equal to youth organisations commonly labelled as 'transnational gangs'. Names such as Latin Kings, Nietas, Black Panthers, Vatos Locos, and Mara Salvatrucha were present in the area and seemed to connect the local gang situation to the American urban ghetto. But it was not clear whether these were only 'labels' or 'branches' related to their 'Motherland' (be it Chicago, Quito, or Tegucigalpa).

Members of these groups mainly are Latin American, in particular Ecuadorian, but with an important percentage of natives, or even members, coming from non-Latin countries such as Morocco, Russia or Equatorial Guinea. The majority are male, but an important number are female. These groups seem to be stable over time. In relation to the Eurogang definition, we cannot say that the involvement in illegal activities is part of their group identity. The fact that some of them may be involved in illegal activities is not connected to membership, but to the street policy and economy to which these adolescents and young adults are mostly subordinated. The reason these groups exist can firstly be understood through the feeling of membership that links these adolescents together in a structure of sociability, resembling a *second family*. The use of the word *hermanito* ('little brother') shows the dimension of brotherhood in an organisation whose main goal is not to commit crimes, but to provide some help through the fact of sharing their difficult daily life in terms of protection, identity construction, and feelings of affection (Brotherton and Barrios 2003; Cannarella *et al.* 2007; Feixa *et al.* 2006). Latin Kings and Nietas in Barcelona represent a social reference in construction of an identity and allowing them to feel their own presence in a dynamic context.

To be a member means feeling part of 'a family, with our own rules, our own structure, our own constitution' (interview of a local leader of Latin Kings).

The relationship of the researchers and authorities with those groups helped them to become youth associations, and they were recognised by the Catalan government in August 2006 (Latin Kings) and February 2007 (Nietas). This means that those two groups agreed to refuse violence, elaborated 'statuses' to be presented to the authorities, collaborated with other institutions (such as churches and migrant adult associations), accepted mediation by the police and social workers when problems arose, and promoted cultural activities such as sports and hip-hop concerts. This process was followed with great interest by several international institutions and news media (such as the BBC the *Chicago Tribune*, *Le Monde*, etc.). As participant observers, we are now investigating the modalities and consequences of this process.

The construction of Latin Gangs by the media

The fear of violent youth street gangs is already a reality.
(*La Vanguardia*, 2 November 2003)

The role played by the media in this scenario is extremely important. As we mentioned, in the case of Barcelona, the issue of Latin gangs was unveiled due to Ronny Tapias' death. This tragic event became a suitable element for them to generate a body of news about gangs. First of all, it should be taken into account that mass communication media are a powerful tool for configuration of social imaginaries. They have the power to choose the images and to decide how they approach every different subject. The media have helped to create a particular idiom and a particular image of the migration process and, in this particular case, they have created a distorted image of Latin American youth, since basically they have offered information about criminal events that threaten citizens' security. It also needs to be taken into account that those are people who have been through a migration process, so the stigmatising factor is more important, as the group of poor immigrants have already gone through a process of media construction that identifies them with social exclusion and conditions of social danger. In the words of Queirolo Palmas (2005), there is a process of stigmatisation (violent groups), ethnic discrimination (immigrants), and symbolic violence.

Although Ronny Tapias' murder is usually taken as a referent, the first news related to Latin gangs was published in Madrid and Barcelona in early 2003. Small incidents attributed to these groups (fights between groups of young Latin Americans) were used by the media to construct and represent a certain image of gangs to form public opinion. A stereotype was being created about the groups of young Latin Americans that were allegedly occupying public spaces in big cities. In September 2003, one month before Ronny Tapias' death, some news was released about the existence of Latin street gangs in Barcelona. The news came from the police and warned the public: 'A dangerous youth gang has been identified by the Barcelona police. Local and region police state that the gang recruits young people and commits aggression' (El Periódico, 10 September 2003). At the same time, certain news reports explained what the gang was like, and this description has been a crucial element in the creation of gangs by the media: it presented a young man with a black bandana wrapped around his head, dressed in gold, black and blue, listening to hip-hop music, and tattooed with a crown (in the case of Latin Kings). This way it was easy to identify the members of these groups. Beyond the looks, organisational aspects were also reported (hierarchic and pyramidal structure) as well as their violence (towards the members of their own gang, towards members of rival gangs, and towards other people). The death of Ronny Tapias fostered an increase in news about gangs. On the one hand, news reports described the facts (how Ronny died, who killed him, and what caused the crime); on the other hand, some editorials about gangs were published: 'The growth of youth gangs increases the need for police presence. Secondary schools that have both immigrant and native children are undertaking a huge task on their own, without any support or social recognition, by turning these teaching centres into laboratories for coexistence and dialogue' (El Periódico, 30 October 2003).

Later, the interest in gangs increased due to three events: the murder of a 23-year-old Venezuelan in Sants in November 2004 (attributed to one of the Latin gangs in the city), a fight between Latin American youngsters in La Sagrera in December 2004, and the beginning of the trial in Ronny Tapias' case in April 2005. The media reporting contributed to build a certain image of gangs in several ways. First, media information is based mainly on police and court sources: 'The police have observed a growth of rival street gangs in the last months. A few months ago, urban policemen seized from a car the diplomas that the gang LK [Latin Kings] award their members after taking an oath and undergoing a series of ordeals' (El Periódico, January 2004).

Such reporting has obviously reinforced the relationship between gang and offence. In a world where the perception of insecurity is increasing, this fact only further stigmatises these young people. We found different approaches, according to the political and ideological tendency of each media outlet, but they all promote an image of Latin-American street gangs as a new form of youth violence that is starting to trouble our society and that is becoming a public security problem: 'The danger of gangs. Barcelona is becoming an insecure city for its inhabitants' (20 Minutos, November 2004).

Second the media give the image of a newly arrived youngster who cannot fit in the receiving society. So the image citizens get is that of a misfit and antagonistic young person who is scaring native young people and taking over public spaces: 'Young people with serious problems of social integration, coming from dysfunctional families with a high rate of school dropouts evidence lack of control and absence of rules of behaviour' (El Mundo, July 2004). The role played by free newspapers distributed Monday to Friday in key centres of the city (the underground, central squares) cannot be underestimated. These are places frequented by commuters, so those newspapers reach many people, even the ones who do not usually buy any newspaper. This type of press tends to give very short, tabloid-style pieces of information, which can easily contribute to creating an even more negative image of these groups of young people: 'Six of the gangs in Barcelona, share the aim of "conquering territory"' (Qué! 18 January 2005), or 'They move following the underground railways and they fight for the control of stations' (20 Minutos, 14 February 2005). Finally, the role of certain sensationalist private TV shows, similar to reality shows, is also significant, as police hypotheses are taken as facts. This subject has attracted the attention of the Sunday issues of serious newspapers (such as El País Semanal) and even erotic magazines (such as Interviu). This creates a permanent doubt: it seems difficult to deny the existence of these groups, but it is important to question the role of the media in spreading the news and in magnifying the phenomenon. In short, apart from reproducing the facts, the media also reinterpret and create a reality that has consequences in the real world in terms of social, employment, and relational opportunities for youth, and effects on self-perception and the construction of identity.

Linked to the idea of 'Latin gangs' is an ignored reality: the thousands of boys and girls of Latin American origin who have been coming to Barcelona since the late 1990s through different processes of family reunification, exiled from their hometowns and social networks at one of the most difficult moments in their life (the always complicated transition to adult life), facing alarmed adults at their destination (over-employed mothers, often absent fathers, insecure teachers and social workers, and fearful neighbours), and being placed on the edge of crime. Latin American migration to Spain increased in the 1990s with a female-dominant composition. Those women first travelled alone and created transnational families. After 1999, thanks to a new reunification state policy, their sons and daughters, educated in their countries of origins with grandmothers and other family members, arrived in Spain. This presence becomes disturbing when linked to new forms of youth identities, crossing geographical borders, that we still confuse with traditional gangs; identities with subcultural pasts, nomad present and a future to be constructed.

Latin American young people in Barcelona

They came here looking for a better future, running away from the ghosts they left behind.
(Speech by the public prosecutor in the Ronny Tapias trial)

Members of these alleged gangs come from different Latin American communities of origin settled in Barcelona since the mid-1980s. At that time, Spain became one of the most important destinations for immigrants, most of them coming from its former colonies. Among the factors that foster the arrival of Latin American immigrant contingents, most of them Andean and Caribbean, are the internationalisation of the Spanish economy; the profound socio-political changes; the globalisation of its main cities, Barcelona among them; and the restructuring of the labour market. The beginning of the twenty-first century would be marked by the migration from different Latin American countries with women as the first step of the migration chain. This feminisation turned migration into a transforming process with profound implications for family structure. In an international migrating context, there is a readjustment in the generation and gender relationships affecting the negotiation of ties within the domestic unit and influencing the modalities of family reunification and the experiences of children from migrant families, both at the places of origin and the places of settlement.

Between 2001 and 2004, the number of immigrants in Barcelona multiplied by two or even three, depending on nationalities.

Nowadays, Ecuadorians are the most representative group (about 32,000), along with Colombians (13,000), Peruvians (13,000), and Dominicans (7000). The largest adolescent immigration comes from South America (about 12,000 under 14 years old and about 15,000 15–24 years old), although there has been an increase of Caribbean youth, especially those 15–24 years old (about 25,000). If we add up the ones living in dormitory areas in greater Barcelona, we can assume that there are over 50,000 Latin Americans under 25 living in the city and its surroundings. But this is not a homogeneous group, since it includes women and young people with individual migration stories, and younger boys and girls, and adolescents reunited with their parents. Generally speaking, some deficiencies in the host system can be observed at school, in employment, at the leisure level, etc. Situations of traumatic schooling processes, difficulties in accessing the labour market, lack of involvement in sports or leisure facilities, etc., are often found. Furthermore, there is a lack of space in their houses, and they lack both access to other spaces and a viable legal status. Consequently, the marginalisation of these groups is alarming, especially considering that those teenagers are arriving at an age on the borderline between compulsory education and the minimum age for employment; they are legally in Spain, but are not allowed to work (they usually have a residence permit, but not a work permit). Integration policies developed by local administrations in this sense do not seem to go beyond declarations of intention and have not managed to fill the gaps for minor-aged immigrants.

In the life histories of young people, the feeling of uprootedness is reflected in a sort of nomad story based on the contrast between here and there. Unlike other stories from diasporas, essential in this case is that the decision to migrate was not made by the subjects, but by their families, and it is often an imposition that breaks primary socialisation networks. The young interviewees describe their experiences as students, as workers or simply as paperless in a foreign country, comparing their experiences here and their experiences there. Living here in limited housing contrasts with their description of their former houses, always with patios or little gardens with trees, where they could play. Another element of divergence arising during the interviews is the difficulty they find in adapting to the Catalan educational system. The need to re-create a similar community to the one they left behind is strong, and all the young interviewees agree that they search for their friends among Latin Americans. Besides, they feel it is a betrayal to leave their own community to 'integrate' in the local community:

There were three of us and then Rolando started to drift apart ... I don't understand him; he's got like ... he doesn't like to be seen like an Ecuadorian. He pretends he's from here. For instance, he started to dress like ... the typical Spaniard, with close fitting clothes, thin, all white, with this pointy hair ... he chose this way of dressing, this style. I don't know; I know he's not really like this, but he started to pretend. He also changed the way he talked and started talking like the people here; he changed his friends too. Now he only goes with Spaniards. (interview with J., a boy from Ecuador)

The search to be identified and recognised as Ecuadorians and to feel different from the Catalan or Spanish young people is constant. For Javier, for instance, wearing baggy clothes and a bandana tied round his head is a sign of being an Ecuadorian. This is why certain looks or musical tastes should by no means be identified with delinquent or violent attitudes. A common element in some of the interviews is that the spectacular cultural, bodily and musical demonstrations of these young people were created in the host country, and not in their country of origin. Interviews show that young Latin Americans move in and take over the public space, creating and interpreting an identity that distinguishes them from the rest of the young people and characterises them as members of their community. This process does not mean that these young people are members of gangs, or that their attitudes and lifestyles are particularly violent or criminal. In fact, there are cases when their arrival in Catalonia is a chance to gain awareness of the role that gangs play in their communities of origin in order to leave behind their most negative effects.

From interviews, it can be inferred that there are different types of insertion of these young people into their current socio-cultural environments. First, their migration process can either be voluntary or forced by a relative; they can follow regular (legal) or irregular (illegal) ways of family reunification; it could happen in the late 1990s or more recently; at an early age (under 12) or during adolescence (during their secondary education) or in their youth (without the possibility of school integration), etc. One young girl explained to us, as a way of complaint, 'I didn't decide, my mother did.' Second, they have different family situations: they can live with their parents who look after them or only with their mothers; in a house on their own or sharing a house with other families; with social networks of support or isolated; etc. Third, their host environment can be in neighbourhoods mainly inhabited by immigrants, or mixed; they can go to school or not; they can see their stay at school as a bonus or as a punishment; they can be legal immigrants or not; they can work in the legal economy or the underground economy, or not work at all; etc. Finally, they may belong to a street organisation, or they may have belonged in the past, or they may not belong to any. They can be active members or just sympathisers; participate in activities or live full-time within the group; subscribe to a symbolic universe or just share some iconographic elements; have a relationship with local boys and girls or just with immigrant young people; etc. The crossroads of each of these possibilities can lead to different subcultural solutions.

Subcultural traditions, hybrid identities

> Our aim is to protect and to ensure the cultural existence of the Latin people and our ancestors.
>
> (Latin King Bible)

The cultural identities of the young people we just described emerge in a border area where, on top of the hegemonic culture and the parental cultures, various subcultural traditions meet. These are hybrid identities that correspond to the youth cultures in the age of information, where local and global, American and European, face-to-face and virtual traditions meet in the same path. Among them, we can outline four basic patterns of transnational youth sociability (Brotherton and Barrios 2003; Matza 1973; Nilan and Feixa 2006), which can help us to construct theoretical references to understand and explain Latin hybrid street organisations in Barcelona.

First there is the *North American tradition*, which includes the experience of the street organisations and whose origin can be found in the gang model. This one is historically linked to the urbanisation process of the USA and the process of symbolic recovery of the original ethnic identity by second and third generations of young people whose parents or grandparents migrated. All of this was translated into a model of the territorialised gang, highly structured and basically masculine, studied by classical urban ethnographers (Thrasher 1927; Whyte 1943). Over time, there has been a change towards more complex and non-territorial forms of sociability (Klein et al. 2001; Vigil 2002).

Second, there is the *Latin American tradition*, represented by the model of the *pandillas*. *Pandilla* is the Spanish word for 'gang': this could be a criminal or marginal organisation, but also an informal, innocuous group of friends. The *pandillas* have a specific way of inhabiting the cities; they live in neighbourhoods with precise geographical borders. They are born and develop in the middle of exclusion and discrimination (racist, cultural, classist), openly denouncing them. They react to silenced and denied conflicts through criminality, defying the established order. Paradoxically, they are also an emotional structure: they are structured for everyday meeting and dialoguing, facing loneliness and fear. They cannot be reduced either to heroes (or victims) or to villains (or criminals). The *pandilla* constitutes basically a social group that displays regularly two kinds of behaviours: aggressive confrontations and material and/or symbolic solutions for their members. These solutions are extreme in response to the amount of strain derived from unsatisfied basic needs and the persisting processes of stigmatisation (Reguillo 1991; Salazar 1990; Valenzuela 2002).

Third is the *transnational tradition* represented by subcultural youth styles, known as *urban tribes* in Spain. Although these young people might have had access in their places of origin to some of these styles already internationally diffused (like punk or hip hop), it is after arriving in Barcelona or Genoa that they became associated with the globally mediated youth scene. They meet the local tradition, represented by existing neighbourhood gangs and more or less traditional youth associations. Yet, on the connections and disconnections between migrant youth cultures from different origins, so far we have information on conflict interactions only, not creative exchanges (Feixa 1998; Queirolo and Torre 2005).

Fourth is the *virtual tradition* represented by youth identity models circulating on the Internet. In this case, more than subcultural (or cybercultural) traditions, strictly speaking, they happen to be new communicative spaces that become the message and the means at the same time. On the one hand, the Internet is a space for information and consumption that disseminates and amplifies those new identity discourses: from telephone boxes in the neighbourhoods where these youngsters live (shared with adult immigrants and native young adults), they can access Latin Kings websites, Web logs about *'la vida loca'*, and forums about gangs. On the other hand, the Internet has globalised gangs, allowing them to become logos that, like brands (e.g. Nike or Levi's), transcend legal consumption borders (franchises) and illegal ones (mafias). Those 'post-industrial gangs' are no longer strictly territorial groups with a fixed structure, but 'nomad' identities that mix cultural elements from the origin countries, the host countries, and the transnational styles circulating on the Internet and the media generally (Hagedorn 2001).

The Latin Kings appeared in Chicago at the end of World War II when different, smaller Latin American gangs amalgamated. The gang network – a complex confederation of local groups – was renamed in 1986 in Collins Correctional Facility (New York State) as *Almighty Latin King Nation* by Luis Felipe ('King Blood'); in 1991, a female version, the *Latin Queens*, was added. A series of cultural productions was created – manifestos, magazines, websites – and the group moved from a primarily prison base to the streets of American cities. By the 1990s, the *Latin Kings* had evolved from a criminal to a political organisation, focused on the claiming of Latin identity and the condemnation of police brutality. International expansion followed national diffusion – Latin America and then Europe. The original Latin Kings had become a sort of transnational franchise with multiple 'glocal' connections (Brotherton and Barrios 2003; Cannarella *et al.* 2007; Kontos 2003). In the 1990s, the Latin Kings gang was established in Ecuador and other Latin American countries (for example, Colombia and the Dominican Republic), due to gang members returning to the country of origin and the compulsory repatriation of Latin American immigrants from USA. After 2000, they arrived in Madrid, Barcelona, Genoa and other south European cities, following the transnational migration and family reunification processes. The Latin King nation was reborn in Spain and its transformations in this new land have also affected its origins; for instance, the recognition process in Barcelona generated different reactions in Quito and Chicago.

Conclusions

In the context that we analysed, 'gangs' can be considered a symptom of personal or unhealed social injuries and also of symbolic resistance to assimilation (or even healthy efforts of self-organisation). Both young people and organisations face the reactions from alarmed adults with whom they coexist daily: mothers and fathers exhausted after long working days, overstressed educators who do not know about the school system in their places of origin, and neighbours threatened by their haunting presence in parks and squares (the neighbours who also used the same urban spaces, today paved in asphalt, when they were young). Latin gangs cannot be considered as representative of the new Latin American generation in Europe, but their presence in Barcelona is undeniable, although there is not yet enough information to appreciate their nature, significance, and scope. The press, the public educators and professionals who deal with young people do not seem to share the same point of view.

On the one hand, certain commonplace assumptions remain unquestioned: gangs are criminal associations comprised of young immigrants; it can be inferred from this that to be young, with darker and indigenous features, and therefore immigrant, means to be suspected of sympathising with a gang, and therefore to be a thief or a murderer. On the other hand, there are many doubts, unknowns, and questions about the strategies of action as well as about the real scope of the phenomenon. Current research provides evidence that there are different modalities of identification with the gang: to look for cultural referents to express and represent youths' own identity as Latin without getting totally involved in the organisation; to join as a full member and follow the group's rules and patterns; or to become involved in criminal activities thanks to the action of agents external to the group, often adults involved in drug trafficking or other illicit activities.

Besides, the later experience of Latin Kings and Nietas in Barcelona as legal youth associations opens new perspectives and poses many questions about their political and cultural aspects, not always considered under the label of 'gang'. Are those groups, then, gangs? The question is open. It is these young and adult people, their organisations, their fears and their hopes, with which our research aims to deal in the future. This research will not be able to reproduce the stagnant models of the old community studies, as it will have to experiment with transnational, networking ethnography, and it will have to be able to look into the flow of life in twenty-first-century cities. Thus far, our material shows ambiguity, symbolic contradictions and cultural conflicts with respect to the groups' identity and to the institutional reactions. It is too early to conclude whether those groups are *real* gangs or what we may call *gangs-in-process*.[4]

Notes

1 The research was promoted by Barcelona City Council – Prevention Services. The results are published in Feixa (dir.), Recio and Porzio (eds) (2006). We are grateful to the peer reviewers for their comments and to James Diego Vigil for his help in adapting the text to an international academic audience.

2 The second phase of fieldwork, conducted in 2006–7 and at present under way, is focused on the main youth street organisation (the Latin Kings and Queens), collecting several life histories, in-depth interviews, questionnaires, gang literature, etc. This second phase, focused on the process of becoming a 'legal' association, is not analysed in this chapter and will be the topic for future articles.

3 'Any durable, street-oriented youth group, whose involvement in illegal activities is part of their group identity' (www.umsl.edu/~ccj/eurogang/euroganghome.htm).

4 This idea has been proposed by J.D. Vigil (personal communication).

References

Berger, P.L. and Luckmann, T. (2005) *La Construcción Social de la Realidad*. Buenos Aires: Amorrurtu.

Brotherton, D.C. and Barrios, L. (2003) *The Almighty Latin King and Queen Nation: Street Politics and the Transformation of a New York City Gang*. New York: Columbia University Press.

Cannarella, M., Lagomarsino, F. and Queirolo Palmas, L. (eds) (2007) *Hermanitos: Vita e Politica della Strada tra i Giovani Latinos in Italia*. Verona: Ombre Corte.

Feixa, C. (1998) *De Jóvenes, Bandas y Tribus: Antropología de la Juventud*. Barcelona: Ariel.

Feixa, C., Porzio, L. and Recio, C. (eds) (2006) *Jóvenes Latinos en Barcelona: Espacio Público y Cultura Urbana*. Barcelona: Anthropos.

Hagedorn, J.M. (2001) 'Globalization, gangs, and collaborative research', in M.W. Klein, H.-J. Kerner, C.L. Maxson and E. Weitekamp (eds), *The Eurogang Paradox: Street Gangs and Youth Groups in the U.S. and Europe*. London: Kluwer Academic Publishers, pp. 41–58.

Klein, M.W., Kerner, H.-J., Maxson, C.L. and Weitekamp, E.G.M. (eds) (2001) *The Eurogang Paradox: Street Gangs and Youth Groups in the U.S. and Europe*. London: Kluwer Academic Publishers.

Kontos, L. (2003) 'Between criminal and political deviance: a sociological analysis of the New York chapter of the Almighty Latin King and Queen Nation', in D. Muggleton and R. Weinzierl (eds), *The Post-Subcultures Reader*. London: Berg, pp. 133–50.

Matza, D. (1973) 'Subterranean traditions of youth', in H. Silverstein (ed.), *The Sociology of Youth: Evolution and Revolution*. New York: Macmillan, pp. 252–71.

Nilan, P. and Feixa, C. (eds) (2006) *Global Youth: Hybrid Identities and Plural Worlds*. London: Routledge.

Queirolo Palmas, L. and Torre, A.T. (eds) (2005) *Il Fantasma delle Bande: Giovani dall'America Latina a Genova*. Genova: Fratelli Frilli Editore.

Reguillo, R. (1991) *En la calle otra vez: Las Bandas: Identidad Urbana y Usos de la Comunicación.* Guadalajara: ITESO.

Salazar, A.J. (1990) *No Nacimos Pa Semilla: La Cultura de las Bandas en Medellín.* Bogotá: CINEP.

Thrasher, F.M. (1927) *The Gang: A Study of 1,313 Gangs in Chicago.* Chicago: University of Chicago Press.

Vigil, J.D. (2002) *A Rainbow of Gangs: Street Cultures in the Mega-City.* Austin, TX: University of Texas Press.

Valenzuela, J.M. (2002) 'De los Pachucos a los Cholos: Movimientos Juveniles en la Frontera México-Estados Unidos', in C. Feixa, F. Molina, and C. Alsinet (eds), *Movimientos Juveniles en América Latina: Pachucos, Malandros, Punketas.* Barcelona: Ariel, pp. 11–34.

Whyte, W.F. (1943) *Street Corner Society: The Social Structure of an Italian Slum.* Chicago: University of Chicago Press.

Chapter 6

Gangs, migration, and conflict: Thrasher's theme in The Netherlands

Frank van Gemert and Jantien Stuifbergen

Introduction

Lonsdale is an English brand of sports clothing. Currently in The Netherlands, these clothes are worn by youngsters in street groups, a number of whom sympathise with the extreme Right. The first reports on Lonsdale groups stem from the mid-1990s. In recent years, these groups are mentioned in relation to clashes with ethnic minority groups and antimigrant actions such as the arson of mosques. Since the mid-1980s, Moroccan boys have been over-represented in police statistics, and there have been repeated reports of gang formation among this group. These Moroccan gangs seldom pick fights with other groups. On the other hand, they are known to come into conflict easily with people around them. Therefore, apart from individual criminal activity, the main problems these groups pose are related to nuisance. These are the two, quite different, faces of street gang problems in The Netherlands. Other kinds of gangs may exist, but it is safe to say that, to date, they are less manifest.

In his monumental study of gangs in Chicago, Frederic Thrasher ('The Gang', 1927) provides an interesting perspective for new research questions to study these phenomena and their relation to migration. He speaks about gangs as 'interstitial groups', meaning a group that finds itself in a gap between bigger entities. This concept can be interpreted in several ways. First, Thrasher, as a representative of the Chicago school, points to the spatial distribution of crime over the city. 'Gangs flourish in the areas that are interstitial to the more settled, more stable and more organised parts of the city' (Thrasher 1927: 22). Next, he mentions adolescence as 'a manifestation of the period of readjustment between childhood and maturity' (Thrasher 1927: 37). This is a phase where youths find themselves in a social interstice between the institutions of home, school, and work. Migration can be seen as a third interstice, which leaves people accommodating between two worlds and easily fits into his reasoning. In early-twentieth-century Chicago, and elsewhere, migrants constituted an important factor in the gangland population.

According to Thrasher (1927), because of their interstitial nature, most gangs are in a state of unstable equilibrium. They easily come into conflict with other gangs because they challenge each other's privileges, goods, or turf. Conflicts with society arise because the gang does not abide by conventions (Thrasher 1927: 26). These conflicts pose a threat to the gang, but they can also strengthen group cohesion. In the process of conflict, members unite and boredom vanishes. 'Conflict with other gangs and the world about them furnishes the occasion for many of their exciting group activities' (Thrasher 1927: 37). Not surprisingly, the core of Thrasher's (1927: 57) definition refers to these elements: 'A gang is an interstitial group originally formed spontaneously, and then integrated through conflict.' Even though Thrasher was one of the first gang researchers, and his work has been superseded by an enormous amount of diverse gang research, his concepts are still useful. The perspective of gangs as interstitial groups in conflict raises new research questions.

This chapter about street gangs in The Netherlands focuses on the conflicts these groups experience. Two basic questions, 'conflicts with whom?' and 'conflicts about what?', make it possible to come to a typology. The central question, however, is about distribution. Why are specific types of groups in conflict found in certain contexts? This issue is in two ways related to migration. First, migrant youth play a dominant role in gangs in The Netherlands (conflicts with whom?). Second, the conflicts in which these groups are involved, often, directly or indirectly, relate to migration issues (conflicts about what?). In the final paragraph, we will discuss whether these groups conform to the Eurogang definition of a gang.

To answer the central question of the distribution of different types of gangs, we rely on several different sources of data. We refer to criminological publications and to other sources that shed light on gangs and youth groups in Dutch cities. Apart from scientific accounts, a large number of newspaper articles and over a dozen policy reports constitute the data on which this chapter is based.

Gang typologies and conflict

Several gang typologies have existed in American gang literature. Cloward and Ohlin (1960) made a distinction between criminal, conflict, and retreatist gangs. Yablonski (1962) talked about gangs as being of a delinquent, violent, or social type. Rosenbaum and Grant (1983) mentioned fighting and moneymaking gangs. Huff (1989) introduced the types hedonistic, instrumental, and predatory. Taylor (1990) spoke of scavenger, territorial, and corporate gangs. Maxson and Klein (1995; see also Klein 2001) designed a typology with traditional, neotraditional, compressed, collective, and speciality gangs. These typologies derive from research by different methods, and all attempt to define relevant and workable categories of gangs. The Netherlands lacks a tradition of gangs; youth groups do not seem to exist for a long period, as do some of the American counterparts. Furthermore, scientists and policymakers use the term *jeugdbende*, the Dutch equivalent of 'gang', only with reluctance (van Gemert 2007). When groups are identified, it seems like a Pavlov response to state immediately that 'these are not like American gangs'. Because people tend to refer to false American stereotypes, Klein (2001) labelled this 'the Eurogang paradox'. A typology to use in this chapter should serve the purpose of describing the distribution of groups in conflict and help explain links with migration. Simply adopting an existing American frame will not work. Keeping in mind Dutch reality, as we know it, we use Thrasher's principles as a theoretical starting point.

To understand gangs, fundamentally one must consider that they are groups (Klein and Maxson 2006). Thrasher referred to group dynamics when he said that gangs integrate through conflict. He did not have in mind quarrels that individual members are engaged in, but he meant the process in which cohesion between group members grows as a result of a common adversary outside the group. Groups are a social phenomenon and, as a consequence, always dynamic. Transformations can occur through which groups end conflict, or move from one conflict to another. Conflicts with whom? Conflicts about what? To answer these questions, to a certain extent, we have to generalise and portray groups in conflict in a way that may seem static. This is a result of the fact that the transformations are not rapid changes that occur daily. On the contrary, conflict brings cohesion and stability, and groups focus on certain conflicts. Who is the enemy? This is may be the most relevant question when it comes to gang formation, and this is what Thrasher underscored. The conflicts in which gangs are involved make them stronger, and more active, and shape group identity.

Gangs fight other gangs. The well-known 1957 musical *West Side Story* by Bernstein offers a clear example of fighting gangs. In the story, the established American gang, the Jets, is confronted by the Sharks, a Puerto Rican gang of newcomers. Probably better known among youth today are the conflicts between Crips and Bloods. These stereotypical West Coast gangs also fight each other, but neither of the two can claim to have been there first. The conflict of which the musical offers an example puts forward a clear difference between the two rivals: seniority. The established group is challenged, may feel threatened, and can lose its dominance to the newcomers. 'Things will not be the same anymore.' It is likely that they also resist the idea of having to share, but as we see it, the key issue is not just material but also emotional. It is about fear and feeling unsafe. Newcomers are unwelcome, and according to the first group they are inferior and should have fewer rights (compare Elias and Scotson 1976). The second conflict is a clash between equals: between groups that are alike, of the same kind. These rivals know each other, and typically symbols that stress difference become important. Here, seniority plays no role. The central issue is material by nature. It is about scarcity, be it of turf, girls, or drug income. The first conflict can be called 'White versus Black', while we, because of the biblical similarity of fighting brothers, refer to the second as 'Cain versus Abel'. The White-versus-Black-type can include groups with racial differences, but we aim for an abstract and more general distinction between the conflicting groups.

Gangs fight gangs, or they can have conflicts with other parties. In some publications, gangs are described as part of the community in which they play a positive role. They are portrayed as a social club and may get involved in local politics (Whyte 1943), or they may guarantee security and act as a militia (Jankowski 1991). More often, however, the relation with the neighbourhood is negative. Gangs may commit violent acts, and demand protection money, and some have been described as scavenger gangs (Taylor 1990). These gangs claim or stand up to authority. Although other conflicts, especially the Cain-versus-Abel type, include parties from outside the neighbourhood, here we see a 'conflict within the neighbourhood'. This is how we label the third type.

It may be clear that the first two types are easy to recognise, in so far as they involve two fighting groups and the result may be violence. A large number of international cases that fit the first two types have been documented (e.g. the non-American accounts by Björgo 2005; Bradshaw 2005; Lien 2005; Mares 2001; see also other chapters in this volume). The third type does not necessarily have a link to violence, and it seems as though it is found less often.

It can be argued that the three types cannot comprise the whole spectrum of gangs in conflict. What about gangs that have specialised in certain criminal activities, such as breaking and entering, or street robberies? What to think of gangs that use illegal drugs or have political goals that they achieve through illegal means? We think that nowadays in European countries other types also exist. 'Speciality gangs' and 'cultural rebels' may be additional types to complete the typology. The question of whom these groups are in conflict with points in a different direction. These are not fighting gangs, and the enemy is not tangible. Both types can be considered to have, on a more abstract level, a conflict with society. The cultural rebels are seen as expressive and their activities are related to leisure time. The speciality gangs, on the other hand, are composed of members who specialise in certain illegal acts; they are instrumental in nature. In this chapter, however, we merely introduce these typologies in order to bring across and explain the most prominent features of Dutch gangs. The typologies are not definitive, and we emphasise the first three types (Table 6.1).

In the last decade, youth groups have drawn additional attention in The Netherlands. In the mid-1990s, gangs calling themselves Crips, whose members committed mainly violent street robberies and rip deals, were identified in The Hague and Rotterdam (van Gemert 1998a; van Stapele 2003). Recently, in the cities of Amsterdam, Tilburg, and Leeuwarden, new groups have surfaced that call themselves 'Bloods' and make fierce statements on the Internet. Even though American West Coast gangs offer attractive role models, and media attention is extensive when gang symbols are displayed, it seems that the type of Cain versus Abel is far less prevalent than the other two conflict

Table 6.1 Typology of groups in conflict (with whom? about what?)

Types	Cain vs Abel	White vs Black	Conflict within neighbourhood	Speciality gangs	Cultural rebels
With whom?	Groups that are alike, equal	Groups that are different, unequal	Citizens, police, shopkeepers	Society	Society
About what?	Scarce goods	Fear, safety	Authority	Instrumental	Expressive

types. In the following paragraphs, two phenomena that are specific to the current Dutch situation will be described in more detail.

Moroccan nuisance

Youth groups that hang around the street can cause problems. One might argue that these youngsters do what they have always done, and that being on the street cannot be considered a crime. There is no denying this logic, but, on the other hand, and especially in recent years, Dutch citizens have made it clear again and again that they perceive youth groups in their neighbourhoods as a very serious problem that deserves police priority (Bervoets 2006; Hoenson 2000; SAMS 2004; Wittebrood 2006). To understand this, one must know more about the details of this nuisance, as well as about the context in which this has emerged.

In Diamantbuurt, a neighbourhood in Amsterdam, a group of Moroccan boys that used a small square as their hang-out had a number of quarrels with a couple who lived in a house on the corner of the square. The couple, who later became known as Bert and Marja, were getting frustrated, but they were also afraid, because their complaints about litter, loud noise, and impolite behaviour were met with intimidating threats or worse. Their car was vandalised, their windows were smashed, and their house was burgled. The police and municipality were informed, but no effective measures were taken. Because they felt there was nothing else to do, in October 2004 Bert and Marja went to *De Volkskrant*, a national newspaper, and offered for publication the diary in which they had written down every incident, from day to day. The media exposure that followed was massive, but personal help for the couple was small. As intimidation increased, they felt unsafe and decided to move. Ever since, the Diamantbuurt case has been a *cause célèbre* when it comes to Moroccan groups that clash with citizens on a neighbourhood level. The dynamics of conflicts like these include nuisance and intimidation, but also social isolation and group processes (De Jong 2007; van Gemert and Fleisher 2005).

Moroccan boys are disproportionately involved in conflicts such as these. This became clear after an inventory was made of youth groups and gangs in Amsterdam (van Gemert 2005). In the Eurogang expert survey, 85 groups were found, 39 of which can be considered gangs according to the Eurogang definition. From the estimated total number of members in all 85 groups, 56 per cent were Moroccan boys. The percentage of Moroccan members was even higher in the 39 gangs: 63 per cent (ibid.:163). This is by no means a reflection of the number of Moroccan inhabitants in the city, which is around 10 per cent (www.os.amsterdam.nl/tabel/10153/). These Moroccan members were sometimes found in groups of mixed ethnicity, but more often they belonged to groups mainly composed of Moroccan males.

Not just in Amsterdam but also throughout The Netherlands, Moroccan boys have become known for their involvement in these conflicts within neighbourhoods. Slotervaart in West Amsterdam was the scene of a disturbance in February 1998, and ever since the whole western part of the city has been associated with problems related to this ethnic group (de Jong 2007). The same association applies to the neighbourhood of Kanaleneiland in the city of Utrecht, and, to a somewhat lesser extent to Schilderswijk in The Hague, and to neighbourhoods in the city of Gouda (Bervoets 2006).

The conflicts are focused on nuisance, which means that, according to the law, this aspect of group behaviour cannot be considered a serious crime. Still, it is clear that these incidences have a strong impact on the citizens involved. Furthermore, the fact that Moroccan boys are involved so often in these conflicts becomes more significant when coupled with another phenomenon. In the mid-1980s Moroccan boys drew attention because of high crime rates (Junger 1990), figures which have been confirmed repeatedly on national and local levels ever since. Ethnographic studies have documented social context, cultural elements, and group processes that help explain this phenomenon (de Jong; van Gemert 1998b; Werdmölder 1990). Members of these groups often have criminal records, and are known to the police (de Jong 2007; van Gemert and Fleisher 2005). The conflict, however, is mainly about nuisance.

So, the large number of reports on neighbourhood conflicts, together with persistent high crime rates, has put Moroccans on the spot. Nowadays, it is not uncommon that Dutch politicians in public debate explicitly mention Moroccans when it comes to youth crime. In March 2002, not realising the microphone was still recording after a formal interview, the Amsterdam alderman Rob Oudkerk used the word *Kutmarokkanen*. The reactions to this very derogatory expression, which can probably best be translated as 'fucking Moroccans', were diverse. Of course, there was no denying that he used the word, so he apologised in public. More interesting was what Mayor Job Cohen added, expressing his concern: 'They are our *kutmarokkanen*.' Shortly afterwards, a rap song with the same title by Raymzter entered the charts and was a number one hit for weeks. *Kutmarokkanen* became a term for young Moroccans. This is but one example in a sequence of incidents that have become subject to public debate. Frustration, but probably also a search for excitement, motivated Moroccan boys that became violent in a demonstration against the war in Iraq (April 2002). On a later occasion they vandalised houses and looted shops after a demonstration that was organised when a Moroccan man was killed by a police bullet (August 2003). More recently, when the Moroccan soccer team played against The Netherlands, Moroccan youngsters stormed the field and vandalised the stadium (May 2007).

Key incidences of a different nature include the killings of two public figures. Pim Fortuyn was a new politician, who, in the aftermath of 11 September 2001, was the first Dutch politician to present a democratic-nationalist and antimigrant agenda. According to the polls, he was very successful in the campaign for the national elections, when he was shot in May 2002. A common first reaction was, 'I hope it was not a Moroccan.' It was not. The Dutch environmental activist Folkert van der Graaff killed Pim Fortuyn. Relief did not last long, however. Theo van Gogh was killed in November 2004. As a columnist, van Gogh had been very critical of Islam, and he directed the film *Submission*, an anti-Islam cinematographic statement written by Ayaan Hirschi Ali. Mohammed Bouyeri, a young man from Moroccan decent born in Amsterdam, shot van Gogh and ritually slit his throat before he was arrested. Later it became clear that he was part of a radical group, but the killing of Theo van Gogh seems to have been a solo action.

A number of Moroccan boys commit crimes and fuel conflicts – this much is clear – but probably a much bigger number do not get involved in such things at all. However, on a national level, Moroccan boys as a group are stigmatised. In some Dutch cities more than others, conflicts within neighbourhoods are being labelled an ethnic problem: a Moroccan problem. Most Moroccan families live in poor neighbourhoods and their unemployment rate is high. Therefore, there clearly is an element of class in the problem, and in pointing to the Moroccans, one is 'blaming the victim'. This is probably true, yet, in The Netherlands, from a pragmatic standpoint, policymakers and others have looked for specific approaches to tackle the problem.

As stated, conflicts within neighbourhoods are mainly a matter of nuisance, and criminal law is ill-suited to minor offences. This complicates matters for the police, who, as law enforcers, seem almost powerless. Some cities introduced local arrangements, such as fines on drinking or smoking cannabis in public, to reduce the number of complaints by citizens and shopkeepers. In a different approach, the police tried to close the gap to the Moroccan community by improving communication, in hopes that this would also improve information gathering. Over the years, many policemen have enrolled in courses on intercultural communication, and a number even went to Morocco to get a 'feel' for where these boys come from. It is very hard to pinpoint the benefits of these efforts to broaden the horizon of policemen.

Over the years, local policymakers have introduced a large number of projects, ranging from simple shelters in which groups can hang out to the hiring of numerous youth workers, who were told to focus especially on Moroccan boys (van Gemert and Wiersma 2000). One specific initiative can be mentioned because of its Moroccan flavour. In 1998, a group of Moroccan fathers in West Amsterdam voluntarily started surveillance in their neighbourhood. These *Buurtvaders* ('neighbourhood fathers') hoped to impose social control by speaking to the Moroccan youths that hang out on the streets and trying to direct them to school or community centres for useful leiure activities (van Gemert 2002). This initiative won national and an international prevention prizes, and it has been replicated in many cities ever since, with the financial support of local government. In West Amsterdam the *Buurtvaders* are no longer out on the streets. As a daily routine, this is asking too much from volunteers. In December 2006 in West Amsterdam 'street coaches' have taken over the surveillance task. Unlike the neighbourhood fathers, these persons have no relation to the neighbourhood; they were selected because they possess different qualities. They are kick boxers, free fighters, or successful practitioners of other martial arts and therefore have 'street cred'. They are employed to be out on the street, to keep it calm, and to report problems. As a follow-up on their surveillance, a social worker can visit the home of (mostly Moroccan) children that have drawn attention in a negative way.

In summer 2007, there was a discussion in parliament about nuisance by youth groups in neighbourhoods. The proposed measures seem to have become stricter. Parents with children that cause trouble on the street may be forced to take a course in bringing up children. If they refuse, they get a financial sanction and lose part of their family allowance. Furthermore, the possibility of curfews in neighbourhoods was looked at, as was the introduction of instruments like the British ASBO (Anti-Social Behaviour Order). Even boot camps were mentioned.

Lonsdale

The recent phenomenon of youth groups that wear Lonsdale clothing and have extreme Right sympathies has its roots in the early 1990s. Then, a new youth style surfaced in The Netherlands: gabber. The word 'gabber' is derived from Hebrew and means 'friend'. Gabbers are different from other youth groups in appearance and music preference. Central to the emergence of this new style are dance parties where loud, monotonous electronic music is played with many beats per minute. This music is referred to as 'hardcore', and gabbers are known for endless dance sessions with quick repetitive movements: 'hakken'. In the beginning Ecstasy (XTC) was the popular drug on these occasions. Later the substance of these pills changed when more amphetamine was added to allow people to keep dancing for hours. Gabbers shaved their heads, and it is said they did so to avoid overheating during dance parties (van Wijk et al. 2007). They wore tracksuits of the brand Australian, bomber jackets, and Nike Air Max shoes. The peak of this gabber style was in 1997. It did not disappear, but nowadays it is less prominent. A certain group still likes hardcore, and they continue to use drugs.

Gabber style is typically a Dutch phenomenon, and maybe for this reason gabbers wear a Dutch flag on their coats or jackets. This flag was interpreted as a sign of sympathy for the political extreme Right, but it is unclear whether this initially was its purpose (Schoppen 1997; van Wijk et al. 2007). Later, the connection to the extreme Right became evident. A limited number of gabber youth started to wear other, more explicit symbols, such as swastikas and certain combinations of numbers that have an extreme right connotation (88 = HH = 'heil Hitler'). Wearing clothes of the Lonsdale brand, in The Netherlands, has also become an important mark of this orientation (AIVD 2005; van Donselaar and Rodrigues 2004). Youths claim that the brand name stands for 'Laat Ons Nederlanders Samen De Allochtonen Langzaam Elimineren' ('Let us Dutch together slowly eliminate ethnic minorities'). Nowadays, people mostly mean teenage gabbers with extreme Right or even racist ideologies when speaking about 'Lonsdale youth' or 'Lonsdale groups' (Cadat and Engbersen 2006). These Lonsdale groups can be seen as stemming from gabber style in the early 1990s (van Wijk et al. 2007).

The relation between the extreme Right and Lonsdale groups is complex and not always clear. van Donselaar and Rodrigues (2006) point to a process of radicalisation through which gabber youth may grow into separate groups of neo-Nazis. In comparison to Lonsdale groups in general, these neo-Nazis are better organised and have a more explicit extreme Right ideology, which allows the use of violence to reach its goals. This ideology focuses on positions in society, and sees migrants as newcomers that bring false competition to the labour market and introduce inferior cultural elements (compare Chapter 5, this volume).

Lonsdale groups seem to use a 'light version' of this ideology that is specially related to the arena of free time and to public space. In reports, Lonsdale youth state that they feel hampered and even besieged by migrant youth. The latter form groups that make them feel secure and they radiate an attitude that intimidates Dutch youth. Indeed, in recent research, Lonsdale youth repeatedly point to behaviour in public space. 'They are always in a group. They will bump into you on the street. They look jealous and they are frightening. They behave like they are more, like they are everything.' And also, 'they make a call, and then a whole group shows up. I am afraid of how they will react. It is like a party and a friend is going to bring two others. But then it turns out that when you get there, he has brought 30' (van Lith 2007). Moreover, Lonsdale respondents say migrant boys go after Dutch girls, while Muslim girls seldom enter discotheques in Dutch cities. Migrant youths also visit hardcore parties, but they do not come to dance to the music; they come to 'score' girls (van Wijk *et al.* 2007).

Gabber lifestyle and Lonsdale groups are about youth, but they cannot simply be defined as youth cultures. For youth cultures, in general, opposition to the older generation is a key element. Youth culture goes hand in hand with generation conflict. This does not fully apply to Lonsdale groups, however, because these youth and their parents seem to agree when it comes to migrants (Homan 2006; van Wijk *et al.* 2007). This became apparent after the killing of Theo van Gogh in 2004, an event that fuelled a very critical attitude to Muslims. Shortly after this tragic incident, mosques and Islamic schools in several cities went up in flames. Probably as retaliation, within days, a few churches and (non-Islamic) schools were also set on fire (Witte *et al.* 2005). The initial deeds of arson showed links to Lonsdale groups. For example, in Rotterdam, 'Lonsdale' was painted on a mosque before the fire started. The Dutch generally rejected these criminal acts, but it cannot be denied that interethnic tension was growing. On the one hand, this became visible in confrontations between youth groups (AIVD 2005). Lonsdale groups picked fights with migrant groups. On the other hand, public debate changed and, as stated above, politicians took more extreme standpoints. The right-wing politician Geert Wilders, for example, with a sharp sense of actuality, spoke about 'a tsunami of Islam'.

Lonsdale groups can vary in size, but there seems to be disagreement about their nature. They are said to cause nuisance and to have a fairly stable composition (Pardoel *et al.* 2004), or they are portrayed as unorganised, fluid networks (AIVD 2005). Lonsdale groups have been reported in Rotterdam, but most authors stress that they are mostly found in small cities and in the countryside (Cadat and Engbersen; van Donselaar and Rodrigues 2006).

In The Netherlands, there is an agency, Monitor Racism and Extremism, that since 1977 has published seven reports on the national situation (www.monitorracisme.nl). From 2001 to August 2005, researchers counted 125 Lonsdale groups and over 200 incidents, about 140 of those of a violent nature. Common acts of violence include abuse (41) and confrontations between native Dutch and migrant groups (50). In many of these confrontations, the difference between victim and offender is unclear. Often there have been a number of incidents with actions that provoke reactions (van Donselaar 2005). Most recent data show a decline in racist violence in general, but racist violence by extremist groups has risen strongly (van Donselaar and Wagenaar 2007).

As a whole, Lonsdale groups throughout The Netherlands have an estimated total number of 100,000–500,000 members (AIVD 2005). A small percentage is in favour of nationalism and extreme ideologies, and so come into conflict with migrant groups (van Donselaar and Rodrigues 2004; van der Sluis 2005). In the last two years, Lonsdale has become less attractive as a style. Newspapers do not report it so much anymore, and young people choose different brands. But some of the young people may have become more radical and joined groups of the extreme Right (van Donselaar and Wagenaar 2007).

To tackle the problem, it is important to analyse the underlying reasons for tensions between groups. If groups have a tendency to further radicalisation, practitioners in their vicinity can be instructed. Information about the actual conduct of these groups can be valuable, and must be shared with different partners (Moors *et al.* 2005).

In December 2004, the Ministry of Integration installed four intervention teams. Forum, an institute for multicultural development, is coordinating the work of these teams. Every team is composed of a number of experienced specialists with diverse expertise. One of the teams has a special assignment to interethnic conflicts, and it has targeted a number of cases where Lonsdale groups were involved (Forum 2007). The team is not taking over the directing role of the municipality, but will advise organisations on how to approach the problem.

Distribution of conflict types

The central question in this chapter is, why are specific types of groups found in conflict in certain contexts? We have focused on two types that nowadays probably are most prevalent in The Netherlands, 'conflict within the neighbourhood' and 'White versus Black'. Moroccan groups that clash with the neighbourhoods where they hang out fall into the first type. Conflicts between Lonsdale groups and migrant groups are examples of the second type (Table 6.2).

The links with migration are obvious. First, migrants play an important role, either because they, especially Moroccans, participate as groups in neighbourhood conflicts or because they are the targets of Lonsdale groups. This relates to 'conflicts with whom'. The answer to the second question, 'conflicts about what?,' is more complex. Conflicts these groups get into relate, directly or indirectly, to migration issues. The extreme Right ideology of Lonsdale groups, even though it may be expressed in a 'light version', is nationalist and antimigrant. The conflicts within neighbourhoods, that Moroccan boys are so often involved in are about authority. With the influx of new groups, social cohesion in neighbourhoods is not a given. Moroccan boys use public space a lot. They do so because they often come from big families that have small dwellings, and consider the house the domain of women. From an early age, boys are found on the streets, while their sisters are not. To a certain extent, they claim the street.

Even though Moroccan boys in The Netherlands had high crime rates and caused nuisance well before 2000, in public debate these two things have become entangled with other developments that started later. The planes that hit the Twin Towers and the Pentagon, and the killings of two well-known Dutch men, need to be taken into account in understanding both types of conflict discussed in this chapter. The stigmatisation of Moroccan boys reflects a growing, very critical, attitude to Muslims. This critical attitude is also a characteristic of Lonsdale groups. It makes clear that the historical context, in the sense of national and international political developments, helps to explain why we see these conflicts now.

Table 6.2 Typology of groups in conflict (where?)

Types	Cain vs Abel	White vs Black	Conflict within neighbourhood	Speciality gangs	Cultural rebels
Where?	Low prevalence in The Netherlands	Small cities, countryside	Especially bigger cities		

Geographical distribution is another matter. As far as we know now, the Lonsdale groups are mainly found in smaller cities and in the countryside, while Moroccan boys mostly cause conflicts within neighbourhoods in the bigger cities. The explanation may lie in concentration. Migrants mostly live in the big cities. Moroccan 'guest workers', as well as those from Turkey, Italy, Greece, etc., were recruited in the late 1960s and 1970s to work in Dutch factories (see Chapter 2, this volume). Then these factories were situated mainly in the big cities. This is still where most of these migrants live, in poor neighbourhoods. Thus, the neighbourhood conflict has to do with demographics.

But, although spatial distribution of the neighbourhood conflicts can be understood through demographics, this does not apply to the Lonsdale groups. Generally, the Dutch countryside has quite a homogeneous, White population. Here, we see a paradox. Is it not strange that a conflict with, or more aptly about, migrants is found where these people are mostly absent. Young people from the countryside are not very familiar with migrants. They come into contact with them more frequently when they leave their native soil to go to secondary school in a city. Here they meet migrant youth that they did not grow up with, but that they heard a lot about. This lack of experience and knowledge, combined with negative stigmatising reports in the media, are important ingredients in the conflicts that evolve (Cadat and Engbersen 2006; van Lith 2007). It is fear of what one does not know, of what may happen. In our view, Lonsdale groups should not be seen as isolated extremist organisations, but rather as a reaction to insecurity and a changing context.

These may be explanations for the emergence of two most prevalent types, but why other types are lacking is an interesting question that is yet unanswered. Especially the absence of the Cain-versus-Abel type begs for an explanation. The fact that European gangs are less territorial than American gangs (see Chapter 2, this volume) fits this pattern. Some plain facts on guns and drugs can further clarify the specific Dutch situation. In The Netherlands, guns are rare, but cannabis is sold in coffee shops. As a consequence, inter- or intra-gang use of firearms seldom occurs, and drug trade (sales of marijuana and hashish) is not an economic activity of Dutch gangs. This means that the obvious reasons for competition, as well as the violent modus to participate in this competition, are different from most other countries. It certainly is different from the USA, where the Cain-versus-Abel type is omnipresent, where guns are common, and where drugs are sold in the streets of poor neighbourhoods.

Are these Dutch groups gangs, according to the Eurogang definition? A number of them certainly are. The Moroccan groups in the big city neighbourhoods are criminally active and, maybe also because of the stigma, this has become part of their group identity. Ethnographic research points in this direction (van Gemert and Fleisher 2005). Are Lonsdale groups gangs? This depends on their criminal activities. Are they fighting, and violent, and is this part of the group identity? These are important questions to answer.

References

AIVD (2005) 'Lonsdale-jongeren' in Nederland: feiten en fictie van een vermeende rechts-extremistische subcultuur. Den Haag: AIVD.

Bervoets, E. (2006) Tussen respect en doorpakken; een onderzoek naar de Politiële Aanpak van marokkaanse jongeren in Gouda, Utrecht en Amsterdam. Den Haag: Elsevier.

Bjørgo, T. (2005) 'Conflict processes between youth groups in a Norwegian city: polarization and revenge,' European Journal of Crime, Criminal Law and Criminal Justice, 13(1): 44–74.

Bradshaw, P. (2005) 'Terrors and young teams: youth gangs and delinquency in Edinburgh', in S.H. Decker and F.M. Weerman (eds), European Street Gangs and Troublesome Youth Groups. Lanham, MD: AltaMira Press, pp. 193–218.

Cadat, M. and Engbersen, R. (2006) 'Londsdale-clash: radicaliserende jongeren veroveren het verstedelijkte platteland', Tijdschrift voor de sociale sector, 60(3): 8–13.

Cloward, R.A. and Ohlin, L.B. (1960) Delinquency and Opportunity. A Theory of Delinquent Gangs. New York: Free Press.

Donselaar, J. van (2005) Het Lonsdalevraagstuk, monitor racisme & extremisme; cahier nr. 4. Amsterdam: Anne Frank Stichting.

Donselaar, J. van and Rodrigues, P.R. (2004) Monitor racisme en extreemrechts: zesde rapportage. Amsterdam: Anne Frank Stichting/Universiteit Leiden.

Donselaar, J. van and Rodrigues, P.R. (2006) *Monitor racisme en extreemrechts: zevende rapportage*. Amsterdam: Anne Frank Stichting/Universiteit Leiden.

Donselaar, J. van and Wagenaar, W. (2007) *Monitor racisme en extremisme: Racistisch en extremistisch geweld in 2006*. Amsterdam: Anne Frank Stichting/Universiteit Leiden.

Elias, N. and Scotson, J.L. (1976) *De gevestigden en de buitenstaanders: Een studie van de spanningen en machtsverhoudingen tussen twee arbeidersbuurten*. Utrecht: Het Spectrum.

Forum (2007) *Vrijblijvendheid voorbij; eindrapportage interventieteams 2005–2006*. Utrecht: Forum.

Gemert, F. van (1998a) *Crips in drievoud; een dossieronderzoek naar drie jeugdbendes*. Amsterdam: Regioplan.

Gemert, F. van (1998b) *Ieder voor zich; kansen, cultuur en criminaliteit van Marokkaanse jongens*. Amsterdam: Het Spinhuis.

Gemert, F. van (2002) 'Marokkaanse buurtvaders blokkeren integratie', *Socialisme en Democratie*, 59(7/8): 56–64.

Gemert, F. van (2005) 'Youth groups and gangs in Amsterdam; an inventory based on the Eurogang expert survey', in S.H. Decker and F. Weerman (eds), *European Street Gangs and Troublesome Youth Groups: Findings from the Eurogang Research Program*. Walnut Creek, CA: AltaMira Press, pp. 147–69.

Gemert, F. van (2007) 'Gangs: system or madness?', in R. van Ginkel and A. Strating (eds), *Wildness and Sensation: An Anthropology of Sinister and Sensuous Realms*. Amsterdam: Spinhuis Publishers, pp. 141–56.

Gemert, F. van and Fleisher, M. (2005) 'In the grip of the group; ethnography of a Moroccan street gang in The Netherlands', in S.H. Decker and F. Weerman (eds), *European Street Gangs and Troublesome Youth Groups: Findings from the Eurogang Research Program*. Walnut Creek, CA: AltaMira Press, pp. 11–30.

Gemert, F. van and Wiersma, E. (2000) *Aanpak groepscriminaliteit: een inventarisatie van preventie- en interventiemaatregelen gericht op groepen*. Den Haag: Ministerie van Justitie (DPJS).

Hoenson, L. (2000) *Bevolkingsonderzoek in wijkteamgebieden 2000*. Amsterdam: Politie Amsterdam-Amstelland.

Homan, M. (2006) *Generatie Lonsdale: extreem-rechtse jongeren in Nederland na Fortuyn en Van Gogh*. Amsterdam: Houtekiet.

Huff, C.R. (1989) 'Youth gangs and public policy', *Crime and Delinquency*, 35(4): 524–37.

Jankowski, M.S. (1991) *Islands in the Street: Gangs and American Urban Society*. Berkeley, CA: University of California Press.

Jong, J.D.A. de (2007) *Kapot moeilijk: een etnografisch onderzoek naar opvallend delinquent groepsgedrag van 'Marokkaanse' jongens*. Amsterdam: Aksant.

Junger, M. (1990) *Delinquency and Ethnicity: An investigation on Social Factors Relating to Delinquency Among Moroccan, Turkish, Surinamese and Dutch Boys* Deventer/Boston: Kluwer.

Klein, M.W. (2001) 'Resolving the Eurogang paradox', in M.W. Klein, H.J. Kerner, C.L. Maxson and E.G.M. Weitekamp (eds), *The Eurogang Paradox: Street Gangs and Youth Groups in the U.S. and Europe*. Dordrecht: Kluwer Academic, pp. 7–19.

Klein, M.W. and Maxson, C.L. (2006) *Street Gang Patterns and Policies*. New York: Oxford University Press.

Lien, I. (2005) 'Criminal gangs and their connections: metaphors, definitions and structures', in S.H. Decker and F.M. Weerman (eds), *European Street Gangs and Troublesome Youth Groups*, Lanham, MD: AltaMira Press, pp. 31–50.

Lith, W. van (2007) *Gabbers, maar niet met iedereen; Brabantse Gabber Groepen van het Platteland en uit de Stad in Zwart-wit conflicten* (Master thesis). Amsterdam: Vrije Universiteit Amsterdam.

Mares, D. (2001) 'Gangstas or lager louts? Working class street gangs in Manchester', in M. Klein, C. Malcolm, H.J. Kerner, C. Maxson and E. Weitekamp (eds), *The Eurogang Paradox: Street Gangs and Youth Groups in the US and Europe*. Dordrecht: Kluwer Academic, pp. 153–64.

Maxson, C. and M.W. Klein (1995) 'Investigating gang structures,' *Journal of Gang Research*, 3(1): 33–40.

Moors, H., Pardoel, K. and Bruinsma, M. (2005) 'Lastpakken in groepsverband,' *Secondant*, 19(2): 14–17.

Pardoel, K., Bruinsma, M., Moors, H. and Enck, E. van (2004) *Vervelend jong: aanzet tot een gerichte aanpak van overlastgevende jongerengroepen*. Tilburg: IVA.

Patrick, J. (1973) *A Glasgow Gang Observed*. London: Eyre Methuen.

Rosenbaum, D.P. and Grant, J.A. (1983) *Gangs and Youth Problems in Evanston*. Report. Evanston, IL: Northwestern University, Centre for Urban Affairs and Policy Research.

SAMS (2004) *Minder bevreesd: andacht voor gevoelens van onveiligheid in de stad*. Rotterdam: Stedelijke Adviescommissie Multiculturele Stad.

Schoppen, H. (1997) *'Het zijn onze feesten': jeugdculturen en geweld tegen allochtonen in Nederland*. Utrecht: Willem Pompe Instituut.

Sluis, R. van der (2005) *Van vreemde smetten vrij? Een quickscan naar rechts-extremisme onder jongeren in Zaanstreek en Purmerend*. Zaandam: Bureau Discriminatiezaken Zaanstreek/Waterland.

Stapele, S. van (2003) *Crips.nl; 15 jaar gangcultuur in Nederland*. Amsterdam: Vassalucci.

Taylor, C.S. (1990) 'Gang imperialism', in C.R. Huff (ed.), *Gangs in America* Newbury Park, CA: Sage, pp. 103–15.

Thrasher, F.M. (1927) *The Gang: A Study of 1,313 Gangs in Chicago*. Chicago: University of Chicago Press.

Werdmölder, H. (1990) *Een generatie op drift: De geschiedenis van een Marokkaanse randgroep*. Arnhem: Gouda Quint.

Whyte, W.F. (1943) *Street Corner Society: The Social Structure of an Italian Slum*. Chicago: University of Chicago Press.

Wijk, A. Ph. van, Bervoets, E.J.A. and Boers, R. (2007) *Trots op Nederland: Achtergronden, kenmerken en aanpak van het Lonsdaleverschijnsel in Venray, Zoetermeer en Aalsmeer.* Politieacademie: Apeldoorn.

Witte, R., Brassé, P. and Schram, K. (2005) *Moskeebrand in Helden: evaluatie van de aanpak en lessen voor de toekomst.* Utrecht: Forum.

Wittebrood, K. (2006) *Slachtoffers van Criminaliteit: Feiten en achtergronden.* Den Haag: Sociaal Cultureel Planbureau.

Yablonsky, L. (1962) *The Violent Gang.* New York: Macmillan.

Chapter 7

Origins and development of racist skinheads in Moscow

Alexander Shashkin

Introduction

This chapter examines the situation of racist skinhead groups or gangs in Moscow and describes the structural, cultural, and political conditions that influence the particular cultural choice of young people to be racist. Appearing in the late 1980s to early 1990s as a 'product' of cultural globalisation, racist skinheads soon became the centre of public fears, media attention, and policy concerns. The existence of hate-based violence was virtually ignored by public officials, police, and scholars, and it was mainly journalists and human rights activists that attracted attention to this phenomenon. According to the latter, skinheads in Russia number close to 70,000 people; in Moscow and the surrounding suburbs, this amounts to 12,000–15,000 people, which is three times higher than in 2005. These figures notably contrast with the police statistics: law-enforcement agencies registered 147 skinhead groups with about 10,000 members in Russia.[1]

Western countries have a long tradition of studying violent youth cultures and gangs. The first studies on skinheads were conducted in Britain in the 1970s (e.g. Clarke 1976; Hebdidge 1979). Later, they appeared in many other European countries, including Germany (e.g. Wahl 1995; Watts 2001); France (e.g. Peralva 1994; Petrova 1997, 2005), Norway (Bjørgo 1997), Finland (e.g. Perho 2001; Puuronen 2001), Sweden (e.g. Lööw 2000), and the United States (e.g. Dobratz and Shanks-Meile 1995; Gerstenfeld 2004; Kleg 1993).

The discussion about racism in Russia began only toward the end of the 1990s (Sokolovskiy 2002; Voronkov et al. 2002), with the most recent and comprehensive studies on racism in Russia conducted mainly in the early 2000s (e.g. Malahov and Tishkov 2002). Youth cultures attracted more attention from scholars (for the most comprehensive examples, see, Omelchenko 2004; Pilkington *et al.* 2002), but Russian scholars have rarely focused research on violent youth cultures and street gangs. Among the few were studies of youth gangs or the 'Kazan phenomenon' (e.g. Ovchinskiy 1990; Prozumentov 1993; Salagaev 1989, 1997; Shashkin and Salagaev 2002) and skinheads (Kaznacheev 1998; Likhachev 2002; Sedov 2002; Tarasov 2000; Verkhovsky *et al.* 1996).

Studies of skinhead groups, whether in Western countries or Russia, are mainly ethnographic and qualitative. Our study, 'Violent Youth Cultures in Moscow', is no exception: according to the research design, narrative interviews with experts or practitioners dealing with violent young people were accompanied by in-depth, semistructured interviews with the members of skinhead and football hooligan groups (two major troublesome youth groups in the Russian capital). The study was supported by the International Association for the Promotion of Co-operation with Scientists (INTAS) of the New Independent States of the Former Soviet Union. The data collection among young people was not yet finished at the time of this writing, so this chapter is based on 20 interviews with experts and practitioners. Interviews were conducted in the autumn and winter of 2004. The experts include four academics who write or work on violent youth, xenophobia, or extremism; three policemen (especially those who deal with young people themselves and are familiar with the situation in their region); five journalists who write about skinheads and football hooliganism; four youth workers; and four human rights activists.[2]

The interviews with the experts were not formal: the experts were asked to speak in an informal way about the past, present, and future of skinheads or football hooligans. At the end, the discussions mainly focused on the following questions: (1) why did these groups appear in Russia?; (2) why did they shortly become so popular and attractive for young people?; (3) what is their current situation?; (4) how will things develop further and what kind of policy – suppressive or preventive – is and will be utilised? In the current chapter, we narrow our interest and particularly address the first two questions in relation to racist skinheads, bearing in mind mainly structural, not individual, conditions.

From working-class resistance towards cultural participation: theoretical and methodological issues

Although groups of young people that pursue delinquent and violent activities have existed for centuries, socio-cultural interpretations of this phenomenon were not offered until the 1920s by the scholars of the Chicago school (see Shaw *et al.* 1929; Thrasher 1927). The first theorists viewed 'deviant subcultures' as a way of acquiring commonly targeted social goals (Merton 1957), as a result of a conflict between social groups (Vold 1958), or as a product of labelling and stigmatisation (Becker 1963). The Chicago school's conceptualisation of 'subculture' was further developed in the frameworks of the Birmingham Centre for Contemporary Cultural Studies (CCCS) (see Hall and Jefferson 1976). The concept of 'subculture' based on cultural Marxism was broadly used to interpret post-war youth cultures as hot spots of working-class resistance to the dominant institutions of British society (see Clarke 1976; Cohen 1972; Hebdidge 1979).

This concept of 'subculture' was criticised for the excessive attention paid to the structural conditions instead of the meanings given by young people themselves (e.g. Hoikkala 1989; Muggleton 2000). Later accounts of youth cultures inspired by the CCCS (the 'British post-subcultural approach') have tried to discover the meanings that young people give to their cultural attachments and actions (e.g. Hodkinson 2002; Redhead *et al.* 1997; Thornton 1995). However, 'post-subcultural theorising' does not engage adequately with youth cultural practices outside the economically developed countries, and terms such as 'postmodern subcultures' or 'neo-tribes' have geopolitically limited explanatory power (see Pilkington 2004). Western subcultural studies have been oriented routinely towards the symbolic transformation of consumer goods and their incorporation into patterns of style-based resistance. Such work has little relevance in the Russian context, where access to consumer goods is gradually restricted, and the youth stage in general is experienced differently because of the low level of economic development (see Lagree 1997). The emergence of the violent youth culture on which our study is focused relates to cultural globalisation, but it does not mean that the 'core' narratives of globalisation should be taken for granted (see Pilkington *et al.* 2002).

We regard skinheads as a violent youth culture and clearly distinguish them from any political, extremist, racist, or nationalist groups, parties, or movements organized by adults, even if they consist of young people. At the same time, it is very hard to separate

99

these groups in real life, as various right-wing parties and movements are constantly trying to work with skinheads, organise them, and foster their political involvement. Such a situation is very similar to the American one, where skinheads first appeared as a reactionary element of the American punk rock scene, but since the mid-1980s they have been recruited by more established racist groups (e.g. Blazak 2001). Groups of skinheads that we will discuss in this chapter consist of young people (average age in the early twenties) and are durable (normally exist for over 1–2 years), street oriented (spend a lot of group time outside home, work, and school), and involved in illegal activity (especially group fights). The last is a part of the group's identity (not only an individual self-image of group members): the basic ideology and culture of these groups is structured by the idea of 'Russia for Russians', which is manifested in violence against people who belong to non-Slavic ethnic groups. In this regard, we consider groups of skinheads to be street gangs according to the definition developed by the Eurogang research network (see Maxson and Klein 1995).

The overwhelming majority of Russian skinheads are racist or neo-Nazi. We use the terms 'Nazi-skins' and 'racist-skins' interchangeably because the differences between them have no principal significance for our work. They copy and adopt the image of Western skinhead as shown in the news media and movies but the ideology and discourse are mainly rooted in a local soil. The main goal of this chapter is to analyse structural, cultural, and political conditions of the appearance and rapid growth of youth racist skinhead gangs in Russia.

The appearance of skinheads: global patterns on Russian soil

Skinhead culture was discovered for the first time in Russia in the early 1990s when about ten young people in the Moscow city centre 'shaved their heads' and began to call themselves 'skinheads'. They probably knew about Western skinheads from the Soviet media during Gorbachev's perestroika, when it was fashionable to report on British, German, and later Czech groups of the same kind (Tarasov 2000). At first, Russian skinheads were mostly oriented towards the skinhead culture (music and style) and were not initially racist, violent, and organised. The ways leading to this particular form of cultural participation were almost similar to those of punk, rock, or hippie cultures: the flow of information about the subcultural styles of Western youth after the fall of the 'Iron Curtain' led to copying and imitation. Our experts agreed that skinheads were the product of cultural borrowing:

> *Komsomolskaya Pravda*, for instance, as I remember, devoted a double-page article to skinheads. Can you imagine how huge the circulation of this newspaper was at that time? We should consider the fact that the majority of mass media had critical attitudes towards the Soviet period so that such materials were given without any evaluation or author's opinion.... Thus some teenagers realised that such a fashionable phenomenon did exist, and they knew the basic information – what skinheads looked like, how they dressed. (Alexander Tarasov, Centre for the New Sociology and the Studies of Practical Policy 'Phoenix', Informational Expert Centre 'Panorama', Moscow, 2004)

As the same expert asserted, the main information that came from the media was about Nazi skinheads in the West. He connected this with the phobias of everything associated with 'red' or left-wing that were present in Russian society in those days: 'Only the information about Nazi-skinheads was published.... Out of the variety of skinhead groups, our journalists reported exclusively about Nazi-skins.... Teenagers started to view extremely racist ideas as something fashionable. I can understand that red skins were not in fashion those days' (Alexander Tarasov).

Once planted in Russian soil, the 'skinhead seed' started to grow in original ways. It became increasingly popular to be a racist skinhead in Russia then. Another expert supposed that besides cultural borrowings, there were 'home-grown' groups of racist youth who later called themselves 'skinheads': 'There were two ways in which skinheads appeared in Russia. The first was just copying Western skinheads, and second was home-grown. Some people imitated the leaders of this movement in the West. Others were more advanced; they read about some figures – Hitler, for example.... But the skinheads in the street knew only "Russia is for Russians, Moscow is for Muscovites"' (Dmitry Sokolov-Mitrich, journalist of *Newspaper*, Moscow, 2004).

We could suppose that this expert is mixing historically different phenomena – the first skinheads appeared after the initial flow of information about Western youth and those Nazi skinheads who came later did so because of specific Russian cultural, social, and economic conditions.

It is important to note that the experts tend to believe that Russian skinheads are a subcultural phenomenon, but not a political grouping or movement. There is ample evidence that groups of skinheads lack the organisational structure, management, and discipline essential for the political structure (e.g. Tarasov 2000). Here is the typical opinion in this respect:

> To tell the truth, I do not have a clear understanding of where they came from. Maybe they grew out of groups of ... football fans ... Maybe not. ... It seems to me that they appeared in the mid-1990s relatively spontaneously. I am far from thinking that somebody was behind them, such as the secret services, but I have heard such opinions. (Grogoriy Punanov, news editor of *Izvestiya*, Moscow, 2004)

The question of why the racist scene was chosen by young people for cultural participation is central to our further analysis. The idea of associating or connecting the appearance of skinheads with working-class resistance and/or the economically and socially subordinate position of young people is rather popular in contemporary literature (e.g. Mac an Ghaill 1999: 141–3; Watts 2001: 611). These kinds of explanations might be appropriate for societies with relatively stable political and economical systems, as well as class structure. Analysing the expert interviews, we came to the conclusion that in transitional countries, such as Russia, 'youth racist choice' is more associated with political, social, and economic transformations, than with working-class struggle or social pressures on an economically deprived population. The next quotation from an expert interview clarifies the main differences of our approach and serves as a prologue to the following discussion:

> Initially the movement came from Moscow: movies, music. ... All this fell upon the unstable economic and political situation in Russia, 'the shoe fit well', as in 1993 to 1994 even Russian foreign policy was rather specific with relation to the national interest. Here we can add the appearance of a huge number of migrants from the former republics of the Soviet Union and other countries. All this contributed to the rise of extremist elements, and the skinhead movement in particular. (Andrey Smirnov, journalist of the newspaper *Tomorrow*, Moscow, 2004)

In the next part of the chapter, we try to single out the preconditions of the rise of racist skinhead culture and the creation of skinhead gangs. Following our experts, we trace recent events in Russian history, specific policy developments, political changes, and failures in the transition to market economy that influenced and are still influencing the choice of particular ways of youth cultural involvement related to racism, nationalism, and xenophobia.

Why racist? Why violent? Preconditions of the rapid growth of racist skinhead movement in Moscow

When talking about the origins of racist skinhead culture and the conditions of the rapid growth of its popularity in Russia, our experts tended to stress not individual, but structural factors and conditions. Generally speaking, they connected the development of racist attitudes among Russian youth with the collapse of the Soviet Union as well as the political and economic situation of the early 1990s. Some single factors that were named do not make much sense in relation to the development of racist youth gangs, but they start to 'work' when combined with other factors and conditions. The discussion below is organised around the specific themes mentioned by experts at least once during the interviews.

The economic crisis of the early 1990s

The economic recession that began in 1991 had a strong impact on the economic and psychological state of the Russian people. Millions of people suddenly became unemployed, and those who were employed (for instance, in the armaments industry or in the public sector in general) did not receive any pay for several months or even years. During the Soviet times, the majority of people were not wealthy, but they had a stable income; in the 1990s, they simply became destitute. All of this led to psychological catastrophe, as people were used to guaranteed employment, state paternalism in education and health services, and other welfare programmes of the Soviet state (e.g. subsidised prices for the basic necessities, children's needs, community services, public transport). The economic disaster led to a situation where more and more parents were forced to work several jobs and thus had no time for their children:

When the economic catastrophe occurred, parents were not able to spend time with their children; they were busy with money making. It was a widespread situation during that time, when people worked on two, three or even four jobs at the same time. They went out early in the morning and came back at night with the sole goal of maintaining the same level of well-being they used to have. Much more effort was needed for that, and their children appeared to be left to themselves. (Tarasov, Centre for the New Sociology and the Studies of Practical Policy 'Phoenix', Informational Expert Centre 'Panorama', Moscow, 2004)

Collapse of the Soviet system of education and upbringing

The collapse of the education system went hand in hand with the economic crisis. The entire school system in the Union of Soviet Socialist Republics (USSR) was public; therefore, it started to fail when the state income was substantially decreased. For financial reasons, 400–450 schools were closed annually in Russia (Tarasov 2000).

In the 'struggle against totalitarianism', the private education (or fosterage) of young people was banned, and in the experts' eyes this was a major factor in the growth of youth crime and delinquency. In the USSR, the idea of youth upbringing was connected with the Komsomol and Pioneer organisations that not only dealt with ideological matters, but also were responsible for youth hobbies and activities, such as art, music, sport, and tourism. These organisations were disbanded but were replaced with nothing. The importance of the Komsomol and Pioneer organisations in preventing crime and violence among youth is reflected in the following quotation:

In my view, our school was not financed well during the perestroika time and now the situation is the same. Schools deal with teaching, and not the upbringing of young people. Our children are not organised, but they strive for organisation anyway. ... Let's assume that the Pioneer and Komsomol organisations in the past did organise the children. I am not calling for a return of the communistic times, but ... then the children were united; they discussed whether somebody had committed something. ... One who did something wrong had the feeling of shame and responsibility in front of his classmates. He was ashamed. Nobody is ashamed any more; they are absolutely indifferent. (Tatyana Temerlina, Head of the Subdivision on Minors Affairs, Department of Interior, Tsaritsyno region, Moscow, 2004)

Ideological shift

Our experts connect the 'discursive domination' of Nazi skinheads with a significant ideological turn that happened after the collapse of the USSR. This idea is reflected in the following quotation:

Why did Nazi-skins flourish in Russia? It was because all people at that time were attacking leftist ideas, and denouncing Marxism, Bolshevism, Leninism, socialism, and internationalism in consequence. ... Moreover, the school lessons about the Great Patriotic War [World War II] were abbreviated as much as possible. But the first lessons on subject provide ... discussions about fascism and its social threat. ... And this was not known to the next generation by the definition. History teachers in our country always 'run in front of the locomotive'. In that period, they had already started to claim that Stalin wanted to attack Germany, and Hitler was defending his country; that Soviet totalitarianism is the most dangerous totalitarianism in the world, and so on. Some of their pupils must have concluded, in their black-and-white teenage way of thinking that Hitler was better than Stalin. If Hitler was better than Stalin, Hitler was good. (Tarasov, Centre for the New Sociology and the Studies of Practical Policy 'Phoenix', Informational Expert Centre 'Panorama', Moscow, 2004)

As Tarasov (2000) himself wrote, in the country that lost 35 million people in World War II, fascism was transformed from the object of everybody's hatred and contempt to an enigmatic and fascinating theme for teenagers. Liberals were so excited by their war against the 'red threat' that they did not notice when the fashion for fascism was created.

The next few reasons for the appearance of violent skinhead gangs mentioned by our experts are connected with the use of force and violence by the state, as happened rather often in recent Russian history. In the experts' opinion, it is in this way that violence became an acceptable (and sometimes the only) means of solving all problems.

State violence

One of the first dramatic cases of violence used by the state in the recent history of Russia was the storming of the Russian Parliament building (White House) in October 1993. The struggle between the supporters of President Boris Yeltsin and the Supreme Soviet (former legislative body), under Ruslan Khazbulatov and Alexander Rutskoy, led to a bloody conflict in the centre of Moscow, in which many innocent people were killed. In this case, Yeltsin showed that violence is 'conclusive proof' in any discussion. The following quotation illustrates the connection between this event and skinhead culture in Russia:

> As a rule, the skinheads of the first wave were average or bad pupils at school. ... As it turned out, many of these young people skipped classes in October 1993 to watch the shelling of the White House. They were in a huge crowd, and they were interested. In this sense I am absolutely convinced that the powers that be demonstrated to all the population that violence is a final argument in social and political discussions. And some part of these people, let's say, regarded this as a guide to action. (Tarasov, Centre for the New Sociology and the Studies of Practical Policy 'Phoenix', Informational Expert Centre 'Panorama', Moscow, 2004)

Another key violent event in recent Russian history was the war in Chechnya, which officially started in December 1994. According to Tarasov (2000), the first Chechen war was accompanied by great-power imperialistic and nationalistic propaganda (especially in Moscow) that had an obvious impact on the number of skinheads and their ideological orientations. Our experts usually mentioned the Chechen war as a primary factor in the rise of Nazi skinhead gangs. One reason that it was so important is presented in the following quotation: 'First of all it was Chechen war that somehow or other shifted the limits of things allowed in the society. Besides, about 1.5 million people passed through the horrors of this war, and this is also a considerable factor' (Emil Pain, Director of the Centre for Research in Xenophobia and Counteraction to Extremism, Director of the Centre for Political and Regional Studies, Moscow, 2004).

The events of October 1993 mentioned above were followed by the 'xenophobic campaigns' in Moscow. Moscow was declared a territory of 'special rule', in which police were ordered to stop suspicious people and check their documents, such as registration (non-residents who stay in Moscow should be registered at the local police station) and residence permit. This situation gave rise to 'ethnic cleansings' in which people who 'looked like foreigners' (mainly those from the Caucasus[3]) were targeted. 'It started when the people with Caucasian face type, or Asian face type, were stopped on the street. ... And when statesmen started to tell in the media that all evil came from Chechens and Caucasians' (Andrey Babushkin, Committee For Human Rights, Moscow, 2004).

The situation continued during the Chechen war and was fuelled by terrorist acts in Moscow. Public fear of people from the Caucasus was created in a very short time. Nowadays, the situation continues; everyday one can see the police stop and check people with 'Caucasian appearance' on Moscow streets and in the underground railway. Violent and xenophobic actions performed by the state go hand in hand with everyday racism. The latter was named by the experts as another key factor in the appearance and development of Nazi skinhead gangs in Moscow.

Everyday racism

Everyday racism is not a new phenomena; it exists in almost every country. Racism also is not only a structural or institutional phenomenon or ideology; it can be a part of everyday interaction. The term 'everyday racism' has been defined as interactional practices that position people unequally according to their skin colour or culture (Essed 1991). Everyday racism includes ethnic name calling, ethnic jokes, and other discriminatory practices, such as insulting gestures, facial expressions, gazes, and isolation, which can result in the exclusion and isolation of ethnic minorities in educational institutions, leisure activities, public and private spaces, associations, and workplaces. These phenomena are not usually recognised by the majority as racist and are seen as part of the culture of certain ethnic and national groups. The origins of everyday racist attitudes to people from the Caucasus and their connection with the creation of skinhead gangs are described in the following quotation:

It is such a spontaneous phenomenon that was born in the suburbs, where a lot of people from the Caucasus live, and naturally ... there are everyday conflicts, such as street fights. ... The rumours about such fights spread in the neighbourhood. ... In other words, I am sure that everything comes from below, because there are 14–15-year-old kids from the workers' quarters who have nothing to do, and their parents complain in the kitchen, I am sorry to say, that 'black asses' have occupied all the kiosks. ... That is how everything happens. (Grigoriy Punanov, news editor of *Izvestiya*, Moscow, 2004)

The quotation illustrates that young people became organised and formed street gangs in conflict with their counterparts from other ethnic groups. This again proves the tight connection between the state of conflict and specific group dynamics.

The generalised experts' opinion is that young racist skinheads 'grew' out of their parents' everyday racism. The crucial point in the discussion was raised in an interview with one of the experts. He wondered how everyday racism and xenophobia lead to the formation of organised groups such as skinheads, and what connected racist talks and racist actions.

> The transition from general xenophobia to the organised groups … is a nonlinear process. It is known that in many countries the level of ethnic phobias is traditionally very high, and this does not necessarily lead to any organised groups. The best example is Hungary. … Phobias exist, but organised groups do not. … Thus, this phenomenon demands a special investigation. (Emil Pain, Director of the Centre for Research in Xenophobia and Counteraction to Extremism, Director of the Centre for Political and Regional Studies, Moscow, 2004)

In our opinion, this expert confused two different issues: firstly, everyday racism as a cultural phenomenon, and, secondly, the phenomenon of youth culture that involves a 'we–others' dichotomy and is structured by collective actions, such as fights with 'enemies', joint parties, and attendance at concerts. Skinhead culture as youth culture was not created out of everyday racism. On the contrary, everyday racism, together with other factors mentioned in this chapter, influenced the choice of cultural participation that young people in Russia are making.

Surge of migration

The idea that the appearance of migrants in Moscow not only stimulated everyday racist attitudes, but also catalysed the creation of skinhead gangs was rather common in our experts' discourse. As a capital city, Moscow has always been a magnet for people from Russia and neighbouring countries. Researchers describe three common strategies of actions towards difference: welcoming, opposing, and maintaining (e.g. Back 1997). Skinhead gangs consist of young people who oppose immigrants and ethnic minorities and support xenophobic and racist ideas. Why? As our experts have mentioned, young people tend to connect their economic and social failures with the presence of migrants. 'Intense migration evoked diverse reactions, especially during the period when people connected their personal failures, their economic and social difficulties, with the dominance of foreigners' (Andrey Babushkin, Committee For Human Rights, Moscow, 2004).

Some of our experts view the development of skinhead gangs as a reaction to 'ethnic crimes'. Statistics on 'ethnic crimes' are secret and surrounded by myths, but perpetrators of hate crimes often refer to such crimes as a neutralisation technique. 'Tajiks provide 70 per cent of drug couriers, Gypsies control 15 per cent of drug sales. It is hard for them to vie with Russians, but it is striking that such a small nation of 300,000 consists of 15 per cent drug dealers. In other words, ethnic crimes urge people forward' (Andrey Babushkin, Committee For Human Rights, Moscow, 2004).

Thus, the reasons and factors that experts associate with the development of racist or Nazi skinhead culture and the creation of skinhead gangs in Moscow can be summarised in the following main categories:

(1) economic crisis of the early 1990s that resulted in the impoverishment of Russian population and the collapse of intrafamily education and upbringing;
(2) the collapse of the Soviet state system of education, fosterage, and out-of-school education;
(3) the ideological shift from total domination of communist ideas to condemnation of Soviet totalitarianism;
(4) state violence (in particular, the storming of the Russian Parliament in 1993, the war in Chechnya, and the 'xenophobic campaigns' in Moscow);
(5) everyday racism and negative attitudes to the economic domination of migrants (particularly Caucasians) in Moscow;
(6) the surge of migration that spawned myths about 'ethnic crimes' and the view that the state is too weak to control these processes.

Discussion: how to deal with the expert discourses

At first glance, the expert opinions presented above seem to reflect the real situation in a homogeneous, consistent, and objective way. At the same time, if we look reflectively at the analysis, we see a spectrum of judgements and evaluations offered by the presenters of different discourses with an unequal level of expertise and involvement in the discussed problems. So the main questions here are, how can we deal with these discourses and what can they give us in terms of scientific understanding of the phenomena of Nazi skinhead gangs and racism in youth contexts?

What we propose is not to objectify the experts' suggestions, but to treat them as showing how different practitioners who deal with youth racism, extremism, and xenophobia view the origins of these phenomena in Russian society. As the reader might notice, these views are not always free from racialisation, simplification, and mythologisation. In any case, expert opinions represent only one side of the subject, which is hard to analyse without considering the views of young people themselves. Thus, the idea of the whole study is to analyse the ideas of 'insiders' and 'outsiders', young people and adults, violent and racist youth, and those who struggle against violence and racism. Our goal in this chapter was not to compare such views, but we can say where youth and adult discourses differ and intersect. For example, the significance of the Chechen war in the development of the racist skinhead movement was stressed by both experts and young people (in the interviews we were able to complete at the time of this writing). But the experts, as we have shown in this chapter, discuss the moral limits for the use of violence that were shifted by this war as well as the everyday racist and xenophobic attitudes that developed as a consequence of military operations in Chechnya and terrorist acts in Moscow. Some young people emphasised that their acquaintances, friends, boyfriends, and relatives actually died in this war fighting in the Russian army, and it was for deeply personal reasons that they hate Caucasians and are 'ready to kill them'. Sometimes these particular episodes from their personal life become a driving force for particular forms of cultural participation and organisation that involve violence and racism.

We understand the differences between the agency of young people and the structural factors that might influence the situation in general. But those structural factors mentioned by our experts can also turn into popular myths. For example, members of skinhead gangs are usually presented as 'stupid working-class aggressive young males who live in Moscow suburbs and have nothing to do'. At the same time, about 80 per cent of all skinheads I interviewed (including three girls) had middle-class (or lower middle-class) backgrounds, study at Moscow universities, read a lot, and are interested in history. Of course, we do not justify racist violence, and do not want to present all skinheads as well-educated middle-class, young people. These examples are given to avoid simplified conclusions and emphasise the need for further research. Moreover, nor do we want to deconstruct the importance of the work that was done in this chapter. We hope that a first step was made in understanding the phenomenon of Russian skinheads, and that this will be helpful to all those who are interested in contemporary Russian history, youth cultures, and the prevention of violence, racism, and xenophobia among youth.

Notes

1 Data from the Press-conference of Russian Ministry of Interior (2007) and the RBC Newspaper, www.rbc.ru.
2 The majority of experts are widely recognised in their field due to their publications (either academic or popular), but some were found to employ the 'snowball' method. There are only a few people in Russia who can be regarded as experts in our field of studies. When we selected academic experts, we analysed publications on the topic and took the key specialists; police experts were taken from the regional Subdivisions on Minors Affairs at the Department of Interior, which is the main state body dealing with youth criminality; selected journalists had proven their expertise by writing on the issues of skinheads/football hooligans; youth workers were taken from the most visible NGOs in the area (finally we realised that they very rarely dealt with violent youth cultures and gangs, so their opinions were of little importance to this chapter); human rights activists that were selected as experts for the study had a long history of raising public awareness of youth racism and xenophobia through the interviews they gave, websites they created, and books they published. We also employed a peer validation technique in which each expert was asked to name a few more, and then we interviewed only those who were named most often. These procedures aimed to justify that our experts were a valid and credible source of information. The average expert interview took about 2–2.5 hours. All interviews were recorded and then transcribed. Interviews were usually done at the experts' work places or in public establishments such as educational institutions, parks or cafes.
3 Migration to Russia from ex-USSR republics started after the collapse of the USSR. Economic ties were broken, so the newly formed independent countries experienced crises with high levels of unemployment and multiple industrial lockouts. The most obvious solution for people was to move to Russia where the situation was relatively better, and they all knew the language. Up to now, the following countries lead in migration to Russia: Kazakhstan, Uzbekistan, Ukraine, Kyrgyzstan, and Armenia.

References

Back, L. (1997) *New Ethnicities and Urban Culture. Racism and Multiculture in Young Lives*. London: UCL Press.

Becker, H.S. (1963) *Outsiders: Studies in the Sociology of Deviance*. New York: Free Press.

Bjørgo, T. (1997) *Racist and Right Wing Violence in Scandinavia: Patterns, Perpetrators and Responses*. Otta: Tano Aschehoug.

Blazak, R. (2001) 'White boys to terrorist men: target recruitment of Nazi Skinheads', *American Behavioral Scientist*, 44(6): 982–1000.

Clarke, J. (1976) 'The skinheads and the magical recovery of community', in S. Hall and T. Jefferson (eds), *Resistance Through Rituals: Youth Subcultures in Post-War Britain*. London: Hutchinson.

Cohen, P. (1972) 'Subcultural Conflict and Working Class Community', *Working Papers in Cultural Studies*, 2: 5–70.

Dobratz, B.A. and Shanks-Miele, S. (1995) 'Conflict in the white supremacist/racialist movement in the United States', *International Journal of Group Tensions*, 25(1): 57–75.

Essed, P. (1991) *Understanding Everyday Racism: An Interdisiplinary Theory*. Newbury Park: Sage.

Gerstenfeld, P.B. (2004) *Hate Crimes: Causes, Controls, and Controversies*. Thousand Oaks, CA: Sage.

Hall, S. and Jefferson, T. (eds) (1976) *Resistance Through Rituals: Youth Subcultures in Post-War Britain*. London: Hutchinson.

Hebdige, D. (1979) *Subculture: The Meaning of Style*. London: Routledge.

Hodkinson, P. (2002) *Goth Identity, Style and Subculture*. Oxford: Berg.

Hoikkala, T. (1989) *Nuorisokulttuurista kulttuuriseen nuoruuteen* ('From Youth Cultures to Cultural Youth'). Helsinki: Gaudeamus.

Kaznacheev, P. (1998) 'Billiardniye shary: Skinkhedy – novoe pokolenie Naci?' ('Billiard-balls: Skinheads – new generation of Nazi?), *Novoe Vremya*, 32: 36–9.

Kleg, M. (1993) *Hate, Prejudice and Racism*. Albany, NY: SUNY Press.

Lagree, J.Ch. (1997) 'Youth in Europe: cultural patterns of transition'. Paper based on a research project supported by the Ministère de la Jeunesse et des Sports Français, Direction de la Jeunesse et de la Vie Associative (author's archive).

Likhachev, V. (2002) *Natsizm v Rossii* ('Nazism in Russia'). Moscow: ROO Centre Panorama.

Lööw, H. (2000) *Nazismen i Sverige 1980-1999: Den Rasistiska undergoundrörelsen: Musiken, Myterna, Riterna*. Stockholm: Ordfront Förlag.

Mac an Ghaill, M. (1999) *Contemporary Racisms and Ethnicities: Social and Cultural Transformations*. Buckingham: Open University Press.

Malahov, V. and Tishkov, V. (2002) *Multikulturalizm i transformaciya postsovetskih obschestv* ('Multiculturalism and Transformation of Post-Soviet Societies').

Moscow: Ethnological and Anthropological Institute of Russian Academy of Science.

Maxson, C.L. and Klein, M.W. (1995) 'Investigating gang structures', *Journal of Gang Research*, 3(1): 33–40.

Merton, R.K. (1957) *Social Theory and Social Structure*. London: Collier-Macmillan.

Muggleton, D. (2000) *Inside Subculture: The Postmodern Meaning of Style*. Guilford: Berg.

Omelchenko, E. (2004) *Molodezh: otkritiy vopros* ('Youth: Open-Ended Question'). Ulyanovsk: Simbirskaya kniga.

Ovchinskiy, V.S. (1990) '"Gastrolniye" poezdki antiobshestvennikh gruppirovok podrostkov i molodezhi – noviy phenomen' ('"Tours" of anti-social groups of teenagers and youth – new phenomenon'), in *Kriminologi o Neformalnikh Molodezhnikh Obyedineniyakh* ('Criminologists on Informal Youth Units). Moscow: Juridical Literature', pp. 192–6.

Perho, S. (2001) 'Features of racist (sub)culture among youth', in V. Puuronen (ed.), *Youth on the Threshold of 3rd Millennium*. Joensuu: University of Joensuu, Karelian Institute, pp. 152–63.

Peralva, A. (1994) 'La violence skinhead' ('Skinheads' violence'), in P. Perrineau (ed.), *L'Engagement politique: déclin ou mutation?* ('Political Involvement: Fall or Mutation?'). Paris: Presses de la Fonation Nationale des Sciences Politiques, pp. 94–110.

Petrova, Y. (1997) 'Les skinheads: solidarité de classe ou "combat national"'? ('Skinheads: class solidarity or nationalistic beliefs?'), in *Agora/Debats Jeunesses* 9. Paris: Harmattan, pp. 77–93.

Petrova, Y. (2005) 'Ethnonational or multiethnic identities: the case of skinhead youth subcultures', in V. Puuronen, J. Soilevuo-Grønnerød and J. Herranen (eds), *Youth – Similarities, Differences, Inequalities*. Reports of the Karelian Institute, No. 1. Joensuu: University of Joensuu, pp. 74–88.

Pilkington, H. (2004) 'Youth strategies for glocal living: space, power and communication in everyday cultural practice', in A. Bennet and K. Kahn-Harris (eds), *After Subculture: Critical Studies in Contemporary Youth Culture*. Houndmills: Palgrave Macmillan.

Pilkington, H., Omelchenko, E., Flynn, M., Bliudina, U. and Starkova, E. (2002) *Looking West? Cultural Globalisation and Russian Youth Cultures*. University Park, PA: Pennsylvania State University Press.

Prozumentov, L.M. (1993) *Gruppovaya prestupnost nessovershennoletnikh i ee preduprezhdenie* ('Group Juvenile Delinquency and Its Prevention'). Tomsk: Tomsk State University Publishing House.

Puuronen, V. (ed.) (2001) *Valkoisen vallan lähettiläät: Arjen rasismi ja rasismin arki* ('The Messengers of White Power: The Everyday Racism and Everyday Life of Racism'). Tampere: Vastapaino.

Redhead, S., Wynne, D. and O'Connor, J. (eds) (1997) *The Clubcultures Reader: Readings in Popular Cultural Studies*. Oxford: Basil Blackwell.

Salagaev, A. (1989) 'Podrostkovaya kompaniya i predkriminalnaya gruppirovka kak usloviya socializacii' ('Socialisation in youth company and pre-criminal gang), in *Proceedings of the International Conference, 'Actual Problems of Regional Social Development'* (Barnaul).

Salagaev, A. (1997) *Molodezhnie pravonarusheniya i delinkventnie soobshestva skvoz prizmu amerikanskikh sociologicheskikh teoriy* ('Studying Youth Delinquency and Delinquent Communities Using American Sociological Theories'). Kazan: Ekocentr.

Sedov, L. (2002) 'Golovy, vybritie iznutri' ('Heads shaved from inside), *Levada-Centre Press-Issue* [Internet], 17 July 2002. Available from: www. levada.ru/press/2002071700.html [accessed 30 November 2007].

Shashkin, A. and Salagaev, A. (2002) 'Russian delinquent gangs: gender regime and masculinities construction', in *Kön och våld i Norden* ('Gender and Violence in the Nordic Countries'). Report from a conference in Køge, Denmark [online] (København: Nordisk Ministerråd), pp. 399–409. Available from: www.norfa.no/_img/3._Masculinity=Culture.pdf [accessed 30 November 2007].

Shaw, C., Zorbaugh, F. and McKay, H. (1929) *Delinquency Areas*. Chicago: University of Chicago Press.

Sokolovskiy, S. (2002) 'Rasizm, rasializm i socialniye nauki v Rossii' ('Racism, racialism, and social sciences in Russia'), in V. Voronkov, O. Karpenko and A. Osipov (eds), *Rasizm v yazyke socialnyh nauk* ('Racism in the Language of Social Sciences'). St. Petersburg: Aleteya.

Tarasov, A. (2000) 'Porozhdenie reform: britogolovie, oni zhe skinkhedy' ('Result of reforms: boldheads AKA skinheads'), *Svobodnaya Mysl* ('Free Thought'), 4: 40–53.

Thornton, S. (1995) *Club Cultures: Music, Media, and Subcultural Capital*. Cambridge: Polity Press.

Thrasher, F. (1927) *The Gang: A Study of 1,313 Gangs in Chicago*. Chicago: Chicago University Press.

Verkhovskiy, A., Papp, A. and Pribylovskiy, V. (1996) *Politicheskiy extremism v Rossii* ('Political Extremism in Russia'). Moscow: Institute of Experimental Sociology.

Vold, G. (1958) *Theoretical Criminology*. New York: Oxford University Press.

Voronkov, V., Karpenko, O. and Osipov, A. (eds) (2002) *Rasizm v yazyke socialnyh nauk* ('Racism in the Language of Social Sciences'). St. Petersburg: Aleteya.

Wahl, K. (1995) 'Fremdenfeindlichkeit, Rechtsextremismus, Gewalt', in Deutsches Jugendinstitut (Hrsg), *Gewalt gegen Fremde* (2 Aufl.). München, pp. 11–74.

Watts, W.M. (2001) 'Aggressive youth cultures and hate crime: skinheads and xenophobic youth in Germany', *American Behavioral Scientist*, 45(4): 600–15.

Part III

Ethnicity and street gangs

Chapter 8

The role of race and ethnicity in gang membership

Finn-Aage Esbensen, Bradley T. Brick, Chris Melde, Karin Tusinski and Terrance J. Taylor

Introduction

Youth gangs have received considerable academic and media attention over the years, with a heightened interest stimulated in part by the American late-twentieth-century youth violence epidemic. Much of the literature has included discussion of definitional concerns, including terms such as 'gang', 'gang member' and 'gang crime'. These definitional debates are difficult when carried out within one country but become even more complex when attempted cross-nationally. In 1998, the Eurogang programme of research initiated dialogue among researchers and policymakers interested in the comparative study of youth gangs (Klein *et al.* 2001). The following consensus definition of youth gangs was reached: '*A youth gang, or troublesome youth group, is a durable, street-oriented youth group whose involvement in illegal activity is part of their group identity.*' A youth survey form incorporating questions that allowed for operationalisation of this definition was subsequently developed. In this chapter, we employ the Eurogang definition and measurement of youth gangs to examine: (1) the distribution of gang membership – prevalence and demographic characteristics – in an American school-based sample; (2) the epidemiology of individual offending by gang membership and race/ethnicity; and (3) descriptions of gang characteristics by race/ethnicity[1] of gang members.

Given the perception that American gangs are typically well organised and comprised of young, African-American males residing in single-parent families in urban areas (Esbensen and Tusinski 2007), issues of race/ethnicity are particularly pertinent to policy issues. American policies aimed at gangs and gang-related violence have often been disproportionate to the threat (McCorkle and Miethe 1998) and targeted disproportionately at groups (often erroneously) perceived to be the main source of the problem. Thus, our study examines racial/ethnic differences in gang membership and behaviour as a way of informing policy which disproportionately affects the lives of minority youth.

Demographic characteristics of gang youth

The actual prevalence of youth gangs and gang membership remains somewhat of a mystery. Historically, the emphasis has been on explaining gangs in local contexts. It was not until Walter Miller undertook the first 'national' US youth gang survey in 1974[2] that attention shifted to documenting the presence of gangs and gang members across multiple jurisdictions. In 2002, Egley *et al.* (2006) estimated that there were approximately 731,500 gang members and 21,600 active gangs. Surveys of adolescents report a range of gang membership. According to Klein and Maxson's (2006) review, estimates ranged from 3 to 6 per cent of youths in studies utilising a restricted definition of current gang membership, 13–18 per cent of youths having ever been gang members in studies utilising a restricted definition, and up to 37 per cent of youths being gang-identified in studies where unrestricted definitions were used (Klein and Maxson 2006: 22–31).

There is significant variation in the demographic characteristics (e.g. sex, race/ethnicity, age) ascribed to American gang membership. Much of this divergence can be attributed to methodological issues associated with two things: the source of the information and the specific definition utilised. Law enforcement data and much of the qualitative research focus on older samples of primarily inner-city minority youth and, as such, typically find gang members to be male, racial/ethnic minorities in their late teens and twenties. Household and school-based youth surveys describe gang-involved youth in their early to mid-teens and demographically representative of youth in their communities (e.g. Esbensen and Lynskey 2001; Thornberry et al. 2003). Yet, assessments of the extent to which demographic attributes among gang members are differentially distributed by racial/ethnic groups are sorely lacking. This is an important void, as public perceptions and policies are often shaped by the media (Decker and Kempf 1991), which perpetuate stereotypes of gang members as young, African-American males, operating as part of violent criminal organisations in American cities (Esbensen and Tusinski 2007).

One common myth about gang members is that they are almost exclusively members of ethnic or racial minority groups. Ethnographic studies, conducted primarily in the neighborhoods of large cities with high concentrations of minority residents, and law enforcement estimates have facilitated this image (Covey *et al.* 1997). A recent report from the National Youth Gang Center confirmed this overall assessment but cautioned that the representation of Caucasian gang members was higher in jurisdictions reporting more recent onset of gang activity (Egley *et al.* 2006). It appears that the race/ethnicity of gang members may be closely tied to community size, as whites comprised only 11 per cent of gang members in large cities, but approximately 30 per cent of gang members in small cities and rural counties (Moore and Cook 1999). As research expands to more representative samples of the general population, a redefinition of the racial and ethnic composition of gang members is likely. Esbensen and Lynskey (2001) reported that community-level demographics were reflected in the composition of youth gangs; that is, gang members were white in primarily white communities and gang members were African-American in predominantly African-American communities.

Interestingly, early American gang studies provided a rich source of information about white urban gangs. These early gangs were usually described according to nationality and/or ethnicity, not race. It was not until the 1950s that researchers began to identify gang members by race (Spergel 1995). This change in gang composition is closely tied to demographic changes in neighborhood characteristics where research is conducted (Covey *et al.* 1997: 240). While the race/ ethnicity of gang members has been noted by researchers and law enforcement reports, less attention has been given to the role of race/ ethnicity in behavior and/or gang characteristics. To what extent, for instance, is crime specialisation race/ethnicity-specific? Are these unique group characteristics associated with different racial or ethnic gangs or gang members?

Gang behavior has also been described primarily as a male phenomenon. Law enforcement estimates generally indicate that more than 90 per cent of gang members are male (Curry *et al.* 1994). Recent survey research, however, suggests that females account for more than one-third of American youth gang members (Bjerregaard and Smith 1993; Esbensen and Huizinga 1993; Esbensen and Winfree 1998). Little is known, however, about the intersection of race/

ethnicity and sex. The question thus remains; to what extent, if any, does the sex composition of gangs vary by race and ethnicity?

Gang activities

Gangs and gang members are engaged in a number of activities other than violent crimes. In fact, throughout most of the day, gang members are like other adolescents – going to school, working, hanging out, and eating with family or friends (e.g. Decker and van Winkle 1996; Esbensen *et al.* 1993; Fleisher 1998; Klein 1995). Criminal activity and violence in particular are relatively rare occurrences in the context of other gang activities. Regardless, it is still a widely documented finding that gang members are responsible for a disproportionate amount of crime. Thornberry and Burch (1997), for example, reported that gang members accounted for 86 per cent of all serious offenses in the Rochester Youth Development Study sample. Block and Block (2001), using law enforcement data, also reported a considerable amount and variety of criminal activity of Chicago gang members. Between 1987 and 1990, for example, there were 17,085 criminal offenses classified as street gang-related in Chicago. Of these, 288 were homicides, over half (8,828) were classified as non-lethal violent offences (i.e. assaults and batteries), drug offences (sale and possession) accounted for approximately one-third of the offences (5,888), and the remaining 2,081 offences included all other offence types.

Gang membership has also been found to enhance involvement in delinquent activity of all kinds (e.g. Battin-Pearson *et al.* 1998; Esbensen and Huizinga 1993; Huizinga 1997; Thornberry and Burch 1997). Comparisons of gang and non-gang youths consistently and historically have produced significant differences in both the prevalence and frequency of offending between these two groups. According to self-report surveys, gang youth account for approximately 70 per cent of all self-reported violent offending in adolescent samples (Huizinga *et al.* 2002; Thornberry and Burch 1997). In their research involving 15-year-old youths, Battin and colleagues (1998), for example, report that gang members committed twice as many violent acts during the prior year as did youth who were not gang members but had delinquent friends, and seven times as many violent acts as non-gang youths without delinquent friends.

Gang characteristics

Gangs are often described as highly organised entities with recognised leadership and organisational structure in the form of cliques and sex- and/or age-specific roles for gang members (e.g. Curry and Decker 2003). Additionally, gangs are described as territorial and persisting over relatively long periods of time. Some gangs in Chicago and Los Angeles are described as multigenerational. To accommodate this wide range of gang characteristics, Maxson and Klein (1995) developed a typology of five gang types based upon specific gang characteristics (e.g. duration, size, age composition, territoriality, and crime specialisation). To our knowledge, few efforts to date have attempted to examine the extent to which such characteristics vary by the racial/ethnic composition of the gang (but see Freng and Winfree 2004).

The Eurogang programme: youth survey

The Eurogang youth survey represents the culmination of many years of collaboration. From 1999 through 2004, a working group of researchers discussed, developed, translated, and ultimately pretested a questionnaire that could be administered to youth as young as 11 and 12.

One noticeable aspect of this instrument was the development of a funneling strategy. While most American gang research utilising youth surveys (e.g. Battin *et al.* 1998; Esbensen and Huizinga 1993, Esbensen *et al.* 2001; Thornberry *et al.* 2003) has relied upon a filtering approach (i.e. ask respondents whether they belong to a gang), the funneling approach leads respondents through a series of questions about their group of friends that ends with the question, 'Do you consider this group to be a gang?' Questions measuring gang characteristics believed to be essential defining elements of the group and descriptions of the group comprise this section. In this manner, the researcher can construct or classify gang membership by the defining characteristics of the peer group rather than rely upon the self-nomination technique.[3]

The Eurogang definition (*a youth gang, or troublesome youth group, is a durable, street-oriented youth group whose involvement in illegal activity is part of their group identity*) contains four key definitional elements: stability or durability, street-orientation, involvement in illegal activity, and group identity. To capture these elements, respondents were first asked whether they had a group of friends with whom they did things. Next they were asked about the age of the group, how long it had existed, whether they spent a lot of time hanging out in public places, whether it was OK for members of the group to do illegal things, and whether they did illegal things together. (See Appendix A for actual questions and response categories.)

Current study

Site selection and sample description

The data utilised in this study are part of an evaluation of a school-based, law-related education program. As such, a purposive sample of 15 schools located in nine cities in four US states was selected for inclusion in the evaluation; only schools offering the targeted programme were eligible for inclusion (for more information on the sample, see Esbensen 2005). The programme was generally taught in middle school: as such, our sample consists of students enrolled in grades six through nine.

Active parental consent[4] was obtained prior to survey administration. Based upon prior experience, a strategy for maximising returns and minimising time requirements was implemented; teachers were recruited to assist in the process. Teachers were compensated for their assistance in collecting the signed parental consent forms and students were provided an incentive for returning the consent forms (e.g. key chains or lanyards). This strategy was quite successful, resulting in a return rate of 84 per cent and taking less than two weeks. A total of 2,353 students were enrolled in the 98 targeted classrooms. Of these students, 1,686 (72 per cent) returned permission slips providing parental consent, 291 (12 per cent) returned refusals, and 374 (16 per cent) failed to return consent forms. Pretests were completed by 1,624 (96 per cent) students while 1,499 (89 per cent) students completed post-test questionnaires.

Student questionnaire and survey administration

The post-test data serve as the basis for the analyses presented in this chapter. The group, self-administered questionnaires were collected during the winter and spring of the 2004–5 school year. All students from whom active parental consent had been obtained were asked to complete the confidential questionnaires. At least two members of the research team were present in each classroom to administer the surveys. To reduce the problem of low reading levels among some students, one researcher read the questionnaire aloud while the other researcher assisted students with questions or problems that arose. To reduce sample attrition, researchers revisited schools one or more times to survey students who were absent on the initial day of data collection. This procedure resulted in an overall completion rate of 89 per cent of the active consent sample.

Results

Consistent with the Eurogang definition, we used the following procedures. First, we utilised the funneling approach and restricted our gang sample to those respondents who indicated the following: they had a group of friends with whom they spent time and who were aged 12–25; the group had been around for more that three months and hung out in public places; and, importantly, members of the group believed that it is okay to do illegal things, and they reported committing illegal acts together. Only those youths with valid responses to all the Eurogang funneling questions were categorised as gang or non-gang.

Of the 1,495 respondents, 115 failed to answer all of the defining gang questions. Of the remaining 1,380 youths, 1,266 (92.4 per cent) were classified as non-gang youth and 114 (7.6 per cent) were classified as gang members by this constructed definition. As in other adolescent surveys, there was little difference in gang membership by sex, with 8.8 per cent of boys and 7.8 per cent of girls classified as gang members. Table 8.1 provides descriptive information about the sample as well as a breakdown by gang and non-gang classification. As in other adolescent surveys, we found that girls comprised a sizable percentage of gang-involved youth; in fact, they accounted for a majority of gang members in this sample (51.8 per cent). Consistent with other surveys, and contrary to law enforcement descriptions, gang membership was found among all racial/ethnic groups (7.3 per cent of whites, 8.3 per cent of blacks, 9.0 per cent of Hispanics, and 12.9 per cent of multiracial[5] groups). Gang membership increased with age; only 1.6 per cent of youth under age 12 were classified as gang youth, whereas more than 15.6 per cent of those 14 and older were so classified. Children living with their biological parents reported the lowest representation among gang youth (7.2 per cent), followed by single-parent households (8.2 per cent) and reconstituted families (e.g. a parent and step-parent) (10.6 per cent), while youth living in some other arrangement had the highest rate of gang membership (11.5 per cent). With regard to parental education, those youths whose parents had at least some college education were the least likely to report gang affiliation (7.7 per cent) while those whose parents had a high school diploma had the highest rate of gang membership (12.0 per cent).

Gang member demographics by race/ethnicity

To what extent, if any, do demographic characteristics vary by race/ ethnicity? We found some interesting differences but, for the most part, the patterns are quite similar. With respect to sex of gang-involved youth, for whites, blacks and Hispanics, boys have slightly higher rates of gang membership (8.0, 10.2 and 10.2, respectively) than do girls (6.6, 7.1, and 8.2, respectively). For multiracial youth, however, girls have a prevalence rate more than twice that of the boys (15.8 versus 7.1). As reported in other surveys of young adolescent samples, gang membership increases with age among white, black and Hispanic youth. Among multiracial youth, the rates are elevated early and remain higher at each age than among the other three groups. It is with family structure that interesting differences emerge. While white youth living in two-parent households (biological parents or reconstituted families), report lower levels of gang membership than white youth living in single-parent and other arrangements, this pattern differs for other racial or ethnic groups. In fact, for black youth, the exact opposite is the case; youth living in single parent or 'other' households report the lowest level of gang membership and those living with their biological parents or reconstituted families report the highest. Yet, a different pattern holds for Hispanic youth, for whom single-parent and reconstituted families are the highest rates. The multiracial group is most similar to black youth, with single-parent families having the lowest prevalence rates.

Gang member delinquency by race/ethnicity

Survey respondents were asked to indicate how many times in the prior three months they had committed a variety of delinquent acts,

Table 8.1 Sample characteristics for total sample, Eurogang categories, and racial/ethnic group gang members

Variable	Total sample n	Total sample %	Non-gang n = 1269 %	Eurogang n = 114 %	White* n = 33 %	Black* n = 12 %	Hispanic* n = 53 %	Multirace* n = 11 %
Sex								
Male	688	46.0%	91.2%	8.8%	8.0%	10.2%	10.2%	7.1%
Female	807	54.0%	92.2%	7.8%	6.6%	7.1%	8.2%	15.8%
Race/ethnicity								
White	482	32.4%	92.7%	7.3%	–	–	–	–
Black	162	10.9%	91.7%	8.3%	–	–	–	–
Hispanic	645	43.4%	91.0%	9.0%	–	–	–	–
Multiracial	88	5.9%	87.1%	12.9%	–	–	–	–
Other	109	6.3%	96.1%	3.9%	–	–	–	–
Age								
Under 12	197	13.2%	98.4%	1.6%	0.0%	0.0%	2.5%	6.7%
12	438	29.4%	94.6%	5.4%	4.8%	3.1%	5.5%	12.0%
13	536	36.0%	91.0%	9.0%	5.1%	10.7%	10.5%	12.5%
Over 13	319	21.5%	84.4%	15.6%	17.1%	12.2%	17.0%	19.0%
Family structure								
Mother and father	855	57.3%	92.8%	7.2%	5.8%	11.5%	7.6%	10.5%
Single parent	267	17.9%	91.8%	8.2%	9.7%	4.3%	9.8%	6.3%
Reconstituted family	240	16.1%	89.4%	10.6%	6.3%	10.7%	14.9%	15.0%
Other	129	8.7%	88.5%	11.5%	15.4%	5.6%	7.7%	30.0%

*Percentages reported for race/ethnicity categories are for gang members only

from skipping school to attacking someone with a weapon. In this chapter, we have collapsed these single items into four composite indices: *general delinquency* includes all 14 items; *minor delinquency* consists of four items; *property offences* include four items, and *serious violence* includes three items. In addition to prevalence rates for these four indices, we also report prevalence rates for three single items for the full sample, for all gang youth, and for each specific racial/ethnic gang in Table 8.2. (See Appendix B for the actual items.) Although more than 40 per cent of this sample were 12 or younger, more than 60 per cent of the respondents admitted to committing one or more delinquent acts during the preceding three months, with almost 14 per cent indicating that they had committed a violent act. Among gang youth, these prevalence rates were significantly higher. Virtually all of the gang members (98.2 per cent) reported committing one or more delinquent acts, all of the black, Hispanic, and multiracial gang members indicated that they had done so. Additionally, almost one in three gang members reported that they had been arrested.

Gang youth, regardless of race/ethnicity, reported higher prevalence rates of offending and arrest than non-gang youths. In Table 8.2, we report only gang rates for race/ethnicity to simplify the comparisons. However, in no instance did the non-gang youth of any race/ethnicity report higher prevalence rates than any gang group. The prevalence rates are generally quite similar across race/ethnic groups, although some differences are worthy of note. White gang youth reported a prevalence of violence almost one-third that of black and Hispanic gang youth. Black gang members reported the lowest rates of property offending but the highest rates of drug sales and weapon carrying, 22 per cent indicating that they had carried a gun for protection, but, interestingly, they also reported the lowest rates of arrest.

Gang characteristics by race/ethnicity

Included in the gang section of the survey were a number of questions tapping gang characteristics, including age, sex, and racial/ethnic composition of group members. We also obtained indicators of the group's longevity, whether it was territorial, and the degree to which members specialised in specific crimes. With respect to group size (see Table 8.3), the gang youth tended to belong to larger groups than did the non-gang youth; 39 per cent of the non-gang youth reported five or fewer members compared to only 13 per cent

Table 8.2 Prevalence of delinquent behaviors for total sample, Eurogang categories, and gang members by racial/ethnic group

Variable	Total		Non-gang	Eurogang	White*	Black*	Hispanic*	Multiracial*
	n	%	$n = 1269$ %	$n = 114$ %	$n = 33$ %	$n = 12$ %	$n = 53$ %	$n = 11$ %
Delinquency								
General	896	60.2%	55.9%	98.2%	93.9%	100.0%	100.0%	100.0%
Minor delinquency	586	39.5%	34.4%	88.6%	81.8%	91.7%	94.3%	81.8%
Property	222	14.9%	12.3%	45.6%	45.5%	33.3%	49.1%	54.5%
Serious violence	207	13.9%	10.3%	50.4%	24.2%	63.6%	62.3%	54.5%
Drug sales	61	4.1%	2.0%	28.8%	22.6%	41.7%	28.8%	36.4%
Weapon carrying	164	11.1%	8.4%	44.2%	42.4%	50.0%	44.2%	36.4%
Gun carrying	17	1.7%	1.1%	9.3%	4.5%	22.2%	11.6%	0.0%
Arrested	97	6.6%	4.1%	30.0%	22.6%	16.7%	32.7%	36.4%

*Percentages reported for race/ethnicity categories are for gang members only

of gang youth. At the other extreme, only 8 per cent of non-gang youth reported their groups as having more than 20 members, while 22 per cent of gang youth reported this many members. Among the gang youth, whites tended to report smaller gangs than did the other racial/ethnic groups; only 36 per cent of whites reported more than ten members in their group compared to 58 per cent of black, 68 per cent of Hispanic and 57 per cent of multiracial respondents.

Gangs appear to be more integrated by sex than is often assumed. Fewer than 10 per cent of gang respondents said that their group was exclusively male compared to 14 per cent of non-gang youth; likewise, only four gang members (3.5 per cent) indicated that their group was exclusively female compared with 13 per cent of the non-gang youth. The sex composition of the gangs was quite similar across racial/ethnic groups, with approximately 85–100 per cent of gang youth indicating that their group comprised both boys and girls (Table 8.3).

With respect to racial composition, respondents were asked to indicate how many of the group's members were white, black, Hispanic, or other. For each category, they could indicate all, most, some, or none. For the purposes of this chapter, we have combined responses to the all or most categories. There appear to be slight differences between the racial/ethnic composition of gangs and non-gang groups as well as differences among gangs. Among non-gang youth, 69 per cent of white, 74 per cent of black, and 77 per cent of Hispanic indicated that most or all of the group's members were the same race/ethnicity as the respondent. A similar pattern exists for gang youth with 72, 73 and 90 per cent of white, black and Hispanic gang members, respectively, indicating that most or all of their gang members were of the same race/ethnicity.

We asked survey respondents a number of questions about their group of friends. As we have seen, some of these questions were used to categorise the peer groups as gang or non-gang groups. Among other descriptors, we asked a series of questions to tap the group's territoriality, including whether they had a place of their own, whether or not they allowed others to enter this area, and whether they defended their area. More than twice as many of the gang (70 per cent) than the non-gang (31 per cent) youth indicated that their group had a place of their own, and a majority of gang youth (51 per cent) also indicated that they defended their space compared to only 12 per cent of the non-gang groups. Some differences existed between the gangs by race/ethnicity; whereas only 55 per cent of the multiracial gang members indicated that their group had a place of its own, 67 per cent of white gang members and 75 per cent of black and Hispanic gang youth stated that they had their own place. There were also differences in their defense of these places, with 42 per cent of white, 46 per cent of multiracial, 54 per cent of Hispanic, and 67 per cent of black youth indicating that they defended their space. Territoriality thus appears to be more characteristic of black and Hispanic gang youths than of the white and multiracial gang youths. Yet another question about their territory supports this assessment: when asked whether they let others into their area, 68 per cent of white and 50 per cent of multiracial youths said that they did compared to only 20 per cent of black and 40 per cent of Hispanic youths.

Considerable attention has been given to the diversity of gangs with Maxson and Klein (1995) suggesting a typology of gangs. New or emergent gang cities tend to report smaller gangs with shorter histories. In addition, there is growing evidence that once gangs are established, they do not necessarily persist. They die out and are replaced by others. Our data support this. Twenty-five per cent of all gangs had been in existence for less than one year and only 10 per cent were reported to have a history of 11 years or more. While there were some variations between racial/ethnic gangs, the major difference was between gang and non-gang groups (42 per cent of non-gang youths reported their group had been in existence for one year or less and only 4 per cent had a history of more than ten years).

Respondents were also asked whether they considered their group of friends to be a gang. Surprisingly, although we classified the youth as gang members according to the Eurogang definition, only 37.5 per cent of this group considered their group to be a gang compared to 7 per cent of the non-gang group who believed that their group was a gang. Interestingly, there were significant differences by race/ethnicity. Among those we classified as gangs, 15 per cent of white, 67 per cent of black, 43 per cent of Hispanic, and 36 per cent of multirace youths considered their group a gang. Comparable percentages for non-gang youth were: 4.4, 11.6, 8.2, and 2.8 percent. Thus, it appears that the Eurogang definition may be capturing something more unique to black gangs than to other racial/ethnic groups, or that youths of different racial/ethnic backgrounds may perceive the word 'gang' differently. (See also Esbensen et al. (2006) for more discussion of this measurement issue.)

Table 8.3 Group characteristics for total sample Eurogang categories and gang members by racial/ethnic group

Group characteristic	Total n	Total %	Non-gang n = 1269 %	Eurogang n = 114 %	White* n = 33 %	Black* n = 12 %	Hispanic* n = 53 %	Multiracial* n = 11 %
Group size (plus self)								
5 or less	519	36.4%	39.2%	13.2%	15.2%	25.0%	7.5%	18.2%
6–10	458	32.1%	32.2%	28.9%	48.5%	16.7%	24.5%	9.1%
11–20	315	22.1%	20.7%	36.0%	27.3%	16.7%	43.4%	45.5%
More than 20	136	9.5%	8.0%	21.9%	9.1%	41.6%	24.6%	11.1%
Sex composition								
All male	190	13.3%	13.7%	9.6%	9.1%	8.3%	11.3%	0.0%
Mostly male	263	18.5%	34.8%	21.9%	9.1%	33.3%	20.8%	18.2%
Half male/half female	532	37.4%	34.8%	55.3%	60.6%	33.3%	54.7%	72.7%
Mostly female	271	19.0%	20.2%	9.6%	6.1%	25.0%	9.4%	9.1%
All female	168	11.8%	13.1%	3.5%	6.1%	0.0%	3.8%	0.0%
Age composition								
15 and under	1286	91.2%	92.8%	74.6%	84.8%	50.0%	73.6%	81.8%
16–18	99	7.0%	5.7%	21.1%	12.1%	33.3%	24.5%	9.1%
19 and over	25	1.7%	1.5%	4.4%	3.0%	16.7%	1.9%	9.1%
White composition								
All or most	646	31.1%	31.9%	28.3%	61.9%	11.1%	8.6%	0.0%
Black composition								
All or most	178	14.0%	13.0%	6.2%	9.7%	72.8%	4.4%	33.3%

	N							
Hispanic composition								
All or most	585	43.3%	41.1%	58.9%	6.4%	30.0%	90.3%	80.0%
Other race composition								
All or most	89	7.6%	6.6%	7.7%	6.8%	10.0%	7.3%	12.5%
No adults present	843	59.2%	56.3%	91.2%	93.9%	83.3%	90.4%	100.0%
Drugs present	170	11.7%	7.2%	62.8%	63.6%	50.0%	67.3%	72.7%
In public place	934	65.0%	60.7%	100.0%	100.0%	100.0%	100.0%	100.0%
Place of own	472	34.1%	30.9%	69.9%	66.7%	75.0%	74.5%	54.5%
Let others in**	288	20.3%	18.8%	32.1%	68.2%	20.0%	39.5%	50.0%
Defend area**	218	15.4%	11.9%	51.4%	42.4%	66.7%	54.0%	45.5%
*How defend** *								
Fight	95	6.8%	4.7%	27.3%	18.2%	41.7%	30.6%	27.3%
Intimidate	71	5.1%	4.0%	19.1%	15.2%	16.7%	20.4%	18.2%
Verbal persuasion	25	2.3%	1.6%	2.7%	9.1%	0.0%	0.0%	0.0%
Other	32	2.3%	2.2%	1.8%	0.0%	8.3%	2.0%	0.0%
Group history								
Less than 3 months	101	7.4%	7.9%	0.0%	0.0%	0.0%	0.0%	0.0%
3 months to 1 year	452	33.3%	34.1%	24.6%	27.3%	16.7%	18.9%	36.4%
1–4 years	600	44.2%	44.4%	46.5%	42.4%	41.7%	54.7%	36.4%
5–10 years	144	10.6%	9.8%	19.3%	24.2%	25.0%	15.1%	18.2%
11–20 years	35	2.6%	2.5%	4.4%	3.0%	16.7%	2.8%	0.0%
More than 20 years	24	1.8%	1.3%	5.3%	3.0%	0.0%	7.5%	9.1%
Approve of illegal acts	257	18.1%	10.4%	100.0%	100.0%	100.0%	100.0%	100.0%
Do illegal acts	244	17.1%	9.2%	100.0%	100.0%	100.0%	100.0%	100.0%
Consider group gang	140	9.6%	7.1%	37.5%	15.2%	66.7%	43.1%	36.4%
Ever been in gang	152	10.4%	7.7%	36.3%	15.2%	50.0%	46.2%	27.3%
Gang in community***	807	55.0%	52.2%	81.6%	66.7%	91.7%	84.9%	90.9%

* Percentages reported for race/ethnicity categories are for gang members only.

** Percentages calculated from entire sample including individuals who responded 'No' to having a place of their own.

*** Percentage is calculated including the 'don't know' category.

Group delinquency by race/ethnicity

The last question examined in this chapter asks about the group-level delinquency of these adolescent groups. Survey respondents were asked to indicate whether their group participated in a series of specific illegal activities. We created two composite measures to examine this issue, one a variety index of violent offences (threaten people, fight, rob other people, or beat up someone) for which a group could receive a score ranging from zero (if they did not commit any of the offences) to four (if they committed all four), and one capturing 'gang-like' illegal activity (the preceding four items plus, carrying illegal weapons and writing graffiti) with a range of one to six. Almost half of the non-gang youth (46 per cent and 45 per cent) reported no involvement of their group in either of these indices compared to 5 per cent of gang youths indicating that their group did not engage in these activities. Conversely, 44 and 31 per cent of gang and 6 and 3 per cent of non-gang youths, respectively, reported committing all of the behaviours included in each variety scale. There appear to be slight variations among different racial/ethnic groups, with Hispanic youths reporting the highest scores on both variety indices (49 per cent scored four on the violence scale and 38 per cent on the gang-like activities). This contrasts with only 36 and 27 per cent, respectively, for whites, 42 and 25 per cent for blacks, and 46 and 18 per cent for the multiracial youths. Table 8.4 provides more detail about the actual distribution of scores on these variety scales. Of particular interest, especially in light of the fact that only 15 per cent of the white gang youth considered their group a gang, we find here that 30 per cent of the white youth indicated that members of their group committed two or fewer of the six behaviours included in the gang-like index compared to 11 per cent or less of the other three racial/ethnic groups. While there were some differences reported on the self-reported delinquency measures by race/ethnicity (see Table 8.2), these group-level measures of illegal activity highlight more substantive differences in offending patterns.

Conclusion

Policymakers, often basing their information on media depictions (Decker and Kempf 1991) that American gangs are typically well organised and comprised of young, African-American males residing in single-parent families in urban areas (Esbensen and Tusinski 2007), have developed gang-related policies and statutes often

Table 8.4 Group delinquent activities indices for total sample, Eurogang categories and gang members by racial/ethnic group

Variable	Total n	Total %	Non-gang n = 1269	Eurogang n=114	White n=33 %	Black n=12 %	Hispanic n=53 %	Multiracial n=11 %
Group violence								
0	614	42.8%	46.2%	5.3%	12.1%	8.3%	0.0%	0.0%
1	239	16.7%	17.3%	7.9%	9.1%	0.0%	11.3%	0.0%
2	213	14.8%	15.3%	10.5%	12.1%	16.7%	9.4%	9.1%
3	249	17.4%	15.7%	32.5%	30.3%	33.3%	30.2%	45.5%
4	120	8.4%	5.5%	43.9%	36.4%	41.7%	49.1%	45.5%
Group gang-like acts								
0	595	41.5%	45.0%	5.3%	12.1%	8.3%	0.0%	0.0%
1	230	16.0%	17.0%	5.3%	6.1%	0.0%	7.5%	0.0%
2	189	13.2%	13.9%	6.1%	12.1%	0.0%	3.8%	9.1%
3	171	11.9%	11.5%	11.4%	9.1%	16.7%	13.2%	9.1%
4	99	6.9%	5.9%	18.4%	15.2%	25.0%	18.9%	18.2%
5	81	5.6%	4.1%	22.8%	18.2%	25.0%	18.9%	45.5%
6	69	4.8%	2.6%	30.7%	27.3%	25.0%	37.7%	18.2%

disproportionate to the threat (McCorkle and Miethe 1998), and have targeted disproportionately racial/ethnic minority groups perceived to be the main source of the problem. In this chapter, we have reported findings from a survey of young adolescents in the USA. Utilising the Eurogang definition and questions, we classified respondents as gang or non-gang and then examined the individual and group characteristics of these two groups. We further examined the extent to which differences and similarities emerged among gang youth of different racial/ethnic backgrounds. In general, we can conclude that gang membership provides a similar experience for its members relative to non-gang youth.

Our findings do suggest, however, that researchers and policymakers should be more attentive to racial/ethnic differences in gangs and gang membership. For example, we conclude the following:

(1) Family structure does not exert the same influence on all four racial groups – gang membership is less common, relatively speaking, among single-parent black and multiracial households than among two-parent families.
(2) White youth have significantly lower rates of self-reported involvement in serious violent offending while black gang youth report the highest level of drug selling and weapon carrying.
(3) Black gangs tend to be larger than other racial/ethnic groups and, regardless of race/ethnicity, gangs tend to be comprised of both boys and girls.
(4) Gangs appear to engage in a variety of offences, although white gang youths report less variety in their gang's offending than do the other gang members.

This work should be considered exploratory, laying a foundation for future research. While we have focused on bivariate relationships, the obvious next step is to pursue multivariate examinations. Such research can help uncover the relationships between gangs, violence, and race/ethnicity, thus leading to more informed public policy.

Acknowledgements

This research is funded by the National Institute of Justice, Office of Justice Programs, US Department of Justice, Award #2003-JN-FX-003 (October 2003–December 2008). Points of view in this document are those of the authors and do not necessarily represent the official position of the US Department of Justice.

Notes

1 This chapter uses 'race/ethnicity' categories based upon US census classifications prior to 2000. Four main racial categories were used by the census: (1) White; (2) Black; (3) American Indian or Alaskan Native; and (4) Asian or Pacific Islander. Additionally, two ethnicities were recorded by the census prior to 2000: Hispanic and non-Hispanic. These classifications have recently been expanded. For more information, consult the US census (2007).

2 Miller's (1974) survey included 12 large American cities. Since then, considerable progress has been made (see Curry and Decker 2003), as the National Youth Gang Center conducts annual surveys of law enforcement agencies to assess the distribution of gangs in the US (see Egley *et al.* 2006).

3 This strategy poses difficulties in cross-national research as the word 'gang' cannot easily be translated into all languages and, even when translated, often has a different meaning than in English.

4 Research involving youths under the age of 18 in the USA requires additional procedural safeguards. With few exceptions, youths under the age of 18 are considered dependents, unable to make informed decisions about risks and benefits, and thus in need of adult permission and oversight to enter into research studies. Parents/guardians are responsible for providing this permission. In order to conduct research with youths, researchers must obtain both the consent of the parent/guardian of the youth (i.e. parental approval for researchers to contact their child(ren)) and the assent of the youths (i.e. agreement to participate). Parental consent generally takes two forms: (1) passive parental consent (i.e. the parent/guardian must specifically prohibit their child's participation) and (2) active parental consent (i.e. the parent/guardian must specify that their child is allowed to participate).

5 'Multiracial' refers to youths who indicated belonging to more than one racial/ethnic group.

References

Battin, S.R., Hill, K.G., Abbott, R.D., Catalano, R.F. and Hawkins, J.D. (1998) 'The contribution of gang membership to delinquency beyond delinquent friends', *Criminology*, 36(1): 93–115.

Battin-Pearson, S.R., Thornberry, T.P., Hawkins, J.D. and Krohn, M.D. (1998) 'Gang membership, delinquent peers, and delinquent behavior', *Juvenile Justice Bulletin*. Washington, DC: US Department of Justice, Office of Justice Programs, Office of Juvenile Justice and Delinquency Prevention.

Bjerregaard, B. and Smith, C. (1993) 'Gender differences in gang participation, delinquency, and substance use', *Journal of Quantitative Criminology*, 4(3): 329–55.

Block, C.R. and Block, R. (2001) 'Street gang crime in Chicago', in J. Miller, C.L. Maxson and M.W. Klein (eds), *The Modern Gang Reader* (2nd edn). Los Angeles, CA: Roxbury Press, pp. 186–99.

Covey, H.C., Menard, S. and Franzese, R.J. (eds) (1997) *Juvenile Gangs* (2nd edn). Springfield, IL: Charles C. Thomas.

Curry, G.D. and Decker, S.H. (2003) *Confronting Gangs: Crime and Communities.* Los Angeles, CA: Roxbury Press.

Curry, G.D. and Thomas, R.W. (1992). 'Community organization and gang policy response', *Journal of Quantitative Criminology,* 8(4): 357–74.

Curry, G.D., Ball, R.A. and Fox, R.J. (1994) 'Gang crime and law enforcement record keeping', *NIJ Research in Brief.* Washington, DC: US Department of Justice, Office of Justice Programs, National Institute of Justice.

Decker, S.H. and Kempf, K. (1991) 'Constructing gangs: The social definition of youth activities', *Criminal Justice Policy Review,* 5(4): 271–91.

Decker, S.H. and Van Winkle, B. (1996) *Life in the Gang: Family, Friends, and Violence.* New York, NY: Cambridge University Press.

Egley, A., Jr., Howell, J.C. and Majors, A.K. (2006) *National Youth Gang Survey, 1999-2001.* Washington, DC: US Department of Justice, Office of Justice Programs, Office of Juvenile Justice and Delinquency Prevention.

Esbensen, F.-A. (2005) *Process Evaluation Report: Evaluation of the Teens, Crime and the Community and Community Works Program.* Washington, DC: US Department of Justice, Office of Justice Programs, National Institute of Justice.

Esbensen, F.-A. and Huizinga, D. (1993) 'Gangs, drugs, and delinquency in a survey of urban youth', *Criminology,* 31(4): 565–89.

Esbensen, F.-A., Huizinga, D. and Weiher, A. (1993) 'Gang and non-gang youth: differences in explanatory factors', *Journal of Contemporary Criminal Justice,* 9(2): 94–116.

Esbensen, F.-A. and Lynskey, D.P. (2001) 'Youth gang members in a school survey', in M.W. Klein, H.-J. Kerner, C.L. Maxson and E.G.M. Weitekamp (eds), *The Eurogang Paradox: Street Gangs and Youth Groups in the U.S. and Europe.* Amsterdam: Kluwer, pp. 93–114.

Esbensen, F.-A. and Tusinski, K. (2007) 'Youth gangs in the print media', *Journal of Crime and Popular Culture,* 14(1): 21–38.

Esbensen, F.-A. and Winfree, L.T., Jr. (1998) 'Race and gender differences between gang and non-gang youth: results from a multi-site survey', *Justice Quarterly,* 15(4): 505–26.

Esbensen, F.-A., Winfree, L.T., Jr., He, N. and Taylor, T.J. (2001) 'Youth gangs and definitional issues: when is a gang a gang and why does it matter?', *Crime and Delinquency,* 47(1): 105–30.

Esbensen, F.-A., Melde, C., Tusinski, K. and Brick, B. (2006) 'Measuring gang membership'. Paper presented at the Annual Meeting of the Western Society of Criminology (Seattle, WA).

Fleisher, M. (1998) *Dead End Kids*. Madison, WI: University of Wisconsin Press.

Freng, A. and Winfree, L.T., Jr. (2004) 'Exploring race and ethnic differences in a sample of middle school gang members', in F.-A. Esbensen, S.G. Tibbetts and L. Gaines (eds), *American Youth Gangs at the Millennium*. Long Grove, IL: Waveland Press, pp. 142–62.

Huizinga, D. (1997) 'Gangs and the volume of crime'. Paper presented at the Annual Meeting of the Western Society of Criminology (Honolulu, HI).

Huizinga, D., Weiher, A.W., Espiritu, R. and Esbensen, F.-A. (2002) 'Delinquency and crime: some highlights from the Denver Youth Survey', in T.P. Thornberry and M.D. Krohn (eds), *Taking Stock of Delinquency: An Overview of Findings from Longitudinal Studies*. New York: Plenum Press.

Klein, M.W. (1995) *The American Street Gang*. New York: Oxford University Press.

Klein, M.W. and Maxson, C.L. (2006) *Street Gang Patterns and Policies*. New York, NY: Oxford University Press.

Klein, M.W., Kerner, H.-J., Maxson, C.L. and Weitekamp, E.G.M. (eds) (2001) *The Eurogang Paradox: Street Gangs and Youth Groups in the U.S. and Europe*. Amsterdam: Kluwer.

Maxson, C.L. and Klein, M.W. (1995) 'Investigating gang structures', *Journal of Gang Research*, 3(1): 33–40.

McCorkle, R.C. and Miethe, T.D. (1998) 'The political and organizational response to gangs: an examination of moral panic in Nevada', *Justice Quarterly*, 15(1): 41–64.

Moore, J.P. and Cook, I.L. (1999) *Highlights of the 1998 National Youth Gang Survey*. Washington, DC: US Department of Justice, Office of Justice Programs, Office of Juvenile Justice and Delinquency Prevention.

Spergel, I.A. (1995) *The Youth Gang Problem*. New York: Oxford University Press.

Thornberry, T.P. and Burch, J., II (1997) 'Gang members and delinquent behavior', *Juvenile Justice Bulletin*. Washington, DC: US Department of Justice, Office of Justice Programs, Office of Juvenile Justice and Delinquency Prevention.

Thornberry, T.P., Krohn, M.D., Lizotte, A.J., Smith, C.A. and Tobin, K. (2003) *Gangs and Delinquency in Developmental Perspective*. New York: Cambridge University Press.

US Bureau of the Census (2007) *Racial and Ethnic Classifications Used in Census 2000 and Beyond*. Available online at: http://www.census.gov/population/www/socdemo/race/racefactcb.html.

Appendix A. Core items from the Eurogang youth survey

1. In addition to any such formal groups, some people have a certain group of friends that they spend time with, doing things together or just hanging out. Do you have a group of friends like that?

   1. No   2. Yes

2. Which one of the following best describes the ages of people in your group?

   1. Under twelve
   2. Twelve to fifteen
   3. Sixteen to eighteen
   4. Nineteen to twenty-five
   5. Over twenty-five.

3. Does this group spend a lot of time together in public places like the park, the street, shopping areas, or the neighborhood?

   1. No   2. Yes

4. How long has this group existed?

   1. Less than three months
   2. Three months to less than one year
   3. One to four years
   4. Five to ten years
   5. Eleven to twenty years
   6. More than twenty years

5. Is doing illegal things accepted by or okay for your group?

   1. No   2. Yes

6. Do people in your group actually do illegal things together?

   1. No   2. Yes

Appendix B. Self-reported delinquency measures

Minor delinquency

Skipped classes without excuse.
Lied about your age to get into some place or to buy something.

Property

Avoided paying for things such as movies, or bus or subway rides.
Purposely damaged or destroyed property that did not belong to you.
Illegally spray-painted a wall or a building.
Stole or tried to steal something worth less than $50.
Stole or tried to steal something worth more than $50.
Went into or tried to go into a building to steal something.

Serious violence

Attacked someone with a weapon.
Used a weapon or force to get money or things from people.
Been involved in gang fights.

General delinquency

Preceding 13 items plus the following three:
Carried a hidden weapon.
Hit someone with the idea of hurting them.
Sold marijuana or other illegal drugs.

Chapter 9

Weapons are for wimps: the social dynamics of ethnicity and violence in Australian gangs

Rob White

Introduction

Ethnicity is central to group formation and to the gang phenomenon in contemporary Australia. This is true both at the level of popular image – as reflected in media fixations with 'ethnic youth gangs' – and in regards to the social activities of large groups of (mainly) young men at the local neighbourhood level. Who you are, in terms of social identity, is largely determined by ethnicity, class background, and gender. Who you hang around with is likewise shaped by ethnicity, among other social factors. Whether or not you are considered a member of a 'gang' is partly a matter of perception (and, indeed, whose perception). It also very much depends upon the extent of engagement in group activities that are illegal and/or seriously antisocial. Violence is a major shaping factor in the genesis of youth gangs. It is also a major defining feature of the activities of these groups.

The aim of this chapter is to explore the social dynamics of ethnicity as this pertains to Australian youth gangs and gang-related behaviour. The link between ethnicity and violence is at the heart of the gang phenomenon in this country. Group identity, group formation, and group activity that is specifically associated with gangs tend to be founded upon and reinforced by physical and verbal conflicts between rival groups of young people.

Gang membership is heavily tied in with group violence. However, this violence is manifest within a wider context of social marginalisation and exclusion based upon ethnicity. Antagonisms on the street – between groups of young ethnic minority youth and authority figures such as the police, and between diverse groups of young people – are constantly reinforced by negative stereotyping, media moral panics, and the day-to-day racism experienced by the young people.

The durability of gang formation is influenced by ongoing violence, generally in public spaces, that is collective in nature and that involves serious assault. It is this intertwining of ethnicity and violence in the lives of young men from particular ethnic minority backgrounds that makes for the constitution of street gangs in the Eurogang sense – a durable, street-oriented youth group whose own identity includes involvement in illegal activity. Nevertheless, there are complexities here that need to be unravelled. Violence is ubiquitous among young ethnic minority men, yet not everyone is regarded by others or by themselves as gang members. To put it differently, racism and racist violence are basic features of life for certain ethnic minorities. It is this, in turn, that provides the ground for the emergence of specific group formations in which street violence, as such, becomes a central defining feature.

Gang research in Australia over the last decade and a half has pointed to the importance of ethnicity in how gangs are socially constructed in cities such as Sydney, Melbourne and Adelaide (Collins *et al*. 2000; Foote 1993; White *et al*. 1999). This research has been of a qualitative nature, generally involving interviews and observation as key techniques of data collection. The research has also been sensitive to the impact of diverse immigration histories and experiences on different ethnic minority youth. In addition, it has tended to frame issues in terms of community relationships as a whole, rather than specific individuals or particular groups abstracted from their local community context (White 2006a).

By and large, media 'moral panics' (Cohen, 1973) have been directed at ethnic minorities in Australian cities, although the specific minority group has varied depending upon location and time period (Poynting *et al*. 2004). For example, in Sydney today, the 'folk devil' of concern tends to be Muslim and Arabic youth, whereas in the 1970s it was young people of Italian and Greek backgrounds. In Melbourne and Perth, it is 'Asian' young people who feature in the newspaper headlines and around whom gang discourse is wrapped. Gang descriptors have generally been linked to specific waves of immigration as new groups have settled into Australia in significant numbers (e.g. Mediterranean migrants in the 1960s and 1970s; South-East Asian migrants in the late 1970s and early 1980s; Muslim and

Arab migrants in the 1990s; African migrants in the 1990s and 2000s). Gang descriptors have also been based upon specific types of crimes, which are linked in the public eye with particular immigrant groups (e.g. drugs with 'Asians'; terrorism with Muslims).

Whether or not the tag of 'gang' is warranted is subject to dispute; yet the perception and image of 'the gang' are, with very few exceptions, racialised through their associations with specific minority groups. The negative perceptions of these youth also plays a part in generating varying forms of resistance on their part, including the use of violence, as a means to bolster group solidarity and enhance personal self-esteem. How this resistance occurs is nevertheless contingent upon both local context and the specific ethnic group in question.

This chapter acknowledges that social perceptions and social dynamics relating to gangs vary greatly depending upon city locale and ethnic background. For present purposes, however, the focus will be on gang processes in Sydney, and in particular the western suburbs of Sydney. I wish to illustrate the complexities and the intriguing social patterns that are characteristic of group behaviour in a relatively impoverished part of this city. Sydney is comprised of some seven million people and lies on the eastern coastline of Australia. My concern is to probe the specific nature of group interaction at a local level, in order to highlight the particular significance of ethnicity and violence in the formation of groups and in actual group behaviour.

Transforming difference into deviance

Young people in the western suburbs of Sydney, particularly areas such as Bankstown and Lakemba, have featured prominently in media reports and academic study in recent years. From the media and politicians' point of view, young Muslim men – of 'Middle Eastern appearance' – have become the *bête noir* of sensationalised reportage and political intolerance (see Poynting *et al.* 2004). From rape gangs to terrorists, the public discourse has vilified Lebanese (Australian) young men in particular. This has been occurring for a number of years, at least since the first Gulf War in the early 1990s. Indeed, for many years, not only have state elections in New South Wales been largely based upon 'law and order' issues, but these have featured racialist discourses that vilify particular ethnic minorities. The Muslim and the Arab in particular have become the contemporary societal scapegoats, the alleged source of the state's crime problems and social ills.

Public denigration and negative generalisation about, for example, the Lebanese community have been reinforced by specific events in which individual members of the community have committed crimes. Without going into detail here, a social process has occurred over a number of years in which social difference has been transformed into social deviance (Figure 9.1). That is, even though most of young men in the area were born in Australia or have been here since little children, they are treated as 'outsiders'. Already subject to economic disadvantage and social marginalisation, a generation of young people has grown up in a social atmosphere that is very hostile to their culture, to their community, to their religion, and to their very presence. This has not been a linear process, but has involved complex transactions that have gradually fed back into the overall transformation of social relationships. The direction of change, however, has tended toward the social construction of the 'Arab Other' (see Poynting *et al.* 2004).

The outcome of this 'othering' process has been captured in previous academic study of these young people and their neighbourhoods. For example, Collins *et al.* (2000) observe that for many young people the way to overcome marginalisation and alienation is to find other ways to affirm their social presence – namely to form or join a gang. From this vantage point, gang membership is significant, not because of presumed criminality but because it provides a means to 'valorise' their lives and empower the young men in the face of outside hostility, disrespect, and vilification. Yet, the very definition of gang rests upon some degree of identification with criminality rather than ethnicity per se. It is the interplay between gangs, violence, and ethnicity that makes for complicated 'readings' of who is in a gang and who is not. When violence comes to dominate the lives of particular group members, and the group itself, then the group can be said to constitute a street gang.

The process of transformation from 'difference' to 'deviance', and the violence associated with this transformation that has implications for all of the young people concerned, is illustrated in recent events in Sydney. For example, Lebanese-Australians featured prominently, initially as targets and then later as protagonists, in the beach riots of December 2005. These occurred at Cronulla beach in south Sydney, the nearest beach suburb to the Bankstown and Lakemba neighbourhoods. The event saw several thousand people, mainly white Anglo Australians, rioting, damaging property and violently

social difference and community stigmatisation
[ethnic concentration; ethnic mix; emphasis on non-conformity;
relative powerlessness; social marginalisaton]

moral panics and ethnic targeting
[naming; media reports, variations depending upon time period, and
which ethnic minority group depending upon city]

building a reputation
[where you hang out; specific incidents]

importance of social identity
[one's place, resisting authority, masculinity and identity,
social valorisation]

social difference as social deviance
[marginalisation, criminalisation, vilification]

social transformation
[impact of Othering process, search for meaning, dealing with oppressive
conditions – potential for extreme violence]

Figure 9.1 Dynamics of deviancy

attacking anyone who had a 'Middle Eastern' appearance. Many participants wrapped themselves in Australian flags. Many, too, shouted, 'Fuck the Lebos' in unison, as a common theme to the aggression.

The next day saw reprisal attacks. Dozens of carloads of people from the community targeted the previous day retaliated – by engaging in similarly 'random' violence throughout the beachside suburbs. The point here is that there exist highly volatile relations between the 'Lebanese' and other young people across major parts of the city. This negativity has been brewing for a number of years, in part fostered by the territorial segregation of particular groups into racialised patterns of disadvantage (Jakubowicz 2006). Where one belongs is increasingly socially constructed in relation to specific 'ethnic locales', areas defined by particular combinations of economic, social, and cultural characteristics. Social ecology thus gives rise to the phenomenon of youth gangs, in so far as it provides the preconditions for the emergence of violence-oriented, street-present young people who band together as an identifiable group.

What recent studies and recent events have demonstrated is the potential for extreme aggression and mass violence stemming from a highly charged and racialised social environment, and profoundly oppressive social circumstances. Racism permeates the lives of many of the young Muslim men, as it does the lives of other ethnic minority groups, such as Vietnamese-Australians, in Sydney and elsewhere (Human Rights and Equal Opportunity Commission 2004). When this is coupled with economic, social and political marginalisation, it is no wonder that violence of varying kinds features prominently in the lives of these young people.

The central paradox for these young people, however, is that the more they try to defend themselves, the more likely they are to be targets. The more they resort to membership of street groups and engage in fighting to assert themselves, the more they will be treated as 'outsiders' and as deviant (see White and Perrone 2001). Out of this cauldron of generally violent relations emerge specific youth groups – the street gangs – whose *raison d'être* is shaped by their immediate social circumstance. Thus, while not all Lebanese-Australian young people end up joining a gang, each is nevertheless affected by the violence directed at their community as a whole. For some, gangs provide a means to deal with this violence. But, as we shall see, gang formation and membership embody their own particular dynamics and impetus towards violence.

The processes of social inclusion and social exclusion are not only forged at the level of broad societal resources and structural disadvantage. Nor are they just constituted by ideological and political processes of separation and differentiation. Exclusion and inclusion are 'made' in the crucible of the everyday, in the mundane activities and relationships of young people as they negotiate their daily lives. The remainder of the chapter explores how young people define who they are by considering how different groups engage in the world around them. As part of a national youth gangs study, we interviewed 50 young people in the Bankstown area of Sydney. The interviews were arranged and carried out by local youth and community workers, who had been briefed on the process and interview schedule. Those interviewed either were identified as being a gang member or were perceived by others to be a gang member. Three main groups of young people were interviewed: Lebanese (Australians), Samoan (Australians), and Vietnamese (Australians). The sample also included a couple of migrant youth from Fiji and Jamaica. Five young women were interviewed as part of the sample, but while they were associating with 'gangs', none were identified as being a gang member. The stories of each main group provide interesting insights into gang formation, group identity, and ethnicity and violence. Although most public and academic attention has focused solely on young Lebanese people, the stories of other young people in the same neighbourhood adds further complexity and richness to our understanding of gangs and gang-related behaviour.

Friends and enemies

To understand gang formation and gang activities, we first need to appreciate the nature of group dynamics in the local area. Gang members are simultaneously members of particular gangs and of diverse social groups, and there is some overlap between the two. How different groups relate to each other has implications for how gangs are formed, the nature of gang membership, and the kinds of violence associated with different gangs. Group membership hinges upon shared ethnicity, language, and culture. It also very much depends upon locale, age, and activities. Each group of young people more or less said that 'anyone' could be a member of their group. However, in practice, membership is highly selective and exclusive to their particular ethnic group. In part, this simply reflects family connections and basic things such as 'speaking the same language' – both literally and figuratively vis-à-vis religion, origins, and shared understandings of manners, honour, and relationships.

Although the primary group connection is to one's specific ethnic group, there are other connections that are also very significant. Some of these are based upon activities, some on simple geography. For example, Samoan and Lebanese young people generally shared an interest in rap music. Rapping together was OK, and was one activity that was generally very inclusive of people regardless of ethnic background.

Living in the same area also was meaningful, even if the young people did not hang around together in the same groups. Many of the youths commented on the negative 'bad' reputation of the area, yet most were proud to live there and wished to remain there in the future. Identity was in fact often constructed both in terms of ethnicity and in terms of locality.

> The FOB's [Fresh Off the Boat] and the Lebo's like they've come together around Bankstown ... smoke weed with the Lebo's. And help us in fights. ... but it's mostly them that bring the trouble. Like they always call us to come and help 'em and that. Against other Lebo's and the – Asians. (C, Samoan young man)

Living in an area of relative economic disadvantage and high levels of unemployment also meant that group membership has specific class dimensions that cut across ethnic belonging.

> To belong to our group you're either an Arab or an Islander, you know, you can't belong – you've gotta be from here. From Bankstown. You can't be one of them rich Arabs that live up that way in, you know, their fathers and brothers they buy them cars and stuff. We don't hang out with them much with them pretty boys that, you know, spend all their time running after girls and stuff. You can't be a, pardon me, wuss. (B, Lebanese young man)

Social difference and social belonging were not only constructed in terms of material advantage. There were fairly strong antagonisms expressed by Lebanese and Samoan young people against 'Asian' young people, although there was relatively little contact, including gang fights, between the groups. The latter category includes, among others, Vietnamese and Chinese young people. The problem here often begins at school. Time and again, the Lebanese and Samoan young people talked about racist teachers and being treated in a discriminatory way by others at school. By contrast, they thought that teachers favoured 'Asians'. They were also conscious that 'Asians' tended on the whole to do better academically than they. Their own negative experiences of schooling tended to be manifested in bullying and dislike of the 'Asian' students.

Each group tended to have particular 'enemies' and potential allies. In some cases, these were one and the same. For example, generally speaking, the Vietnamese did not particularly like the Chinese (reflecting antagonisms stemming from long-standing conflicts between the countries of origin). Yet, on occasion, for example at school, the two groups would get along, due in no small part to being lumped together as 'Asians' and being subjected to racism by others. On the other hand, the category 'Islanders' includes a wide array of nationalities, yet most of the Samoans interviewed were very antagonistic toward the Tongan young people. This was reflected in gang talk and gang gear – the Bloods (Samoans) wear red, the Crips (Tongans) wear blue, and other Islanders (such as a Fijian young man in our sample) were caught between conflicting loyalties.

Ethnicity was largely seen as establishing the boundary of membership, whether this was in regards to a social group or to a gang. The ways in which friends and enemies are socially constructed at the local neighbourhood level, and in respect to ethnicity generally, provide the first filters in the sifting out of who is 'eligible' and who is not for specific gang membership.

Nonetheless, group membership and friendship networks involve many different points of belonging and connection, which vary according to circumstances and activities. Many of the young people who were interviewed had friends from other ethnic backgrounds. They were all familiar with the other groups who lived in their neighbourhood. The variables that constituted the basis for making social connections are presented in Figure 9.2.

Different groups would collaborate or have alliances with each other, particularly the Samoan and Lebanese groups, depending upon what was happening in the neighbourhood at the time. They might share in drug taking (e.g. smoking weed), in music making (e.g.

Wider territory
Other familiar locales

Size of group   Music

Ethnic identity
Masculinity
Criminality   **Group activity**   Religion
Social class
Friends

Locale

Other friends   Acquaintances

Other familiar groups
Wider ethnic affiliations

Figure 9.2   The basis for making connections

rapping together), or even fighting (e.g. combining against a third force). In some instances, the neighbourhood connection was stronger than ethnic identity as such, as when 'outsiders' from a similar group (such as an outside Lebanese gang) entered the shared geographical area in order to battle it out with local Lebanese youth.

In other cases, as with the Samoan young people, the local 'gangs' are part of larger ethnic networks and subgroups, incorporating large geographical areas and relationships across distances. For example, there were connections across the city (i.e. different groups of 'Bloods', which sometimes had additional local names as well), as well as across the Tasman Sea (i.e. back to New Zealand, from where many families had migrated).

In the end, while group membership is exclusive, individual friendship is not. And groups can combine in varying ways to protect territory, reputation, and specific individuals. Social connection within the context of gang formation and membership thus has a number of different dimensions. Specific 'gangs' as defined by Eurogang standards do exist (i.e. durable, criminally oriented groups), but they emerge from and are blended with youth groups identified by certain social descriptors (i.e. relating to ethnicity, illegal activity such as cannabis use, rap music, antagonism toward other groups, and so on). This makes it hard at times to distinguish the street gang from the non-gang group, particularly from an outsider's perspective. Violence and illegality tend to feature in each type of group's behaviour and activity. However, when someone says, 'I am a gang member', this is meaningful from the point of view of the type and extent of violence in which they engage (see White and Mason 2006). Thus, group identity is still crucial to the key focus of group activity.

Gangs and street fighting

Although everyone who was interviewed mentioned fighting, the nature and dynamics of fighting varied depending upon social background. Conflicts occurred within groups and between subgroups, as well as between identifiable 'ethnic' conglomerations. The latter refer to instances when literally up to 100 or more young people would travel outside their area, usually into the city centre. Inevitably this type of 'swarming' (White 2006b) would result in some kind of group punch-up. Many of the young people also mentioned occasional fights involving members of their immediate social group. In other instances, the fighting was intracommunal, involving different groups from within the same ethnic minority community – for example, Vietnamese fighting Vietnamese.

The nature of the violence, and in particular the attitude towards and actual use of weapons, varied greatly according to distinct ethnic group. Some young men were reluctant and seemed to regret having to carry weapons. Their logic was that if everyone carries weapons, then everyone has to.

> It's for show – yeah. Fuck man – why do a lot of people carry? 'Cause the streets are getting rough these days man. Fuck everyone's carrying these days. So fuck everyone has to get strapped man. That's why they carry. (I, Samoan young man)

Weapons use was associated with a graduated learning experience. The idea is that, depending upon age and experience, one progresses to different types of weapon use.

> Usually like before you fight with poles. Before that you fight with hands, but then you fight with poles, and then comes the machetes. After that, nowadays, you know, once you get older, you mostly do it with guns and that ... 'cause say when you're young, you know, you don't know nothing about guns, you know what I mean, all you know is how to hold something and just wack 'em with it, you know what I mean, like a baseball bat or something – yeah. But then that's only going to give 'em a bruise and this and that. But when you get a bit older, you go 'All right. I'll use a knife' you know what I mean. 'I can cut 'em and make 'em bleed.' You know what I mean it's more effective than maybe a baseball bat, you know, you can slice people. In nowadays like when you get older, you know, you're thinking 'Oh man, these guys, you know, they're using machetes on me.' You've gotta use a gun to protect yourself 'cause most older people these days are all holding guns. (A, Vietnamese young man)

This 'progression' varies, however, depending upon with whom you talk. For example, some interviewees said that it was mainly the older young men who handled the guns and/or used them. Others, by contrast, said that it was the younger boys – those around 15 and 16 years of age – who used guns to impress others around them. The older boys in fact had 'matured' and gone beyond the need to 'put on a show'.

Among the sample, it was the 'Asians' who were most associated with weapons use. In fact, the other two main groups, the Lebanese and Samoans, were disdainful of the generalised use of weapons on the streets. For some Vietnamese, the use of weapons was intrinsically tied to body size.

> Maybe 'cause we small people you see and the other ones they're so big. If you fight by hand you can't win. (D, Vietnamese young man)

But there is more to this than just body size. It also has to do with the specific 'culture' surrounding the body. Some sense of cultural difference is provided in the following observation:

> Well if you fight with Asians all right expect to have knives chucked at you and if it is – this is how it is race based all right. The Samoans are guaranteed to have a good fight one on one – fist to fist. If it's Lebo's guaranteed to have every family down on you flat. If it's Asians get ready to have everything – every knife you've seen in your life. (K, Samoan young man)

Physicality is directly related to ethnicity. This takes the material form of different body sizes and shapes. For example, the Samoan young people tend to be heavier and more thickset than the Vietnamese, who are of slighter build. The physical body is also the site of cultural construction. Every Samoan young person who was interviewed said that he had played rugby (either rugby union or rugby league). Many of the Lebanese young people likewise had experience in playing rugby or engaging in contact sports such as boxing. The Vietnamese, if they played a sport, tended to pick basketball or martial arts. It was clear from the interviews that the Samoan young people in particular really enjoyed the physicality – the roughness, the aggressiveness, and the body pounding – of their chosen sport.

Consideration of the intersection of ethnicity and class as this relates to the body helps us to understand the quite different perceptions of weapon use and masculinity, which vary according to social background. It is generally acknowledged that being tough and putting one's bodily integrity at risk is associated with traditional, working-class male culture. Matters of physique and the physical have been central to working-class forms of aggressive masculinity that celebrate strength, speed, agility, and ability to withstand pain (Connell 1995, 2000; White 1987/8). Those young men who are socialised into experiencing, and enjoying, more brutalising forms of contact sport are more likely to favour violence that tests their physical prowess in some way. Those who do not share these experiences or whose physical size limits their ability to engage in unarmed combat are derided by those who 'can do.'

> They can't do bitches – they can't fight with their fists. (F, Lebanese young man)

Translated: weapons are for those who can't or won't fight. They are for wimps.

> I don't know. I reckon they just don't have the balls to throw fists – use their fists. That's mainly with my group we never – we hated like – hated guns and we hated weapons and, I don't know, we just liked our fist and that. (M, Samoan young man)

Interestingly, there was some suggestion in the interviews that those young men who adopted this kind of attitude were also those most likely to (1) enjoy fights as a form of recreation and fun, and (2) resort to violence as a 'normal' and first reaction to conflict. Fighting, for these young men, is 'naturally' enjoyable and a 'natural' part of their everyday life. They do not even think twice about resolving an argument by 'giving 'em a smack'. It is an ingrained reflex into which they have been socialised – at the neighbourhood level, at home and in sports. Fighting is fun precisely because of its physicality and the adrenaline rush accompanying such violence.

> Oh we love fights, smoking up and drinking and girls. (G, Samoan young man)

> I knocked a guy last year for being a racist. ... He just walked past me and he just said 'Yeah, you black shit.' So I broke his nose. I broke his nose and shit and broke his jaw. (N, Samoan young man)

Thus, violence is not only made natural by its prevalence in the lives of boys and men, but in many cases it is an important source of pleasure. It represents meaningful attempts to transgress the ordinary (Hayward 2002). It is in fighting (which is, in fact, a very conventional, 'ordinary' phenomenon) that many of these young men can find the excitement that transforms the mundane (see Jackson-Jacobs 2004). It parallels experiences of the physical in pursuits such as sports, yet offers a different way in which to vent aggression, passion, and emotional angst. Violence is desirable because it can and does offer pleasure, for some people, for some of the time (Schinkel 2004).

Analytically, the importance of this observation is that it implies that violence may be at the core of social action, and that the 'gang' may be merely the mechanism through which violence can perhaps best be expressed. As mentioned, fighting is widespread among the young men in this study. But, for some, joining a gang may well provide the social vehicle through which the desired collective violence can ensue.

Interpreted in this way, it is not (only) that the violence of the neighbourhood (or of racism or economic marginalisation or social inequality) leads to the gang, but also that violence is attractive because it provides its own reward, a reward that is enhanced by combining with others who share similar urges. Whatever the answer, it is important to acknowledge that group formation and group violence are complex phenomena that require sensitivity to a wide range of factors and dynamics. There are myriad motivations for particular individuals to engage in violence or join gangs.

The type of group formation in which one is involved also plays a major part in how violence manifests itself. For example, masculinity in a group context was very much constructed in terms of toughness and being manly. It also included notions of loyalty to the gang and of members to each other, of courage and fearlessness, and of mutual protection.

> These days it's about all muscle and people in our group – some of 'em are big and some of 'em have courage like as in if somebody swears to 'em they'll come back at 'em. ... They wish to be all big and strong and if anyone swears to you or says something about your mum, you go bash 'em and this and that. (D, Lebanese young man)

Being a member of a gang was intrinsically linked to doing violence in the name of the gang, and supporting other gang members at any time or in any circumstance. Being tough was more than just about appearances: it demanded performance.

Conclusion

This chapter has explored the social dynamics of ethnicity and violence by examining how young people from different ethnic minority backgrounds view and participate in specific types of groups and gang-related behaviour. The youth gangs in Sydney tend to be homogeneous in terms of ethnicity and sex, and the boundaries of gang membership are basically set by a combination of social factors. Ethnicity (i.e. a distinct cultural identity) forms the core of the social relationships, but then intersects with variables such as geography (e.g. specific locality), age (i.e. mainly teenagers, but up to mid-twenties), size (i.e. sheer number of people who congregate at any point in time), affiliation (i.e. with people from similar cultural backgrounds), and familiarity (i.e. of one's immediate neighbours, peers, and acquaintances).

The contours of gang violence vary depending upon ethnic affiliation. Here a crucial difference in gang-related behaviour relates to the physicality of the young people involved – the size and shape of their bodies, the cultural context within which they use their bodies, and the circumstances under which violence occurs. The material and ideological basis of group activity includes different social constructions of what constitutes 'fun' and the enjoyable.

This analysis of ethnicity and violence raises certain questions that warrant further attention. For example, does intergroup fighting promote weapons use generally, given that some groups rely on weapons more than others? Street fights among gangs that share similar attitudes towards and understandings of 'bare fist' fighting would necessarily be different from those involving gangs that utilise weapons other than fists. Does use of specific weapons result in differences in violence rates or lethality for different groups? If certain types of weapons are associated with particular groups, does this translate into avoidance tactics on the part of potential protagonists who do not use such weapons? Or does it increase the overall use of weapons on the street, as gangs strive to even the odds in fight situations?

In other words, to what extent do ethnic differences, paradoxically, create the ground for uniformity and escalation in the nature of violence on the streets? There are complexities and contradictions here that once again reinforce the fact that social context is crucial to understanding the nature of gang formation and gang behaviour.

References

Cohen, S. (1973) *Folk Devils and Moral Panics*. London: Paladin.

Collins, J., Noble, G., Poynting, S. and Tabar, P. (2000). *Kebabs, Kids, Cops & Crime: Youth, Ethnicity & Crime*. Sydney: Pluto Press.

Connell, R. (1995) *Masculinities*. Sydney: Allen & Unwin.

Connell, R. (2000) *The Men and the Boys*. Sydney: Allen & Unwin.

Foote, P. (1993) 'Like, I'll tell you what happened from experience… perspectives on Italo-Australian youth gangs in Adelaide', in R. White (ed.), *Youth Subcultures: Theory, History and the Australian Experience*. Hobart: National Clearinghouse for Youth Studies.

Hayward, K. (2002) 'The vilification and pleasures of youthful transgression', in J. Muncie, G. Hughes and E. McLaughlin (eds.), *Youth Justice: Critical Readings*. London: Sage.

Human Rights and Equal Opportunity Commission (2004) *Ismae – Listen: National Consultations on Eliminating Prejudice Against Arab and Muslim Australians*. Sydney: HREOC.

Jackson-Jacobs, C. (2004) 'Taking a beating: the narrative gratifications of fighting as an underdog', in J. Ferrell, K. Hayward, W. Morrison and M. Presdee (eds), *Cultural Criminology Unleashed*. London: Glasshouse Press.

Jakubowicz, A. (2006) 'Hobbits and orcs: the street politics of race and masculinity', *Australian Options*, 44: 2–5.

Poynting, S., Noble, G., Tabar, P. and Collins, J. (2004) *Bin Laden in the Suburbs: Criminalising the Arab Other*. Sydney: Sydney Institute of Criminology.

Schinkel, W. (2004) 'The will to violence', *Theoretical Criminology*, 8(1): 5–31.

White, R. (1987/8) 'Violence and masculinity: the construction of criminality', *Arena Magazine*, December–January: 41–4.

White, R. (2006a) 'Youth gang research in Australia', in J. Short and L. Hughes (eds), *Studying Youth Gangs*. Walnut Creek, CA: AltaMira Press.

White, R. (2006b) 'Swarming and the dynamics of group violence', *Trends and Issues in Crime and Criminal Justice*, no. 326. Canberra: Australian Institute of Criminology.

White, R. and Mason, R. (2006) 'Youth gangs and youth violence: charting the key dimensions', *Australian and New Zealand Journal of Criminology*, 39(1): 54–70.

White, R. and Perrone, S. (2001) 'Racism, ethnicity and hate crime', *Communal/ Plural*, 9(2): 161–81.

White, R., Perrone, S., Guerra, C. and Lampugnani, R. (1999) *Ethnic Youth Gangs in Australia: Do They Exist?* (seven reports – Vietnamese, Turkish, Pacific Islander, Somalian, Latin American, Anglo Australian, Summary Report). Melbourne: Australian Multicultural Foundation.

Chapter 10

Ethnicity and juvenile street gangs in France

Coralie Fiori-Khayat

In a country where the extreme Right has been ready to challenge democracy over the past 15 years, what role does ethnicity play in street violence and especially in juvenile street gangs, who embody the climactic form of street violence in France? This chapter is meant not only to discuss whether juvenile street gangs (under the Eurogang definition) exist in France or not, but also to address the question of what might link juvenile street gangs in Paris suburbs and the ethnic concerns that turn out to be a characteristic feature of suburban areas around Paris and other major French cities. Over the past ten years in France, the issue of juvenile repeat offenders has become a worrying one, among the public as well as policymakers. Although they are far from numerous, they usually commit offences in groups. Thus, examining peer groups as criminal structures for juvenile offenders can be a promising path of research. However, are those groups real 'gangs'? The question is heavily debated, since most French researchers deny the very existence of 'gangs' among juveniles. The implicit reasons for this denial are mostly political: policymakers and experts agree not to claim that France is gradually becoming like the USA and pretend that the situation is under control (e.g. Macé 2002: 33–41; Vilbrod 2000: 9–17), since there seems to be no room for political error; moreover, admitting the existence of juvenile gangs as a new phenomenon might lead to questioning the efficiency of French social workers (Esterlé-Hédibel 2000, 2001, 2002), with political consequences that are unpredictable. Furthermore, the issue of juvenile street gangs in France becomes taboo when the issue of 'ethnicity' is raised in regard to that particular topic (Martiniello 1995; Poutignat and Streiff-Fenard 1995).

One key reason for this issue to be taboo is the heritage of a dark past: as far as France's political history during the second half of the twentieth century is concerned, two major events lead modern policymakers to avoid clear references to ethnic issues. The first is the Vichy regime and the fact that this French government collaborated with the Third Reich, and the second is the war in Algeria, some 20 years after World War II. Neither has ever been fully acknowledged by the French population, which is still ill at ease with slavery in the former French colonies. While extreme Right parties have used ethnic issues as their political battlefield over the past 30 years, it has become difficult to discuss this topic without risking being 'labelled' a member of the extreme Right wing.

Thus, it is not at all surprising to face a complex legal situation when one raises questions about the role of ethnicity within delinquent, juvenile peer groups. In particular, French law distinguishes between French persons and foreigners, but prohibits any distinction between 'French persons of French origin' and 'French persons of foreign origins'. Creating ethnically based files is a felony,[1] and it is particularly important to underscore that such files could not be created or used for the purpose of drafting this chapter. Police do gather what is called 'racial information', to make investigations easier; such files are authorised and controlled by the National Commission on Computer Files and Liberties (Commission Nationale Informatique et Libertés). Using the information in those files for purposes other than investigations, however, would be a felony, and the police officer (or researcher) would be fired and prosecuted. Ethnic differences, segregation, racism, and discrimination can be observed by anybody in France who simply looks around, but creating files based on origin, skin colour, religion, community or other ethnic factor could send the researcher to jail. This is all the more important to underscore as on 15 November 2007, the French Constitutional Court stated that creating ethnically and/or racially based files, even for scientific and research purposes, was (and still is) prohibited by Article 1 of the French Constitution. The court thus declared a part of a bill unconstitutional, as it authorised the gathering of ethnic data.[2] Hence, no official ethnic data will be used here, for legal reasons.

Current study on juvenile street gangs

I conducted field research for six years, including the years I was studying for my doctorate, on teenage peer groups involved in street violence in suburbs around Paris. The primary aim of the study was to determine whether there were (or were not) gangs in the Île-De-France region. To make this research consistent with my past research activities, I decided to consider the same places I had studied during my PhD work. Hence, I studied teenage groups mainly in several suburbs of Les Yvelines, namely Les Mureaux, Mantes-La-Jolie, Trappes, and the numerous small towns around Trappes. For each city, one teenage group (around ten members, including non-permanent ones) with an extensive criminal background, was chosen, and compared with the reactions, behaviours, and answers of a teenage group without a criminal background. The peer groups were found in kick-boxing clubs, as this sport is popular among this population. The study consisted of qualitative interviews and case studies. Each teen was interviewed once for about two hours, with the exception of two teens who decided to stop the interview. The interviews mostly took place in neutral areas, such as sports clubs or around schools, as it was difficult to interview them in their homes or quite near them (due to the pressure from their peers) or in police stations. However, one troublesome group agreed to talk in the police station. After preliminary questions (e.g. age, family structure, school background), I asked them about their 'social network' and the way they chose their friends. I then asked several questions to determine whether the criteria of the Eurogang definition were met.[3] If they were, I explored the ways each teen would interact both with peers and with his community.

This field research led to several key findings, the first being that juvenile street gangs, under the Eurogang definition, do exist in France (Fiori-Khayat 2005: 178–90), especially in Paris suburbs; thus, more precise research on how groups are created and on issues related to ethnicity was possible. Indeed, Paris suburbs are troubled by teenage and/or young adult groups that tend to be long-lasting. Those groups tend to roam the streets. This is not illegal; the problem is that these youths meet mostly in order to commit offences together, or happen to commit offences while they are together. Those offences may be property offences (thefts, arson, burglaries, and robberies), personal offences (rape, assault, and aggravated assault), or even trafficking (mobile phones and drugs). Hence, it seems possible to assert that, in contrast to what most French researchers claim, juvenile street gangs do exist in France, even though the word 'gang' is banned, for political reasons, in the country.

A second important finding is that juvenile street-gang members tend to use ethnicity and ethnic issues as a justification (Mucchielli 2002a: 21–47, 2002b: 38–40, 2003: 325–55) for some, but not all, offences. Roughly, there are two main types of offence: non-political offences, which tend to appropriation, in which ethnicity plays no role in justification; and pre-political or political offences, which do not tend to appropriation but rather to destruction of existing political and social symbols, for which ethnicity is then used by juveniles to justify their actions. Using ethnicity to justify a crime seems surprising; yet, juvenile offenders tend to use this justification as a way to respond to a *feeling* of discrimination. At that point, it does not matter whether that the feeling matches reality (that these young offenders are seen as second-rank citizens) or not. Strikingly, in juvenile street gangs that use ethnically based justifications when committing offences, members have at least two common points. They belong to the same ethnic minority, and they live in the same neighbourhood. One is thus led to wonder whether the key issue is ethnic background or if it is urban segregation. Indeed, some French inner city areas do have one community, such as the black community, that is over-represented (more than 90 per cent of the population, according to City Hall officials), whereas other communities are under-represented, such as the North African community[4] (e.g. Les Mureaux and Yvelines). Remarkably, ten years ago, these populations mixed together. Thus, ethnicity has to be correlated with other factors (Beaud and Pialoux 2002: 215–43), such as urban segregation (Bélorgey 2002: 135–40; Bourdin and Lefeuvre 2002: 143–64; Bidou-Zachariasen 2002: 81–92; Charlot and Madelin 2002: 223–34; De Rudder 2002: 113–20), unemployment, and school failure, that can explain – at least partly – the failure of individually centred, ethnic-diversification strategies.

Ethnicity as a reason for joining a gang

Ethnicity and peer group

Ethnic background in itself does not distinguish juvenile street gangs from non-delinquent peer groups. While studying how deviant and non-deviant peer groups appear, I have noticed that youths from a specific cultural background are more likely to join other youths with roughly the same background than peers who have a different background. The ethnic issue, as it is part of educational, cultural, historical, and sociological frames, exerts a direct influence on peer-group creations. From that point of view, the role of the educational system is particularly important: in primary schools, children gradually join a 'team' of peer friends, and the degree of segregation of each school plays a key role (Sicot 2000: 87–108).

As for peer-group creations, common ethnicity plays roughly the same role for both non-deviant juvenile peer groups and deviant ones (including street gangs). When ethnicity is not perceived by youths as a basis for discrimination, it does not differentiate non-deviant groups, deviant groups, or gangs. It is just a common point that helps people feel comfortable together. In other words, at that stage, young people gather because they have the same educational frames, the same food habits, the same types of relationships with a country where they still have relatives, etc. Interestingly, they feel 'different from other pupils', but they scarcely feel stigmatised or otherwise discriminated against in primary schools.

However, one's ethnicity can also be seen as a basis for a discriminating process (e.g. my failures are due to my skin colour, to my religious beliefs), and then it becomes an important part of a deviant scheme: young gang members explain that they are not responsible for their being in a gang; it is more a consequence of a specific social pattern that has been imposed on them. One of the most climactic examples happened in October–November 2005. After two teens died, the French suburbs saw rioting that lasted two months and led to the implementation of the 'état d'urgence', a discriminatory system under which civil and political liberties are partly suspended; this happens only during major crises, and since the Algerian War it had not been implemented. Rioting teens explained that they were burning their neighbours' cars and houses because they resented the (tough) policy that had been implemented over the past three years by N. Sarkozy, Minister of the Interior at that time.

Ethnicity and juvenile delinquent groups: a feeling of discrimination

When a peer group becomes delinquent and even develops into a gang, ethnicity turns out to be important since it matches another issue: discrimination, be it real or felt. This feeling of discrimination based on ethnic background emerges from or is reflected in the group's experiences of facing common difficulties, living in the same ethnically bound neighbourhoods, and sharing feelings of anger at their treatment by others.

Common obstacles

Juvenile street gang members face common difficulties and obstacles (in schooling, finding a job, etc.), which they explain by ethnic discrimination. From their point of view, they have failed at school because teachers do not care about teenagers of foreign origins. Indeed, the question of school segregation cannot be avoided, nor can the issue of violence in such schools (Baudry *et al.* 2000; Debarbieux 2002). In inner-city schools, teachers are often defensive, tend to fear their pupils (especially in junior high), and may be reluctant to take a few more hours to explain to them what they have not understood. This may be due to the fact that such teachers are beginners and/or are not happy to be appointed to such schools, but a feeling of frustration remains among their pupils. School failure is seen as the first of a long series (Payet 1995); it is followed by unemployment.

Young street-gang members claim that they cannot find a job because of the colour of their skin. This feeling is all the more central, as every day they see school graduates in their communities who cannot find a job for the same reason. In the inner city, graduates often have difficulty in finding a job, and this failure, due to discrimination and a form of racism within French society, tends to deter teens from interest in school (Nicole-Drancourt and Roulleau-Berger 2001). They wonder why they should even try to find a job, seeing it is hopeless (Dubet 1987; Dubet and Lapeyronnie 1994). Drug dealing appears to them to be more profitable. However, some French observers challenge this explanation, as it characterises offenders as victims (Delsol 2006: 57-68).

Some young street-gang members, however, do find a job (Calogirou 1989; Lepoutre 1997). Strikingly, job socialisation does not counterbalance street socialisation. In a case study of a street gang near Paris, I saw that the gang leader, Farid, had found a position in a sandwich shop; less than a month later, he had forced his boss to employ his fellows. 'Forced' is the exact word, as the shopkeeper had been threatened with a gun and decided to hire a dozen employees because he feared for his life. When one of them insulted a client, the employer wanted to fire him right away; Farid called a couple of friends to threaten the boss once more, and the employee was kept. What is surprising in this case study is that not only does job socialisation fail to counterbalance street socialisation, but it also even strengthens gang members' relationships. Such groups turn out to be 'locked', in the sense that, no matter what members do, they belong to the group, and peer socialisation is always stronger than any other.

Common neighbourhoods

Juvenile street-gang members live in neighbourhoods that they depict as ghettos. The term 'ghetto' is not technically correct, as inner city areas in France have nothing in common with the ghettos that were created to separate the Jewish population from the 'Gentile' population and that lasted for centuries in Eastern Europe (Vieillard-Baron 1990), but it is difficult to deny that urban segregation does parallel ethnic and economic ones (Bordet 1998; Boucher 2003a; Boucher and Vulbeau 2003b; Schoffel 1996: 123–33). Everyday life turns out to be much more difficult in such neighbourhoods than in those where the middle class lives (Bachmann and Leguennec 1996; Bourgeois 1996; Castel 1995; Delarue 1991; Stébé 2002; Villechaise-Dupont 1999), but this reality is common to all inner-city inhabitants, be they street-gang members, deviant or non-deviant teenagers. The most obvious difference between deviant and non-deviant peer groups is that the latter try to rise out of the ghetto, by higher education, by working for the state, etc., and the former are too attached to the ghetto to leave. In a way, their ghetto belongs to them; it is not the *place* where they live, but rather a *thing* they own (Bailleau and Gorgeon 2000; Walgrave 1992). This particular feeling explains, at least partly, why relationships between youths and the police are so tense. When they enter the inner city, policemen, firemen, doctors, etc., are seen as 'those from the outside' and tend to be considered foes since their presence limits the youths' power in the space – and when a group sets fire somewhere, it expresses its power. Arson is a powerful means of destruction that immediately forces the population to leave the place. Thus, the neighbours of arsonists are, to some extent, subject to their will and might (Maffesoli 2006: 87–100; Wunenburger 2006: 69–86).

Common feelings of anger

Juvenile street-gang members share the same feeling of anger, which they use to justify their delinquent acts. Their anger targets French Caucasians, who are seen as racist (Wieviorka 1992), especially when they belong to the French administration: social workers, postmen, policemen and judges are seen as racist, as they may be in fact sometimes, but this cannot be generalised.

Juvenile street-gang members are also angry at other minorities; youths who express pride in being 'from North Africa' tend to stay away from youths who are black and may even express racist feelings towards them. Similarly, black youths may also have racist feelings against peers whose families come from North Africa. Each community seems to feel that it is more discriminated against and more victimised than any other.

As regards ethnicity and the creation of deviant peer groups, ethnic background appears to be related to two aspects in the process of group creation. The first aspect involves 'ethnic pride', whereby teenagers of one minority keep a distance from deviant teenagers from other minorities, may even attack them or their families, and may make life a hell for other minorities, just to be the only group that has power in the neighbourhood. This phenomenon happened in inner-city Les Mureaux (15 miles west of Paris), where families from North Africa have all left because teenagers from sub-Saharan Africa were too threatening. In 2002, for example, a group of deviant peers set fire one night to a former warehouse where several homeless men slept – a point of which the group was unaware. The homeless persons were able to escape, but they lost everything they had. The police investigation found that the group (that had existed for several months, was street-oriented and involved in criminal activities) wanted to burn the warehouse because it was thought to be a meeting point for another teen group belonging to another ethnic background.

The second aspect is an objective alliance of deviant teenagers of a given ethnic minority with teenagers of another ethnic minority background against 'predators', that is people, especially the police, who do not belong to the neighbourhood. Although this alliance is rather efficient in the short term, it is not obvious when there is no danger. This aspect turns out to be more frequent, as perceived 'predators' are numerous: the police, of course, but also the fire department, the emergency medical services and postmen, not to mention landlords, social workers, etc. Any person who does not belong to the neighbourhood and, thus, who could potentially disturb or harass group members, can be labelled a 'predator'. Even though these ethnically bound groups fight each other, they tend to become allies when predators are around.

Ethnicity and juvenile street gang activities

Material reaction to discrimination: from destruction of public property to riots

Ethnicity is used as a basis for mobilisation and resistance when these youths feel that they are discriminated against because they belong to a particular ethnic group. This tends to be characteristic of several offences, which target mainly public property. The variety of such offences is quite broad, from graffiti on the walls of public or private buildings, to the arson common during the November 2005 riots. However, they all have a common point, which distinguishes them from non-ethnically based offences: the theme, the expressed message, is always one of anger against, or even hatred of France and its institutions. Such messages tend to suggest that French society is gradually falling apart and that the gap between ethnic communities is broadening.

The hate that young rioters and gang members express is a message in itself (e.g. 'I will fuck France until she loves me', the title of a song that made members of the National Assembly sue the singer). These youths do not see themselves as a part of French society. During field research, I have often heard serious, violent, young street-gang members say, 'Why should I feel French?' They assert that such issues as 'the Muslim veil',[5] job discrimination, and the implicit racism of Caucasians make them think they are rejected (Wieviorka 1992, 1999).

These young people refer to their problems in ethnic and religious terms instead of political and social terms. The separation of church and state has been total since 1905, but some of these young offenders say clearly that French laws are not binding on them since they exclude religious rules. They express anger at France because of the situation of their 'brothers' in Iraq and Palestine, although France has no troops in Iraq and, until the election of Sarkozy, did not support Israeli policy. The issue of ethnicity is thus used to question international political issues, but it does not help them to achieve a political voice (Redeker 2006: 27–36). From that point of view, young rioters have nothing in common with the Black Panthers or Black Muslims in America.

Physical reaction: from insults to assaults

Ethnicity can also be seen as a part of the paradigm of insults. However, insults – including racist ones – tend to become almost a 'common' way of addressing peers, even though this is not specific to France. This situation is then quite different from racism.

In field research in 2003, I saw letters written by a young street-gang member to a friend who was in jail. Here again, both teenagers were members of the same peer group, which was a long-lasting one (more than a year). They would meet daily in the street (they all lived in the same neighbourhood), and committing offences was, in their minds, a leisure activity. The letter started, 'Hi, fucking nigga!' and ended, '"A" [his name], the little *bicot.*'[6] The rest of the letter was extremely kind. 'A' was very sorry to see his friend in jail; he explained to him that he was supporting his family and wrote that he would send him money as soon as he could. It was clearly not a 'racist' letter, yet there were two racist words, the first referring to the reader, the second referring to the writer.

I asked 'A' why he had called his friend 'nigga', and 'A' was astonished. In his mind, it could not be an ethnically incorrect way of addressing a friend, precisely because both were close friends. He even said, 'Well, you know, he's black; I'm brown. He's a nigga and I'm a bicot, what's the matter?' His lawyer was amazed, because he was aware of the racist connotation of the word, but in 'A''s mind everything was simple. 'A' went on to explain that in inner-city the very same word sounds either like a joke (between friends) or like a very serious insult. This suggests that the context of a 'racist insult' matters more than the word itself (Larguèche 2000: 173–92). I have noticed the same phenomenon with serious (but not racist) insults, such as 'son of a bitch' or 'motherfucker,' in other field research.

Insults, however, can also be tied to racism. When the speaker addresses another teen who is not a close friend, when he refers not only to the teen but also to the whole family, or when the entire community is insulted, there is no room for ambiguity. This oral aggression, in their mind, demands a physical response. This situation may then escalate and create what could be called 'ethnically based solidarity' on both sides. The most telling and climactic situation I observed happened in Les Mureaux, a very rough city. It includes four inner-city areas where Caucasians comprise less than 5 per cent of the population (most Caucasians live on the other side of the highway, in highly secure communities); all used to have black inhabitants as well as people from North Africa. Between 1998 and 2000, one of these neighbourhoods lost all its population from North Africa and became almost 100 per cent black. A young North African street gang member, whom I interviewed in a police station, told me about the place, 'This is jungle.' 'Jungle?', I said, as I did not understand what he meant. 'Jungle,' he repeated, 'full of all these fucking niggers! Too many niggers, we ain't gonna live there.' The police officer who was with me replied that he had been living there for a couple of years, and the youth said, 'Yes, I used to. Those niggers made me move out.'

Indeed, ethnic relationships had become so tense between 'black' and 'brown' communities that the latter finally left the neighbourhood and moved to another place, where they made life a hell for the black community that was living there – and made them leave. Such phenomena happen rarely. Generally speaking, they are not very well known, because neither the police nor local authorities (including social workers) hear about the problem. What happens in the inner-city tends to be kept secret. It is thus particularly important to analyse how the black community made life impossible for the people from North Africa and finally made them leave the estate.

According to teens in my research, the problem did not concern the adults at first. It was all about rivalries between teens, for drug dealing and other crimes. For reasons that remain unknown (the police think it was for drug dealing, but nobody dared say a word about it), racist conflict gradually appeared and became more important than rivalries in drug dealing. It was quickly characterised by extensive racist violence that nobody reported to the police. The police started to hear about it when firearms were used, but by then the situation was already out of control. It involved not only teens, but also young adults. As for the parents, they could not do anything to restrain their children. In many black families in Les Mureaux, fathers are in their sixties or seventies while their youngest sons are teens. Most of the elderly in both communities had good relationships with each other, yet a whole community had to move out due to ethnic conflicts among the young people in the neighbourhood.

One should notice that 'racism' as used by inner-city youths has little in common with what is usually referred to as 'racism' linked to extreme Right political parties, the latter meaning that racism is first and foremost a political message. As far as inner-city youths are concerned, there is no political message in their actions.

The absence of a political dimension

Although some authors think the November 2005 riots were a political message (e.g. Mucchielli 2006), there seems to be no clear political dimension in these riots – and neither were there political aspects in past urban incidents. As regards economic and social issues, these teens and young adults generally say 'no' to all governmental actions. They even attribute the war in Iraq to the French government, even though there are no French troops there. They seem to lack opportunities – or willingness – to express proposals on political issues (Kokoreff 2003; Senhadji 2001: 161–4). From that point of view, such movements as 'La marche des Beurs', 'SOS Racisme' and 'Ni putes ni soumises'[7] have never been able to mobilise ethnic minorities and find a 'spokesman'.

Of course, a gang leader is not a political leader. Street-gang members' political knowledge is weak, as is their political consciousness (Redeker 2006: 27-36). Yet, they feel that they can act as a political pressure group, and rap singers such as Joey Starr made this clear in December 2005. The French public was extremely worried about the riots, and the real risk of these riots is that they can lead to a massive vote for the extreme Right. Young street rioters are not likely to use this power in a positive way – to obtain affirmative-action programmes, for example – since their political consciousness is still extremely low. Paradoxically, what young street-gang members do has no political meaning, at least from their point of view. However, due to history and tradition, entrenched racism is wide-spread among the French. This feature, added to street violence, tends to turn the issue of juvenile street crime into a major domestic political issue – and, finally, into a threat to democracy (Redeker 2006: 27-36). Fighting on the battlefield of the extreme Right, pointing out that juvenile street gangs frighten huge parts of the population, and labelling these gang members 'racaille' (the French for 'rabble'), Sarkozy gained votes that won him the 2007 presidential election. During the two polls of the presidential election, Segolene Royal (Sarkozy's opponent) warned clearly that the election of Sarkozy would lead to riots. When the identity of the new president was known, some riots started, but they did not last, as the whole community of policymakers, including the left wing, made it clear that the outcome was the result of democratic elections, and that they would not support rioting.

To predict how the situation will develop with Sarkozy at the head of state is impossible. However, the current political system (in which the president is everywhere and seems to make each and every decision alone; no minister, including the prime minister, is allowed to say anything to the people) could lead to massive reactions in the population, who could make one man a scapegoat for all their problems. Furthermore, continuing to consider street-gang members as 'victims' of the Caucasian part of French society is no solution, since gang members are also offenders. One appropriate reaction could be to listen to them and try to understand why they join gangs and why they commit offences. Doing this, however, would suppose that the French scientific community admits that juvenile street gangs exist – an admission not yet made.

To conclude, it seems important to underscore that ethnicity definitely plays a role both in the creation of juvenile street gangs and in the reaction of the French people to them. Though they are merely one feature among others as regards non-deviant peer groups, ethnically bound, troublesome groups do exist in France – even though it is frequently denied; moreover, ethnically bound paradigms are often used by their members to justify their actions. Paradoxically, such ethnic themes are not turned into political messages or into political groups. What seems to characterise ethnically bound, troublesome groups is a total rejection of France and of its institutions rather than requests for change. Hence, the issue of juvenile street violence has become a major domestic political issue. The two phenomena may explain the success of right-wing theories and tough policies to deal with troublesome teen groups.

Notes

1 Several Acts prohibit direct or indirect references to ethnicity: the Freedom of Press Act (1881) made racist papers and talks illegal; and, more recently, the Gayssot Act specifically punishes denial of the existence of the Holocaust. In the French criminal code, most offences have aggravating circumstances if they have been committed in an ethnically based context. Several job agencies that had created ethnically based files were heavily fined, and the managers who ordered the files were sentenced individually.

2 Conseil Constitutionnel, Décision n°2007-575 DC, of 15 November 2007, *Journal Officiel de la République Française*, 16 Novembre 2007.

3 Examples of these questions were the following: 'For how long have you known such or such person?'; 'Where do you mainly meet your friends?'; 'When you meet them in the streets, do you stay in the streets, or do you go to such places as cinemas, coffee shops, or swimming pools?'; 'When you meet your friends in the street and stay there, what kind of activity do you have?'; 'Are these activities performed on a regular basis?'; 'Do you fight with other groups? If so, can you tell me why?'.

4 By 'black people,' I refer to people whose families come from sub-Saharian Africa; the expression 'North Africa' refers to the three following countries: Algeria, Morrocco, and Tunisia – three former French colonies. In both cases, the population is mostly Muslim.

5 The Muslim veil is the veil that Muslim girls and women are supposed to wear. Its use spread rapidly in the late 1990s. Schoolteachers did not know how to react to teens who refused to take it off during lectures and even refused to take some mandatory courses (e.g. music, biology, sports), arguing that their religion did not allow them to do so. The problem grew over the decade, as policymakers did not know how to react. After a debate in parliament, a law was passed in 2004 banning the veil from primary school, junior high school, and high school up to 18 years of age (the age of civil and political majority in France).

6 *Bicot* is a slang and an extremely racist word to refer to people from North Africa.

7 La marche des Beurs was a huge series of demonstrations in the early 1980s to try to stop both street violence and racism. They led to the creation of the 'SOS Racisme' movement, which aims to stop racism. SOS Racism quickly became a satellite of the left-wing, moderate French Socialist Party and spent more time and energy promoting the Socialist Party's policy than helping discriminated against populations. After several teenage girls were burnt alive in the suburbs (because they had refused to wear the Muslim veil, because they did not want to get married at 13 years old, or because they just wanted to choose for themselves), a group of young women led by Fadela Amara created the movement, 'Ni putes ni soumises'. This movement aims to defend women and girls in the suburbs from sexist violence, and all the leaders of the movement come from the inner-city. In June 2007, Amara became a secretary of state in charge of urban policy.

References

Bachmann, C. and Leguennec, N. (1996) *Violences urbaines. Ascension et chute des classes moyennes à travers cinquante ans de politique de la ville.* Paris: Albin Michel.

Bailleau, F. and Gorgeon, C. (eds) (2000) *Prévention et sécurité, vers un nouvel ordre social?* Paris: Ed. de la D.I.V.

Baudry, P., Blaya, C., Choquet, M., Debarbieux, E. and Pommereau, X. (2000) *Souffrances et violences à l'adolescence.* Paris: ESF.

Beaud, S. and Pialoux, M. (2002) 'Sur la genèse sociale des émeutes urbaines', *Sociétés contemporaines*, 45–46: 215–43.

Bélorgey, J.-M. (2002) 'Quelle politique de la ville?', in G. Baudin and P. Genestier (eds), *Banlieues à problèmes: la construction d'un problème social et d'un thème d'action publique.* Paris: La Documentation Française, pp. 135–40.

Bidou-Zachariasen, C. (2002) 'La dimension territoriale de la crise des banlieues: pour une lecture régulationniste de l'espace urbain', in G. Baudin and P. Genestier (eds), *Banlieues à problèmes: la construction d'un problème social et d'un thème d'action publique*. Paris: La Documentation Française, pp. 81–92.

Bordet, J. (1998) *Les «jeunes de la cité»*. Paris: Presses Universitaires de France.

Boucher, M. (2003a) *Turbulences, contrôle, et régulation sociale: les logiques des acteurs sociaux dans les quartiers populaires*. Paris: L'Harmattan.

Boucher, M. and Vulbeau, A. (eds) (2003b) *Émergences culturelles et jeunesse populaire. Turbulences ou médiations?* Paris: L'Harmattan.

Bourdin, A. and Lefeuvre, M.-P. (2002) 'Le sociologue et les grands ensembles', in G. Baudin and P. Genestier (eds) *Banlieues à problèmes: la construction d'un problème social et d'un thème d'action publique*. Paris: La Documentation Française, pp. 143–64.

Bourgeois, C. (1996) *L'Attribution des logements sociaux, politique publique et jeux des acteurs locaux*. Paris: L'Harmattan.

Brenner, E. (2004) *Lesterritoires perdus de la République*. Paris: Les Mille et Une Nuits.

Calogirou, C. (1989) *Sauver son honneur*. Paris: L'Harmattan.

Castel R. (1995) *Les Métamorphoses de la question sociale*. Paris: Fayard.

Charlot, B. and Madelin, B. (2002) 'La banlieue comme objet de recherche et terrain d'intervention', in G. Baudin and P. Genestier (eds), *Banlieues à problèmes: la construction d'un problème social et d'un thème d'action publique*. Paris: La Documentation Française, pp. 223–34.

Debarbieux, E. (2002) *L'Oppression quotidienne: recherches sur une délinquance des mineurs*. Paris: La Documentation Française.

Delarue, J.-M. (1991) *Banlieues en difficultés: la relégation*. Paris: Syros, Coll. Alternatives.

Delsol, C. (2006) 'Au moins l'éducation leur défendra de tout oser', in R. Drai and J.-F. Mattéi (eds), *La République brûle-t-elle?* Paris: Michalon, pp. 57–68.

De Rudder, V. (2002) 'Banlieues et immigrations. Le social, l'urbain et le politique', in G. Baudin and P. Genestier (eds), *Banlieues à problèmes: la construction d'un problème social et d'un thème d'action publique*. Paris: La Documentation Française, pp. 113–20.

Draï, R. (2006a) 'L'embrasement des cités', in R. Draï and J.F. Mattei (eds), *La République brûle-t-elle?* Paris: Michalon, pp. 15–26.

Draï, R. (2006b) 'Identités bloquées', in R. Draï and J.F. Mattei (eds), *La République brûle-t-elle?* Paris: Michalon, pp. 137–54.

Draï, R. and Mattei, J.F. (eds) (2006) *La République brûle-t-elle?* Paris: Michalon.

Dubet, F. (1987) *La Galère: jeunes en survie*. Paris: Fayard.

Dubet, F. and Lapeyronnie, D. (1994) *Quartiers d'exil*. Paris: Seuil.

Esterlé-Hédibel, M. (2000) 'Délinquance des mineurs: du passé au présent, la concordance des temps?', *Agora Débats-Jeunesses*, 21: 45–60.

Esterlé-Hédibel, M. (2001) 'Délinquance des mineurs: recherches et tendances', *Revue E.M.P.A.N.*, 44: 24–31.

Esterlé-Hédibel, M. (2002) 'Jeunes des cités, police et désordres urbains', in L. Mucchielli and P. Robert (eds), *Crime et sécurité, l'état des savoirs*. Paris: La Découverte, Coll. Textes à l'appui, l'Etat des saviors, pp. 376–85.

Etienne, B. (2006) 'Ban-lieues: essai d'interprétation anthropologique', in R. Draï and J.F. Mattei (eds), *La République brûle-t-elle?* Paris: Michalon, pp. 119–36.

Fiori-Khayat, C. (2005) *Les politiques de lutte contre la récidive et la réitération ches les mineurs délinquants. Approches comparées franco-américaines* (PhD dissertation). Paris: University Paris IV Sorbonne, (to be published as *Mineurs violents: si l'on osait faire autrement*).

Haddad, M. (2006) 'Violence anomique ou violence atavique?', in R. Draï and J.F. Mattei (eds) *La République brûle-t-elle?* Paris: Michalon, pp. 37–56.

Kaltenbach, J.-M. (2006) 'L'impéritie française', in R. Draï and J.F. Mattei (eds), *La République brûle-t-elle?* Paris: Michalon, pp. 101–18.

Kokoreff, M. (2003) *La Force des quartiers. De la délinquance à l'engagement politique*. Paris: Payot.

Larguèche, E. (2000) 'L'Injure chez les pré-adolescents: l'influence d'un contexte', *Jeunes sans foi ni loi, Les cahiers de la sécurité intérieure*, 42(4): 173–92.

Lepoutre, D. (1997) *Coeur de banlieue, codes, rites et langages*. Paris: Odile Jacob.

Macé, E. (2002) 'Le traitement médiatique de la sécurité', in L. Mucchielli and P. Robert (eds), *Crime et sécurité, l'état des savoirs*. Paris: La Découverte, Coll. Textes à l'appui, l'Etat des saviors, pp. 33–41.

Maffesoli, M. (2006) 'La société de consumation', in R. Drai and J.-F. Mattéi (eds), *La République brûle-t-elle?* Paris: Michalon, pp. 87–100.

Martiniello, M. (1995) *L'Ethnicité dans les sciences sociales contemporaines*. Paris: P.U.F.

Mucchielli, L. (2006) *Quand les banlieues brûlent*. Paris: La Découverte.

Mucchielli, L. (2002a) 'L'évolution de la délinquance juvénile: essai de bilan critique', *Vie Sociale*, 3: 21–47.

Mucchielli, L. (2002b) 'La politique de tolérance zéro: les véritables enseignements de l'expérience new-yorkaise', *Hommes et Libertés*, 120: 38–40.

Mucchielli, L. (2003) 'Le rap de la jeunesse des quartiers relégués. Un univers de représentations structuré par des sentiments d'injustice et de victimation collective', in M. Boucher and A. Vulbeau (eds), *Émergences culturelles et jeunesse populaire. Turbulences ou mediations?* Paris: L'Harmattan, pp. 325–55.

Nicole-Drancourt, C. and Roulleau-Berger, L. (2001) *Les jeunes et le travail, 1950–2000*. Paris: P.U.F.

Payet, J.-P. (1995) *Collèges de banlieue. Ethnographie d'un monde scolaire*. Paris: Méridiens.

Poutignat, P. and Streiff-Fenard, J. (1995) *Théorie de l'ethnicité*. Paris: P.U.F.

Redeker, R. (2006) 'Le nihilisme et l'assourdissant silence des émeutes banlieusardes', in R. Drai and J.-F. Mattéi (eds), *La République brûle-t-elle?* Paris: Michalon, pp. 27–36.

Schoffel, Ph. (1996) 'Les conditions de vie dans les quartiers prioritaires de la politique de la ville', in D. Pumain and F. Godard (eds), *Données urbaines*. Paris: Anthropos, pp. 123–33.

Senhadji, L. (2001) 'Dessine-moi la France!', in C. Samet (ed.), *Violence et délinquance des jeunes*. Paris: La Documentation Française, pp. 161–64.

Sicot, F. (2000) 'Enfants d'immigrés maghrébins: rapport au quartier et engagement dans la délinquance', *Jeunes sans foi ni loi? Les cahiers de la sécurité intérieure*, 42(4): 87–108.

Stébé, J.-M. (2002) *La Crise des banlieues*. Paris: P.U.F., Coll. Que Sais-Je

Vieillard-Baron, H. (1990) 'Le ghetto, un lieu commun, impropre et banal', *Les Annales de la recherche urbaine*, 49: 13–22.

Vilbrod, A. (2000) 'Qu'est-ce que la justice fait aux jeunes?', *Agora Débats et Jeunesses*, 21: 9–17.

Villechaise-Dupont, A. (1999) *Amère banlieue: les gens des grands ensembles* Paris: Grasset.

Walgrave, L. (1992) *Délinquance systématisée des jeunes et vulnérabilité sociétale*. Genève: éd. Médecine et Hygiène.

Wieviorka, M. (1999) *Violence en France*. Paris: Seuil, Coll. L'épreuve des faits.

Wieviorka, M. (1992) *La France Raciste*. Paris: Fayard.

Wunenburger, J.J. (2006) 'Imaginaires de la violence: du fondement symbolique au fantasme destructeur', in R. Drai and J.-F. Mattéi (eds), *La République brûle-t-elle?* Paris: Michalon, pp. 69–86.

Chapter 11

Migration background, group affiliation, and delinquency among endangered youths in a south-west German city

Hans-Jürgen Kerner, Kerstin Reich, Marc Coester and Elmar G.M. Weitekamp

Introduction

Since the 1990s, after the fall of the Berlin Wall and the tearing down of the 'Iron Curtain' that had hitherto divided Europe for decades, Germany has had to deal with growing numbers of immigrants from eastern countries. Among literally millions of so-called Germans of Russian descent and similar 're-settlers' from other eastern states who aimed to be repatriated, there were hundreds of thousands of young people. In addition came the fugitives (and victims), along with their children, of the ethnically co-determined war in the Balkans. Those developments added strain to the still not sufficiently answered challenge to the German state, economy, and society. This included the stark challenge of mastering the task of integrating the offspring of generations of so-called guest workers. Accordingly, the situation sparked scholarly interest in the problem of delinquent behaviour among young people of migrant background in general and of violent group or clique oriented activities in particular. Criminological and other social science studies looked, for example, for the potentially specific 'nourishing' conditions with which foreign or repatriated (second-generation) youngsters were being confronted (cf. Förtig 2002; Müller 2000; Oberwittler 2003; Reich 2003; 2005; Schmitt-Rodermund and Silbereisen 2004; Weitekamp, Reich and Kerner 2005). This development added considerable knowledge to the extant youth group or gang-related studies (cf. Farin and Seidl-Pielen 1996; Fuchs 1995; Seidl-Pielen and Farin 1995; Tertilt 1996; Wilfert 1959; Youkhana 1996). Our study adds to this growing body of knowledge by examining whether there are differences in the characteristics and risk factors of migrant and non-migrant youth receiving street work services in a German city.

The underlying study: youth street work in the city of Stuttgart

Stuttgart and its population

The present study was conducted in Stuttgart, the capital of the State of Baden-Württemberg in South-west Germany. Stuttgart has, among other factors, two main characteristics making it interesting for the study of migration, social problems, and crime and delinquency:

1 The city has almost 600,000 inhabitants including adjacent suburbs, and it enjoys a reputation for top-level high-tech industry as well as for innovations. This creates wealth, prosperity, and economic and employment stability.

2 At the end of the year 2005, over 20 per cent of Stuttgart residents were non-native, from almost 180 countries around the world, compared to 8.9 per cent (equalling 7.3 million people) in the Federal Republic of Germany at large (Statistisches Bundesamt, September 2006).

Even in prosperous Stuttgart, migrants had been disproportionally affected until recently by worsening economic trends and the accompanying consequences such as unemployment (cf. generally Statistisches Bundesamt 2007, Part II/12). However, it seems as if the city had been able to contain the relevant problems in a positive manner. Stuttgart has earned national recognition for its creative efforts to develop a multifaceted 'integration policy' for foreigners and repatriates, backed up by its special 'Office for Integration Policy', and by a city-wide 'Alliance for Integration' (Pavkovic and Lavadinhos 2006).

As far as the younger generations are concerned, Stuttgart had been experiencing already in the past cliques, troublesome youth groups, and even a few gangs in the more strict sense of the term (Klein *et al.* 2001; Esbensen and Weerman 2005). Similar problems can be found at present, but Stuttgart has always been active in offering special advice and support to youth in problematic situations. Among the most elaborate and enduring programmes so far has been street oriented mobile youth work.

Street work in Stuttgart: tradition and recent situation

The street work project in Stuttgart was established in 1967 as 'Soziale Jugendarbeit' (literally translated: 'social youth work'). It was primarily influenced by the experiences of the USA and the UK (cf. Specht 1991; 1999). Today associations or neighbourhood offices can be found in 19 of the 23 districts of the city. The mobile youth workers annually take care of about 3,000 juveniles from 10 to 25 years of age. They concentrate on socially disadvantaged youths in danger of becoming socially and economically marginalised, or of drifting towards generalised deviance, or joining troublesome youth groups if not gangs and, eventually, beginning an officially 'recognised' delinquent or criminal career (cf. Bodenmüller and Piepel 2004; Gillich 2005; Srur *et al.* 2005). Street workers' daily endeavours are thus based on the principles of strict confidence and voluntariness.

The study, sample and research questions

Our study, conducted between November 2004 and December 2005, did not and could not aim to contribute much to theoretical issues. Neither was it a truly representative research project on the most pressing aspects of migration, ethnicity and gang formation or gang-related delinquency in Germany. Rather, a unique opportunity was offered by a Stuttgart city parochial organisation that asked us to help them evaluate their street work programme.[1] By doing so, and bound to a tight time frame as well as limited resources, we hoped to get at least some worthwhile insight into troublesome youth groups, their formations, identities, individual factors associated with membership and, perhaps, distinctive differences with regard to differential engagement in repeated and serious offending. We tried to follow at least in part the concepts and definitions of the Eurogang Research Programme. The study sample was recruited from three different districts in Stuttgart that are regarded by the Mobile Youth Work team, due to long practical experience in the field, as 'typical' of different problem profiles in the city:

- a core city quarter with a high percentage of inhabitants with migration background and a daily influx of many, also problematic (young) people from other quarters or suburbs;

- a quarter at the outer ring of the city with rapid recent growth and high-rise buildings, and a comparatively high percentage of indigenous and migrant families, many depending on public welfare subsidies;

- another quarter at the outer ring of the city, characterised by slow growth, rather stable social structures, and nevertheless a remarkable percentage of people/families having a migration background.[2]

The youths (some 200) were contacted either in or via neighbourhood youth clubs run by the mobile youth work teams, or via a special pretraining course programme. Eventually, 157 consented to study participation and delivered correctly filled in questionnaires. The personal and social situation of the young people was very similar in all three living quarters. The total study group can be basically characterised by the following properties:

- *Gender*: male = 56.3%; female = 43.7%.
- *Age*: 11–14 = 14.2%; 15–16 = 37.2%; 17–18 = 42.3%; and 19 and older = 6.3%.
- *Born in Germany*: fathers = 21.3%; mothers = 22.4%; respondent youths = 69.7%.
- *Language spoken at home usually*: German = 55%; foreign language = 45%.
- *Fathers' occupational status*: 88% employed; 12% unemployed or impaired.
- *Mothers' occupational status*: 52% employed; 48% housewives or unemployed or impaired.
- *Respondent youths' occupational status*: still in school of one kind or another = 90.5%; on vocational education = 3.8%; having a job = 2.5%; nothing at all = 3.2%.
- *Living situation*: with parents = 90.5%; assisted living in flats = 5.8%; living fully alone = 1.9%; other solutions = 1.8%.

Fathers of the study subjects originated from 22 different countries, mothers from 19 different countries, and subjects themselves from 13 different countries, with the following contributing the greatest percentages (in order from highest to lowest percentage): Turkey, the former Yugoslavia, the Russian Federation, Italy, Russian Federation countries, Belarus, Greece, Poland and Romania.

In this chapter we deal only with selected issues related to young persons' deviant and delinquent behaviour styles, as connected to family factors, personal characteristics, and their joining troublesome youth groups in their living quarter. From the beginning, the subjects had been selected from the perspective of belonging to a 'special population' of allegedly endangered city youths. Thus, no strictly causal inferences can be drawn about, for example, factors truly decisive for deviant lifestyles, and particularly truly decisive for joining troublesome youth groups or even gangs. The leading research questions were therefore more descriptive in nature:

1 Among already endangered youth in a German city (here, Stuttgart), are young persons with a full migration background more prone to engage in deviant and delinquent behaviour than are young persons with a partial migration background, and perhaps even more so compared to fully 'indigenous' young persons?

2 Would such a distinction also be found with regard to joining troublesome youth groups?

3 Would there be a distinction between basically non-delinquent youth groups (if present at all in the three living quarters as a choice for the young people in the study), occasionally delinquent groups concentrating so far on 'typical youth offences', and 'truly delinquent' groups engaging in a whole variety of minor and major offences as punishable by the penal law, including serious crimes?

Migration background and the relationship to extent and seriousness of individual problematic or delinquent behaviour

The following sections of this chapter will show results of our working with the data set, using SPSS routines. We started with building three subgroups. The first consists of all youths without any direct migration background at all (n = 23 or 14.6 per cent). They are called 'non-migrants', meaning the respondent and both parents were born in Germany. However, indirect or extended migration background might have been present in grandparents or great-grandparents, who may have come from foreign countries. The second subgroup consists of youth with partially direct migration background (n = 90 or 57.3 per cent). They are called 'partial migrants,' meaning that subjects and/or their mother and/or their father were born in a foreign country. The third subgroup consists of youth with full migration background (n = 44 or 28 per cent). They are called 'full migrants', meaning that the subjects and both of their parents were born in a foreign country and immigrated to Germany either together or separately at different ages.

The 85.3 per cent of young persons with migration background indicates a stark over-representation among the study clientele, compared to the normal distribution among Stuttgart's population, so the mobile youth workers association does reach more problematic migrant youths than indigenous youths. Since the street work teams are highly committed and possess intimate, long-standing knowledge of their quarters, it seems plausible that a true higher percentage of young people with than without migration background do drift into personally, socially, and criminally dangerous lifestyles.

The partial migrant youths were living in their quarters longer (79.3 an average of 11.5 years) than their non-migrant counterparts (76.2 an average of 10.9 years), and both subgroups had much longer time to integrate there than did the full migrant youths (57.5 an average of 7.2 years). The full migrant youths were living in larger families ($p < 0.005$; Phi = 0.478), more of them were still living with their parents (88.6) than were the partial migrant youth (86.5), and both migrant groups were more bound to family living than were the non-migrant youth (69.6). This means that possible stabilising factors were differently distributed in each respect.

As shown in Table 11.1, the migrant subgroups reported more contacts or contact possibilities with their parents (especially parental monitoring-type behaviours) than did the non-migrants, whereas the

Table 11.1 Parent–child interactions with regard to migration status

Items youths said to be true at present, per cent of each subgroup	Non-migrant youths	Partial migrant youths	Full migrant youths
I can reach/contact my parents even if not at home	81.8%	90.8%	100.0%
Parents know my whereabouts (apart from home or school)	60.9%	72.45%	74.4%
Parents know whom I am with in free time	72.7%	76.5%	75.6%
I can talk to my parents about anything I want	47.8%	48.8%	50.0%
I am required to be at home at evening at a certain hour	50.0%	57.8%	45.0%
I actually do talk to my parents about my plans	63.6%	56.1%	47.2%
I feel my parents do not understand me really	28.6%	25.6%	41.2%
My parents pick on me	17.4%	29.1%	35.1%

results are more mixed in other respects, indicating that migrants were less well off, considering emotional and substantial issues.

In spending free time apart from having contact with the mobile youth work teams or institutions, the young migrants were considerably less engaged in reading ($p < 0.05$; Phi = 0.229), but considerably more engaged in playing video games ($p < 0.05$; Phi = 0.210) and being active in sports clubs or events ($p < .05$; Phi = 0.263) than were non-migrant youths (Table 11.2). Concerning personal deviance and delinquency, the partial migrant youths showed a whole variety of problems more than either the full migrants or the non-migrants. As shown in Table 11.3, partial migrants did have slightly or even considerably more problems regarding trouble with other inhabitants of their neighbourhood or living quarter, or being

Table 11.2 Leisure time activities with regard to migration status

Items youths said to be true at present, per cent of each subgroup	Non-migrant youths	Partial migrant youths	Full migrant youths
Reading	23.8%	9.0%	2.3%
Playing video games and the like	23.8%	41.6%	38.6%
Doing something out of home with a good personal friend	90.5%	89.9%	84.1%
Doing something outside home with individual girlfriend/boyfriend	42.4%	44.9%	47.7%
Joining sports clubs or common sports events	9.5%	38.2%	50.0%

Table 11.3 Selected troubles of the youths with regard to migration status

Items	Non-migrant youths	Partial migrant youths	Full migrant youths
Trouble with other inhabitants in neighbourhood or quarter	43.5%	55.6%	39.5%
'No-go areas' as imposed by other persons or institutions	21.7%	23.3%	4.7%
Preferred mode of dealing with different opinions: punching or the like	4.5%	18.8%	10.8%
Playing truant	73.9%	75.0%	70.5%

confronted with 'no-go areas' (due to exclusion from school grounds, to abstention orders with certain public places by the police, or to being banned from entering certain buildings; $p < 0.10$; Phi = 0.187). They were also more likely to get into fights with others in cases of difference of opinions and to be truant.

The non-migrant youths, by contrast, were more constant users of alcohol and marihuana (data not shown here). More serious drugs were uncommon with all three subgroups. Part of the difference can be attributed to the fact that the migrant subgroups were composed of Moslem youths to a certain extent.

The migrant subgroups, when asked in a non-specific manner, confessed to have committed more delinquent acts (not known to police) in the four years preceding the study than did the non-migrants. They reported more occasions where they had been stopped by the police 'just on the spot' without any connections to delinquent acts, which might be interpreted as having been discriminated against. However, the highest percentage of those reporting 'trouble with the police' after having committed criminal offences was among the partial migrant subgroup, whereas the full migrant subgroup fell between the non-migrants and the partial migrants (data not shown here).

This peculiar position of the partial migrant youths seems attributable to the amount and the severity of their delinquent behaviour. The subjects were asked in more detail to tell whether or not in the past six months they had committed one or more of 15 different acts punishable by German criminal law, and if so, how often they had committed them. In Table 11.4, we present only the basic results with the category 'ever during that period'. As can be seen, the partial migrants came out on the top position in all but two respects (auto burglary and group fights), sometimes with a quite remarkable percentage difference. The differences are not statistically significant, however, mainly due to the small numbers and the curvilinear distribution.

Are the differences to be considered spurious, therefore? We do not think so, since a recent representative study pertaining to average youths in Münster, north-west Germany, found structurally similar results. The researchers studied in-depth some 1,800 tenth-grade school pupils. Here we refer solely to a special analysis by Walburg (2007: 263) on correlations between self-reported violence and personal or socio-economic factors. Suffice it just to mention the final result of a set of multiple regressions. After controlling for gender, socio-economic family conditions, having experienced parental violence at

Table 11.4 Criminal activity during the last half-year before study contact, by migration status

Item (answer category: ever)	Non-migrant youths	Partial migrant youths	Full migrant youths
Selling illegal drugs	8.5%	18.0%	15.0%
Spraying graffiti	18.2%	26.1%	16.2%
Entering buses, the metro, cinemas, etc., without a ticket	26.1%	54.5%	52.4%
Falsifying age in order to get access to clubs or to rent adult videos or the like	39.1%	60.6%	52.4%
Stealing something worth no more than 50 euros	8.7%	23.6%	16.3%
Stealing something worth more than 50 euros	8.8%	21.8%	11.4%
Attemping to break or actually breaking into a car with the intent to steal	0.0%	9.0%	11.4%
Attempted or completed burglary of a house, flat, etc.	8.9%	14.6%	11.6%
Attempted or completed theft of a car	0.0%	13.5%	9.1%
Assaulting another person (battering or the like)	21.7%	46.0%	36.4%
Intimidating or assaulting another person with a weapon	18.2%	23.6%	13.6%
Engaging in a fight where groups of people were involved	17.4%	43.3%	45.2%
Vandalising in public or otherwise rampaging	34.8%	42.2%	38.6%
Blackmailing	8.5%	18.9%	13.7%
Robbing or threatening another person with weapons	0.0%	11.5%	6.8%

home, and socialising with delinquent peers, migration background still contributed independently ($p < 0.01$) to violent behaviour, in particular to repeated violence.

Neither our small data set nor even the much more elaborated data set as used by Walburg comprises enough variables to allow a convincing explanation of those particularities. In a tentative manner, we assume they are related – to a certain extent in the Stuttgart sample – to the stressful background situation regarding immigration conditions and to the shorter time of living in and adapting to the present neighbourhood as indicated above.

This leads us to the further question whether the three subgroups also differed at all with respect to joining groups in general and, especially, troublesome youth groups or even gangs. This question will be dealt with in the next section.

Migration status and clique-joining, particularly troublesome youth cliques

When asked, 'Do you belong to a group of young people whom you are spending time with, doing things together or just hanging around?', 134 youths (out of 157) or 85.4 per cent answered 'yes'. More non-migrant youths responded affirmatively to belonging to such a group or clique (95.7 per cent) than did partial migrants (83.3 per cent) or full migrants (84.1 per cent). With regard to the Eurogang definitional elements (duration, street orientation and involvement in illegal activities/acceptance of illegal activities), we found that 50 youths (31.6 per cent of the explored youth in Stuttgart) could be described as being a member of a gang according to the Eurogang definition. Of these, five (or 10 per cent) were without any migration background, 31 (or 62 per cent) were partially migrants, and 14 (or 28 per cent) were full migrants.

However, both the full and partial migrants reported a higher average number of group members and more participation of siblings (not shown in table format). Their cliques were predominantly male-oriented and ethnically homogeneous ($p < 0.05$; Phi $= 0.363$); they had, on average, younger members; and they clearly tended to have stayed together for more than two years ($p < 0.05$; Phi $= 0.345$). In addition, they met more often than did non-migrants during the week and on weekends; however, they did not stay out overnight more often than did the non-migrants. Much more elaborated was their tendency to meet primarily on the street, in parks or in playgrounds, and at youth clubs, open youth homes and the like (25 per cent vs 40 per cent vs 42 per cent; the difference was not statistically significant, however).

When asked about their feelings and attitudes toward their groups, non-migrant youths stressed slightly more positive aspects of belonging, mutual support and solidarity with each other, and experiencing 'action' or exciting events in general (Table 11.5). These appear to be more 'emotional' or 'expressive' concerns. By contrast, migrant youth stressed more elements such as getting suitable help with making decisions and learning from others in the clique, seemingly more 'instrumental' concerns. The most decisive difference, however, occurred with regard to the feeling of 'importance' for full migrants, indicating a rather elevated need for psychological or psycho-social compensation.

In the next step of analysis, we looked at involvement of the youths' cliques/groups in delinquent activities. The young respondents had been asked, 'Is it accepted in your group, I mean, is it okay for the group to commit prohibited acts?' Forty-five per cent of the non-migrants answered 'yes', compared to 46.9 per cent of the partial migrant youths and 64.3 per cent of the full migrant youths. When asked then in a generalised manner, 'Does it occur, that several members of your group commit illegal acts together?', a definite 'no' came from 56.5 per cent of the non-migrants, from 33.3 per cent of the partial migrants, and from 31.8 per cent of the full migrants. The remainder was a mixture of either definitely 'yes' or just leaving the answer blank. Field workers' remarks lead us to assume that several youths remained a bit suspicious about confidentiality, and therefore had been very reluctant in particular to implicate their comrades in delinquency.

The young persons were then asked about 14 different specifically clique-related acts. The header was neutrally formulated: 'How often

Table 11.5 Functions of clique/youth group membership, by migration status

Item	Non-migrant youths	Partial migrant youths	Full migrant youths
My group is somehow like a family for me	73.7%	69.7%	75.9%
My group provides me with safety and protection	94.7%	91.7%	93.3%
My group gives me the feeling of belonging somewhere	94.7%	83.6%	81.5%
We support each other and we show solidarity	82.6%	76.7%	70.5%
I experience 'action' or exciting events with my clique	100.0%	94.4%	90.9%
My group partners are helpful in reaching important decisions	73.7%	79.1%	86.2%
I can learn from others in my group	58.8%	73.4%	79.3%
Due to my group I feel important	52.6%	55.1%	75.0%

does your group do the following things?' The answer categories were once, multiple times, never. We experienced basically the same reluctant tendency as with the generalised question. The answers vary slightly from item to item, however, as Table 11.6 clearly shows. For the sake of simplification, we are here combining the answers 'yes, once' and 'yes, multiple times' with the item 'ever.' As one can see, on the one hand, in 10 out of 14 items the non-migrants were the highest percentage of those whose groups *never* do such forbidden acts; on the other hand, they also were at top on 10 out of 14 items in saying that their group committed such acts once or multiple times ('ever').

This at first sight seemingly contradictory result becomes plausible when one considers the amount of missing answers where the subjects left the category in the questionnaire blank. Taking 'ever' and 'blank' together, implying tentatively a disguise of acts actually committed by their group on the part of the migrants, would lead to similar or even higher percentages for them in almost all respects. This can be demonstrated with two items. One is assaulting other persons or engaging in group fights (non-migrants, 73.9 per cent, partial migrants, 67.7 per cent, full migrants, 75.0 per cent). The other is stealing vehicles (non-migrants, 8.7 per cent, partial migrants, 34.5 per cent, full migrants, 34.1 per cent.

Differentiation of cliques' delinquency structure with regard to migrant status

Our results have shown that migration status seems related to problem behaviour and to joining troublesome youth groups or cliques. But differences were not always as high as expected. Furthermore, the differences in the extent of problems were not always linear, contrary to what had been hypothesised. We built new subgroups regarding the extent and intensity of delinquent group behaviour to examine our hypothesis that the full migrant youths joined 'real delinquent' cliques to the highest degree.

By excluding the items, drinking alcohol, using illegal drugs, selling illegal drugs and committing 'other' delinquent acts, we retained ten delinquent acts defined as criminal in the German Penal Code, some of them property related, and some of them violence related. We differentiated three subgroups with regard to criminal behaviour: the first committing only minor acts, without property or violent offences at all ('not committing core criminal acts'); the

Table 11.6 Cliques' delinquent acts (not) reported by youths, by migration status

Group-related item	Non-migrants (ever, never, blank)	Partial migrants (ever, never, blank)	Full migrants (ever, never, blank)
Spraying graffiti	*21.7%*	*15.6%*	*15.9%*
	69.6%	**61.1%**	**56.8%**
	08.7%	23.3%	27.3%
Carrying weapons	*47.8%*	*23.3%*	*22.7%*
	43.5%	**52.2%**	**50.0%**
	08.7%	24.4%	27.3%
Vandalism, criminal damage	*39.1%*	*26.7%*	*31.9%*
	52.2%	**48.9%**	**43.2%**
	08.7%	24.4%	25.0%
Assaulting other persons or fights with other groups	*65.2%*	*44.4%*	*47.7%*
	26.1%	**32.2%**	**25.0%**
	08.7%	23.3%	27.3%
Simple theft	*17.4%*	*20.0%*	*31.8%*
	73.9%	**47.8%**	**38.6%**
	08.7%	22.2%	29.5%
Breaking and entering into a house or flat with intent to steal	*17.3%*	*12.3%*	*13.6%*
	73.9%	**52.2%**	**59.1%**
	08.7%	25.6%	27.3%
Blackmail	*21.7%*	*17.8%*	*13.6%*
	69.6%	**57.8%**	**59.1%**
	08.7%	24.4%	27.3%
Breaking into cars with intent to steal	*00.0%*	*12.3%*	*11.4%*
	91.3%	**65.6%**	**61.4%**
	08.7%	22.2%	27.3%
Stealing vehicles	*00.0%*	*08.9%*	*06.8%*
	91.3%	**65.6%**	**65.9%**
	08.7%	25.6%	27.3%
Depriving others of their property by violence or using weapons	*21.7%*	*15.6%*	*06.8%*
	87.0%	**60.0%**	**65.9%**
	08.7%	24.4%	27.3%
Selling illegal drugs	*17.3%*	*15.6%*	*15.9%*
	73.9%	**58.9%**	**54.5%**
	08.7%	24.4%	29.5%
Using illegal drugs	*39.1%*	*30.0%*	*27.3%*
	52.2%	**46.7%**	**47.7%**
	08.7%	23.3%	25.0%
Drinking alcohol	*78.2%*	*54.4%*	*61.4%*
	13.0%	**21.1%**	**13.6%**
	08.7%	24.4%	25.0%
Other delinquent acts (to be specified by respondent)	*00.0%*	*02.2%*	*06.8%*
	34.8%	**46.7%**	**40.9%**
	65.2%	51.1%	52.3%

second committing occasionally violent or property offences, with a maximum mix of up to five categories such as department store theft and vandalism ('committing youth typical criminal acts only'); and the third engaging in at least six of the ten offences ('fully committing criminal acts'). Against our hypothesis, the migration status of the study youths was not at all related to that differentiation ($p > 0.60$; Phi = 0.145). To put it another way, the 'criminal dimension' seemed to cut across the 'migration dimension.' Irrespective of the migration status of our study youths, we found the following in many respects: the more they belonged to the youth typical and the fully criminal subgroup, the more additional problems could also be found among their group (data not shown here).

Discussion and conclusions

Our study subjects were city youths living under conditions that made them vulnerable to becoming marginalised and eventually delinquent. Accordingly, the association's street workers had as much pertinent contact with them as possible, trying to help them with problems and to enhance elements of stabilisation in their personal and life situation. Due to the whole setting of mobile youth work in the quarters, one could assume from the beginning that no great internal differences might come out in a study of their clientele. The philosophy of street-oriented social work in Stuttgart has always been antidiscriminatory with regard to gender and ethnicity. Actually, we found no gender-related differences at all in our research. Some differences occurred, however, with regard to the migration status of the study subjects. The percentage of migrants among the Stuttgart street workers' clients was definitely higher than to be expected from the population distribution in the whole town. Taking all our impressions and calculations together, we are nevertheless quite sure this had nothing to do with any kind of discriminatory 'lens' among the practitioners dealing with the youths. Whether socio-geographical conditions in the quarters played a relevant role could not be ascertained.

We tried, then, in a 'perspective from within' the scene to look for distinct differences between different subgroups. Since the whole study group was rather small (157 participants), we could not differentiate by individual foreign countries of birth. Instead, we took a more structural approach, and we made a distinction related to the extent of the familial migration background. This resulted in three subgroups:

'full migrants' (subjects and parents born outside Germany), 'partial migrants' (subjects and/or one or both of their parents born outside Germany), and 'non-migrants' (youth and parents born in Germany). On a descriptive level, both migrant subgroups exhibited more problems in a couple of life and behavioural fields than did the non-migrant subgroup (e.g. less communication with parents, less time reading and more time playing video games). Against our expectation, the full migrants were not always worse off (and, in fact, for issues listed in Table 11.3, full migrants were generally 'best off'). On the contrary, in some critical issues the partial migrants dominated the relevant percentages, particularly in regard to individual delinquency involvement (Table 11.4) and other troubles (Table 11.3).

These findings may be in line with others' work on second-generation immigrants (e.g. Vigil, this volume), although our data preclude a deeper examination of such concerns. We assume, as other researchers have found, that a more extended culture conflict situation is at work here, adding strain from divergent parental cultures of origin to the typical strain with which all young migrants (in particular those stemming from far distant cultures of origin) are confronted according to the criteria of culture conflict theory (see Sellin 1938; cf. Auernheimer 1990; Youkhana 1996). Results of recent and methodologically more refined German studies seem to confirm the picture (cf. Boers et al. 2002; 2007). However, there is so far no way to test the assumption empirically, due to the lack of more detailed specific data on concrete living conditions and personal pressures among the young migrants.

The higher amount of violence among migrant youths has long been discussed also in Germany. Among the factors considered to be decisive are family strain, personal strain, adverse living conditions, and other objective elements, but also socio-cultural factors, such as a 'culture of honour' or 'machismo', and respectively rigid gender role attitudes (cf. Albrecht et al. 2007; Babka von Gostomski 2003; Brettfeld and Enzmann et al. 2003; Brüß 2004; Feltes and Goldberg 2006; Weber and Gosch 2005). We saw some of those factors in personal interviews, but do not have quantitative access so far. However, we could detect in our study some indicators that the group context itself, irrespective of ethnic factors, could create dynamics leading to different levels of deviance and crime.

Many studies have shown strong correlations between the delinquent or violent behavioural manners of youngsters and the amount of delinquent behaviour present in their respective circle of friends, in particular during leisure time (see, for Germany, Baier and

Wetzels 2006). Studies in the USA and the UK consistently found that integration in deviant peer groups goes together with a rise in delinquent activity as well as the establishment of delinquent-prone attitudes (cf. Elliott and Menard 1996; Patterson and Dishion 1985; Sharp *et al.* 2006; Thornberry *et al.* 1993, 1994 and 2003). Our comparatively few data would fit this picture if only we could relate clearly the criminal offence spectrum of individual youths to the amount of criminal offences of the subgroup to which they belong. The underlying tendency can also be found in a recent representative study of a very large group of ninth-grade pupils (n = 4,567) in the German State of Lower Saxony. Brettfeld *et al.* (2005) detected there that the amount of self-reported delinquency steadily increased with the increasing number of delinquent friends with whom the pupils socialised. This was true for all kinds of delinquency but came out most clearly for violent acts (assault, wounding, robbery, etc.). Pupils socialising with up to four delinquent friends among their peers admitted more than threefold more violent acts (15 per cent) than did pupils with non-delinquent peers (4.7 per cent). Having five or more delinquent friends among their peers clearly boosted the youngsters' own delinquency by 45.2 per cent violent acts committed.

In conclusion, what kind of underlying reasons lead juveniles in Germany to join troublesome youth groups? We do not have enough specific data to provide an answer to this question. In accordance with Klein (1995), we think that there is surely no mono-causal explanation for gang membership. However, some heavy deficits in interpersonal relations and the need for identity and status (cf. Klein 1995) seem to play a role. For some 74 per cent of those juveniles belonging to the full criminally active subgroup, 'feeling important' was a major factor; among the migrant subgroups discussed, 75 per cent of full migrants (compared to about 50 per cent of the other two groups) listed this aspect. Aggregate factors, such as poverty, inadequate educational processes, population shifts, and ethnic segregation may be relevant to our study population too. In Stuttgart, though, there are rather strong inclusionary policies, as compared to other German regions, that may moderate the extent of negative aggregate influences, at least in terms of differences between migrant and non-migrant youths in our study. Further study of the particular experiences of partial migrants relevant to full and non-migrants is warranted.

Notes

1 We are very grateful to managers and mobile street social workers of the 'Mobile Jugendarbeit Stuttgart e. V.' Association for their close collaboration. Many thanks also to the young persons willing to answer our questions via interviews and questionnaires.

2 We are grateful to Katrin Kampermann and Miriam Wittmann for work done in the study (under supervision of Hans-Jürgen Kerner, Marc Coester and Siegfried Müller). Gerald Warscheid provided useful support with additional SPSS runs.

References

Albrecht, P.G., Eckert, R., Roth, R., Thielen-Reffgen, C. and Wetzstein, T. (2007) *Wir und die anderen: Gruppenauseinandersetzungen Jugendlicher in Ost und West*. Wiesbaden: VS Verlag für Sozialwissenschaften.

Auernheimer, G. (1990) *Der sogenannte Kulturkonflikt. Orientierungsprobleme ausländischer Jugendlicher*. Frankfurt: Campus Verlag.

Babka von Gostomski, C. (2003) 'Einflussfaktoren inter- und intraethnischen Gewalthandelns bei männlichen deutschen, türkischen und Aussiedler-Jugendlichen', *Zeitschrift für Soziologie der Erziehung und der Sozialisation*, 23(4): 399–415.

Baier, D. and Wetzels, P. (2006) 'Freizeitverhalten, Cliquenzugehörigkeit und Gewaltkriminalität', in A. Dessecker (ed.), *Jugendarbeitslosigkeit und Kriminalität*. Wiesbaden: Kriminologische Zentralstelle e.V., 69–97.

Bodenmüller, M. and Piepel, G. (2004) *Streetwork und Überlebenshilfen*. Weinheim: Beltz-Verlag.

Boers, K. and Reinicke, J. (2002) *Informationen zur 3. Schülerbefragung in Münster* [Online]. Münster: Westfälische Wilhelms-Universität Münster, Institut für Kriminalwissenschaften. Available from: www.jura.uni-muenster.de/download.cfm?DownloadFile=2D3038B9-015A-4817-9921F5C1481BD08C [accessed 30 November 2007].

Boers, K. and Reinecke, J. (eds) (2007) *Delinquenz im Jugendalter*, Münster: Waxmann Verlag.

Brettfeld, K., Enzmann, D., Trunk, D. and Wetzels, P. (2005) *Abschlussbericht zur Evaluation des Niedersächsischen Modellprojekts gegen Schuleschwänzen, Forschungsbericht*. Hamburg: Universität Hamburg.

Brüß, J. (2004) 'Zwischen Gewaltbereitschaft und Systemvertrauen', *Psychologie in Erziehung und Unterricht*, 51(3): 201–12.

Elliott, D.S. and Menard, S. (1996) 'Delinquent friends and delinquent behavior: temporal and developmental patterns', in D.J. Hawkins (ed.), *Delinquency and Crime: Current Theories*. Cambridge: Cambridge University Press, 28–67.

Esbensen, F.A. and Weerman, F.M. (2005) 'Youth gangs and troublesome youth groups in the United States and The Netherlands: a cross-national comparison', *European Journal of Criminology*, 2(1): 5–37.

Farin, K. and Seidel-Pielen, E. (1996) *Krieg in den Städten: Jugendgangs in Deutschland*. Berlin: Rotbuch Verlag.

Feltes, T. and Goldberg, B. (2006) 'Selbsberichtete Delinquenz, Viktimisierung und Verbrechensfurcht bei Schülern mit und ohne Migrationshintergrund', in J. Obegfell-Fuchs *et al.* (eds), *Nationale und internationale Entwicklungen in der Kriminologie*. Frankfurt am Main: Verlag für Polizeiwissenschaft, 203–37.

Förtig, H. (2002) *Jugendbanden*. München: Utz, Herbert.

Fuchs, M. (1995) 'Jugendbanden, Gangs und Gewalt an Schulen', *Soziale Probleme*, 6(1): 62–83.

Gillich, S. (2005) *Ausgegrenzt & abgeschoben: Streetwork als Chance*. Gelnhausen: Triga/Verlag.

Klein, M.W. (1995) *The American Street Gang*. New York: Oxford University Press.

Klein, M.W., Kerner, H.J. and Maxcon, C.L. (eds) (2001) *The Eurogang Paradox*. Dordrecht: Kluwer Academic Publishers.

Müller, J. (2000) 'Jugendkonflikte und Gewalt mit ethnisch-kulturellem Hintergrund', in W. Heitmeyer and R. Anhut (eds), *Bedrohte Stadtgesellschaft*. München: Juventa, 257–305.

Oberwittler, D. (2003) 'Geschlecht, Ethnizität und sozialräumliche Benachteiligung', in S. Lamnek and M. Boatca (eds), *Geschlecht – Gewalt-Gesellschaft*, Band 4. Opladen: Leske and Budrich, 269–95.

Patterson, G.R. and Dishion, T.J. (1985) 'Contributions of families and peers to delinquency', *Criminology*, 23(1): 63–79.

Pavkovic, G. and Lavadinhos, I. (2006) *Grundlagen der Integrationspolitik in der Landes-hauptstadt Stuttgart*. Stuttgart.

Reich, K. (2003) 'Delinquent behaviour: one possible response to migration related problems for young male ethnic-Germans?', in F. Dünkel and K. Drenkhahn (eds), *Youth Violence: New Patterns and Local Responses*. Mönchengladbach: Forum Verlag Godesberg, 443–57.

Reich, K. (2005) *Integrations- und Desintegrationsprozesse junger männlicher Aussiedler aus der GUS*. Münster: Lit-Verlag.

Schmitt-Rodermund, E. and Silbereisen, R.K. (2004) 'Ich war gezwungen, alles mit der Faust zu regeln', in D. Oberwittler and S. Karstedt (eds), *Soziologie der Kriminalität*. Wiesbaden: VS Verlag für Sozialwissenschaften, 240–63.

Seidel-Pielen, E. and Farin, K. (1995) 'Straßengangs-Straßengewalt', in K. Hurrelmann, C. Palentien and W. Wilken (eds), *Anti-Gewalt-Report*. Weinheim: Beltz Verlag, 145–65.

Sellin, T. (1938) *Culture Conflict and Crime*. New York: Social Science Research Council.

Sharp, C., Aldridge, J. and Medina, J. (2006) *Delinquent Youth Groups and Offending Behaviour: Findings from the 2004 Offending, Crime and Justice Survey.* Home Office Online Report 14/06) [online]. London: Crown Publishing Group. Available from: www.homeoffice.gov.uk/rds/pdfs06/ rdsolr1406.pdf [accessed 6 December 2007].

Specht, W. (1991) *Die gefährliche Straße: Jugendkonflikte und Stadtteilarbeit.* Bielefeld: Böllert, KT-Verlag.

Specht, W. (ed.) (1999) *Street Children and Youth Work.* Stuttgart.

Srur, N., Meinhardt, R. and Tielking, K. (2005) *Streetwork und Case-Management in der Suchthilfe für Aussiedlerjugendliche.* Oldenburg: BIS-Verlag.

Statistisches Bundesamt (2007) *Datenreport 2006,* Teil II, 12. Bonn: Bundeszentrale für Politische Bildung.

Tertilt, H. (1996) *Turkish Power Boys. Ethnographie einer Jugendbande.* Frankfurt am Main: Suhrkamp.

Thornberry, T.P., Krohn, M.D., Lizotte, A.J. and Chard-Wierschem, D. (1993) 'The role of juvenile gangs in facilitating delinquent behavior', *Journal of Research in Crime and Delinquency,* 30(1): 55–87.

Thornberry, T.P., Lizotte, A.J., Krohn, M.D., Farnworth, M. and Jang, S.J. (1994) 'Delinquent peers, beliefs, and delinquent behavior', *Criminology,* 32(1): 47–83.

Thornberry, T.P., Krohn, M.D., Smith, C.A., Lizotte, A.J. and Tobin, K. (2003) *Gangs and Delinquency in Developmental Perspective.* Cambridge: Cambridge University Press.

Walburg, C. (2007) 'Migration und selbstberichtete Delinquenz', in K. Boers and J. Reinecke (eds), *Delinquenz im Jugendalter.* Münster: Waxmann, 241–68.

Weber, M. and Gosch, P. (2005) 'Inszenierungen von Männlichkeit unter Bedingungen sozialer Randständigkeit', *Kindheit, Jugend und Gesellschaft,* 50(1): 18–23.

Weitekamp, E.G.M., Reich, K. and Kerner, H.J. (2005) 'Why do young male Russians of German descent (Aussiedlers) tend to join or form gangs where violence plays a major role?', in S. Decker and F.M. Weerman (eds), *European Street Gangs and Troublesome Youth Groups.* Walnut Creek, CA: Alta Mira Press, 81–104.

Wilfert, O. (1959) *Jugend-Gangs: Entstehung, Struktur und Behandlungsmöglichkeit der Komplizengemeinschaft Jugendlicher.* Wien: Springer.

Youkhana, E.S. (1996) *Subkultur und Jugendbanden: Überlebensstrategien ausländischer Jugendlicher in Deutschland.* Bonn: Holos-Verlag.

Chapter 12

Respect, friendship, and racial injustice: justifying gang membership in a Canadian city

Scot Wortley and Julian Tanner

Gangs have become an important social issue in Canada. Indeed, a recent survey indicates that over 70 per cent of Canadians feel that street gangs are a serious or very serious problem within their community (Wortley and Tanner 2007). Similarly, most Canadian police agencies believe that youth gangs are increasing within their jurisdiction (Chettleburgh 2007). As in Europe, much of the public discussion about gangs has centred on the risks posed by immigration and racial diversification. The Canadian media frequently run stories about the proliferation of racial minority gangs within urban areas, and both politicians and police officials frequently lament that foreign 'gang cultures' are inconsistent with Canada's traditional values and beliefs (see Henry and Tator 2002). As a result, many Canadians believe that their country's gang problem is largely imported from other countries and concentrated within the 'non-White' population (Wortley 2002).[1] This paper begins with a brief review of previous Canadian research to determine whether immigrants and racial minorities are in fact more involved in gang activity than native-born Whites. We then turn to analysis of data from a recent Toronto study to investigate racial differences in reasons for gang involvement. We argue that racial differences in how gang members explain or justify their gang involvement may help account for why some racial groups are more involved in gang activity than others.

Canadian research on race and gang activity

Much of the existing research on gangs in Canada is at least a decade old and focused on isolated youth groups. Mathews (1993), for example, investigated the gang issue in Toronto by conducting a series of interviews with 12 youths involved in the same street gang (Mathews 1993). Other research has been similarly modest in scope, often employing ethnographic methods to investigate small groups of youth residing in specific geographic locations (see Baron 1997; Delbert and Robinson 1980; Gordon 2000; Martin and White 1993). Although rich in qualitative detail, these studies have made no effort to determine whether gang activity is more prevalent among some racial groups than others.

Official statistics on Canadian gangs are almost nonexistent. To date, police services in Canada do not regularly release data on gang-related crime. However, in 2003, the Solicitor General conducted the first Canadian Police Survey on Youth Gangs (Chettleburgh 2007). More than 264 police agencies from across the nation participated in this study. Between them, they identified 484 different youth gangs operating within Canada and an estimated 6,760 individual gang members. Interestingly, the majority of the police agencies participating in the survey maintained that racial minority youth are grossly over-represented in gang activity: Asian gangs are thought to dominate the west coast, Aboriginal gangs dominate the Prairie Provinces, and Black gangs dominate central and eastern Canada (Chettleburgh 2007: 18–20).

The only other large-scale study of youth gangs in Canada was conducted in Toronto (see Wortley and Tanner 2006). This survey, conducted in 2000, involved a representative sample of 3,393 high-school students. Unlike media accounts, this survey found that immigrant students (5 per cent) were actually less likely to be currently involved in gangs than were Canadian-born youth (7 per cent). Nonetheless, the rate of gang membership was twice as high among Black (13 per cent) and Hispanic youth (12 per cent) than among White (6 per cent) and Asian (5 per cent) youth. It must be stressed that while Black and Hispanic students were more likely to report gang involvement than White students, a large proportion of all gang-involved students (over 40 per cent) were White.

Logistic regression analyses revealed that the impact of race on the probability of gang membership was not reduced after statistically controlling for social class, educational performance, single-parent family background, peer deviance, or self-control. However, the impact of race became statistically insignificant after a variable was introduced that measured respondent perceptions of racial discrimination. In other words, respondents who perceived racism against their own group – with respect to policing, housing, education, and employment opportunities – were more likely to be involved in gangs than those who did not perceive racism. Furthermore, group differences in perceptions of racism seem to explain why our Black and Hispanic respondents are more likely to report gang involvement than either White or Asian students.

In our opinion, these survey results are important. They indicate that, at least in the Canadian context, there may be a strong relationship between experiences and perceptions of racism and the likelihood of gang involvement. However, many critics have argued that we must turn to more qualitative methods to understand why some youth decide to become involved in gangs (Maxson and Whitlock 2002). Compared to survey methods, qualitative interviews allow respondents to use 'their own words' to describe 'lived experiences'. As such, qualitative data can provide depth to statistical results. Thus, in the next section, we attempt to supplement the results of our survey data with findings from a series of qualitative interviews with known gang members. The focus will be on identifying racial differences in the reasons or justifications behind gang involvement.

Methodology

The Toronto Street Gang Pilot Project entered the field in November 2004.[2] Producing a representative sample of gang members is a difficult process. Obviously, there is no existing list of gang members to draw from or a formal gang registry to consult. As a result, most gang researchers in Canada have either conducted detailed ethnographies of specific youth gangs or employed survey methods to determine the extent and nature of self-reported gang activity within the wider population. We decided to take a third approach – detailed qualitative interviews with a large sample of 'known gang members' from a variety of backgrounds and neighbourhoods. The term 'known gang member' is used to describe individuals identified as a gang member by criminal justice officials – including police officers, social workers, probation officers, and youth counsellors.

In order to produce our sample of gang members, we used a two-stage sampling strategy. We first approached a number of local organisations working with youth who had been charged and/or convicted of criminal activity. These organisations included four different probation offices, three shelters for youth recently released from custody, four community centres operating programmes for 'at-risk' youth, and two organisations operating specific 'gang-exiting' programmes. Within each organisation, we identified adult 'informants' who were currently working with youthful offenders. We described the purpose of our study to these 'informants' and asked them to identify youth within their own organisation who were believed to be gang-involved. We then asked our 'informants' to contact these youth and tell them about our study (including the fact that they would be paid a $25 honorarium for their participation). Youth who were interested were given a phone number by the informant and asked to contact a member of the research team to arrange an interview.

Once an interview had been arranged, we asked potential respondents a series of screening questions to ensure that they were or had recently been involved in a gang. In order to take part in the study, respondents had to be 16–24 years of age and report that: (1) they belonged to a gang that consisted of five or more individuals; (2) they had been the member of this gang for at least six months; and (3) that criminal activity was the primary purpose or focus of the gang. At the end of the interview, respondents were also given a card with a contact number. They were then asked to inform other gang members that they might know about the study. We believe that this 'snowball' strategy added only five respondents to the final sample. Many respondents were reluctant to divulge to peers that they had participated in a research project.

By the summer of 2006, the research team had completed 125 face-to-face interviews with gang-involved youth. To the best of our knowledge, this is the largest sample of 'known gang members' ever produced by Canadian researchers. A third of our sample (34 per cent) was reached through probation officers, a third (30 per cent) were reached through gang exiting programs, 24 per cent were reached through community centres, and 20 per cent were reached through youth shelters. We believe that the strength of our sampling strategy was that it identified individuals from 21 different youth gangs from 16 different Toronto neighbourhoods. Thus, compared to ethnographies that focus exclusively on a single gang, the results of this study might be easier to generalise. An obvious weakness, however, is that we were able to contact only gang members who had come into contact with the criminal justice system or with selected community organisations. It is also impossible to determine whether the gang members who agreed to participate in our study were substantively different from those who did not want to be interviewed. In our opinion, these sampling concerns are common to many other gang studies.

Interviews were scheduled for quiet locations close to the respondents' current residence. Confidentiality was guaranteed. Interviews did not proceed without informed consent. All respondents were given the opportunity to ask questions before the interview commenced. Interestingly, despite the sensitive nature of the interview, all respondents agreed to have their responses tape-recorded. These tapes were immediately transcribed by members of the research team and subsequently destroyed. Interviews took between one and three and a half hours to complete (mean: 85 minutes). A structured interview protocol was employed. Questions focused on a variety of topics, including the personal background of the respondents, gang characteristics, reasons for gang involvement, the benefits and consequences of gang membership, criminal and non-criminal activities within the gang context, and the causes of gang-related violence. The interview concluded by asking the respondents about their attitude to the criminal justice system and their opinion of various gang-prevention strategies (see Wortley and Tanner (2007) for a more detailed description of the research methodology).

Respondent characteristics

The vast majority of our gang respondents were male (82 per cent). Almost all came from disruptive family backgrounds: 61 per cent were raised in a single-parent household and 11 per cent grew up within the child-protection system. The majority of respondents were born in Canada (70 per cent) – a finding that challenges the myth of the alleged link between immigration and gang activity. Nonetheless, the sample is racially diverse: 41 per cent of respondents self-identified as Black, 37 per cent were White, 9 per cent were Hispanic, 7 per cent were Aboriginal, 3 per cent were Asian and 3 per cent were of South Asian descent. Interestingly, minority respondents were more likely to be born in Canada (77 per cent) than White respondents (66 per cent). A large number of our White respondents were immigrants from Eastern Europe. Finally, consistent with previous research, most of our respondents grew up under circumstances of poverty and social disadvantage. Indeed, almost two-thirds of our respondents (60 per cent) indicated that they were raised in a public housing project.

Gang characteristics

As discussed above, the youth we interviewed meet the most stringent of gang criteria – including the gang definition established by the Eurogang project (see Esbensen and Weerman 2005). Our typical respondent belonged to a gang or 'crew' that consisted of between 10–30 members. Almost all of the respondents (96 per cent) stated that their gang had a distinct name. In addition, 93 per cent stated that their gang had specific identifiers including colours, tags, tattoos and brandings. Furthermore, almost all of our respondents (93 per cent) stated that their gang had a specific territory that was under their control. All of our respondents were heavily involved in various types of street crime within the gang context: 97 per cent reported that their gang was involved in theft (including car theft, breaking and entering, etc.), 93 per cent indicated that their gang was actively involved in drug trafficking, 73 per cent said that their gang was involved in robbery and extortion, and 36 per cent said that their gang was involved in fraud (including bank-card fraud, passing bad cheques and counterfeiting). A small proportion of our respondents (10 per cent) also stated that their gang was involved in prostitution. Finally, gang involvement appears to be quite durable. Our respondents were involved with their gang for an average of 2.7 years.

The racial composition of gangs

Our results suggest that many of Toronto's gangs are quite integrated. Only 28 per cent of our respondents indicated that they belonged to a gang in which all other members shared the same racial background. By contrast, over 60 per cent indicated that they belonged to a mixed-race crew, and 12 per cent claimed membership in a gang in which most members were from another racial group. It should be noted, however, that our Black and Hispanic respondents were more likely to state that they belonged to a racially homogeneous gang, while White youth were more likely to claim that they belonged to mixed race gang units.

Reasons for gang membership

In this section, we examine factors that may help explain gang membership in Toronto. The findings discussed below stem from responses to two related interview questions. First, why did youth initially become involved with a gang? And second, what are the good things about being a member of a gang? In other words, what are the benefits? An analysis of the transcribed interviews reveals that the pathways to gang membership are complex and often vary from respondent to respondent. Nonetheless, we were able to identify six major themes with respect to how our respondents explained their gang membership: (1) neighbourhood, peer, and family influences; (2) protection; (3) support and companionship; (4) status and respect; (5) money; and (6) racial injustice. Many of these reasons or justifications have been identified by previous gang researchers (Curry and Decker 1998; Decker and Van Winkle 1997; Huff 2002; Maxson and Whitlock 2002; Padilla 1992). However, in our opinion, a unique finding is that racial minority gang members are much more likely to highlight racial injustice and social inequality as reasons for gang membership than their White counterparts. The implications of this result are discussed in the final section of the paper.

Neighbourhood, peer, and family influences

For many respondents, what eventually became a gang often began as an informal friendship grouping of kids who grew up in the same neighbourhood or went to the same school. We could not identify significant racial variations in this theme. It seems that almost all gang youth, regardless of their background, recognise the influence of neighbourhood peers. The following statements are typical:

> I joined 'cause it was like natural. Just what you did in my neighbourhood. You either with the crew or against them. But it was like they did not force me. It was jus' one of them things cause from where I lived and where you hang when you were growing up. (case 121: White male, 23 years old)

> It wasn't too good at home, and so, like, I started hangin' out on the streets. And then I met the wrong crowd. I met a person and he showed me, like, you know, some bad stuff and for some reason I liked it. And then I just started doing it and then I got involved. (case 39: Hispanic male, 17 years old)

> We just grew up together and some of them sold drugs and I needed to make some money so I started selling drugs, and we started hanging out even tighter. They were my friends to start with. I was gonna hang out with them no matter what. It

wasn't because they're a gang. That's not what it was about at all. It was just friends. (case 49: White male, 23 years old)

Some respondents emphasised that the nature of their early lives made it more or less inevitable that they would become involved with gangs. For example, one 19-year-old Black male (case 19) stated that:

I guess there was lots of reasons. But it was just like what ya had to do. I mean these are all the same guys you hung out with when you was small. Like one day you playing on the swings with these guys, and the next day you fightin' and hustlin' with them. It just what you did where I came from. You had no option. If you did not join them ... no friends, no protection, no money.

Protection

The gang as protection was another theme stressed by respondents from all racial backgrounds. Frequently, respondents described the environment that they grew up in as extremely violent. Gangs are often a direct response to such environments. They are attractive because they seemingly afford protection from the local predators:

In my area, man, if you ain't with a crew your gonna get punked and jumped all the time. If ya can't beat 'em join 'em. The gang got your back and people don't mess with you 'cause they know you got backup. (case 52: White female, 19 years old)

Like, my community is rough, man. Somebody always jump you for your money or just beat you for fun. But when you got your own crew, all that shit stops, 'cause people don't want a war, man. (case 93: Black male, 21 years old)

At my school, man, the Black guys used to beat us Indian kids bad. Take your lunch, your jacket. ... So we needed to join up to fight them back. Meet force with force. We needed to protect ourselves from those punks. (case 85: South Asian male, 22 years old)

Man, when I got to high school these White dudes would always like beat me, call me names and like take my money. ... Then I met some brothas at school ... and they said they would have my back. We beat their racist asses bad. They never touched me again. No way I was gonna leave the gang after that. (case 8, Black male, 20 years old)

Social support and companionship

Along with physical protection, gangs were also seen as a valuable source of friendship and support. Our interviews were replete with comments about the emotional comfort, material aid, and companionship that gangs provide. Many respondents, from all racial backgrounds, expressed love and emotional attachment for their fellow gang members. The gang-as-family analogy is evident from the following exchanges:

> That's why lots of people go to gangs because they don't have parents and they don't have any family to love 'em or trust 'em. So you go to a gang where you have a big family, so you stay with them and it's like you're in a gang family. (case 20: White male, 19 years old)

> They would like play basketball with you, they would take you to the store to buy candy or food for you and they would just make you feel like family. They were nice and gave you shit. Yeah – like they are the only real people who care about you. (case 43: Black male, age 22 years old)

> The gang is like my family, man. When you need something like some clothes or some food or some money or a place to crash, they are there. When you need to talk, they are there. When you got a beef, they got your back. I love those guys, man. They are my blood, my heart (case 63: South Asian male, 22 years old)

> Whenever there was a problem, you could count on them to be there, whether it was a violent problem, emotional problem, hell, even a math problem. Somebody would be there, somebody would help you with your problem. So that's what makes you think of them like family. (case 49: White male, 23 years old).

Social status and respect

According to respondents from all racial backgrounds, gangs also provide social status. Some respondents reported that they enjoyed the level of fear that their reputation as a gang member produced. Others claimed that they enjoyed the power and alleged respect associated with the gang lifestyle:

The best thing about being a gang member I would say [is] … the respect you get, basically, the respect you get. (case 30: Black male, 20 years old)

The money, the power, portraying fear unto others, it was an ego thing … people fearing you and recognising who I was. (case 1: White female, 21 years old)

It was just more cool. I like the respect. I like the power. You walk into a place with your boys and people notice you, ladies notice you. Ya got status, you can swagger. People know you ain't no punk. (case 44: Black male, 21 years old).

Several of our male respondents, from all racial backgrounds, stated that the power and respect accorded gang members facilitated sexual conquests:

As I said, you had your shorties, like your girls, know what I'm sayin'? They would like come around and hang with ya and party. Some girls, man, they was like groupies. We would like pass them around for sex and stuff. They jus' liked hangin' with the bad boys. (case 43: Black male, 22 years old)

Man, you always get girls in the gang. Like you always get laid. Girls just love the bad boys, know what I'm saying? One of the good things about the gang is the women all want your jock. (case 86: White male, 20 years old)

Financial motivations

Money was by far the most frequently cited benefit of gang membership. Many saw gang-related crime, particularly drug dealing, as a significant moneymaking opportunity. When asked about the positive aspects of gang membership, many respondents simply responded that it was all about 'making money' (case 39: Hispanic male, 17 years old). Others were more expressive when describing their financial motivations. The following statements are typical:

I personally probably got involved just for the fact of the money. I guess I didn't really like being broke all the time. I wanted to make some money so I could be like all them other kids that go to the movies, you know? In the gang you could sell drugs, you could do all sorts of things to make money. So … I guess that's what really got me. (case 60: White male, 20 years old)

I like it for the money. We made lots of money sellin' drugs and stealin' and rippin' people off. I got to buy stuff I could not get with no job at McDonalds. Money would be my main reason for liking being in a crew. (case 50: Black male, 21 years old)

It was just, like … everybody's like … you see what everybody's doin', like – if I'm goin' to school, right, if this guy's goin' and he's beatin' up people, he's taking their stuff, you see the stuff he has, you see the stuff he's stealin', and you're like, 'Damn, I want that stuff. I need that stuff, too.' 'Cuz my mom's not really that rich … she can't give me no money, you know? (case 29: Black male, 21 years old)

Other respondents expressed the belief that there was more dignity and respect in drug dealing and gang activity than working in low-paying jobs in the service industry. This perspective was particularly prevalent among our Black respondents – who frequently stated that they would refuse to take low-paying, low-status jobs that reminded them of the legacy of African servitude. As the following statements reveal, many Black gang members felt that such dead-end jobs provided low pay and no opportunity for either social status or personal pride.

I'm not workin' at McDonalds or some place like that. That's slavery. They pay you shit and make you dress like a goof and have some punk manager order you around. Nobody respects some guy flippin' burgers. I make real cheddar in the gang, we are our own bosses, and we get plenty more respect from people 'cause of the money we got and because we never sell out. (case 51: Black male, 22 years old)

It's like the only jobs they got for poor Black people is like McDonalds or Wendy's or other bullshit like that. Low, low pay, no respect. You basically just a slave, just a punk, while some fat owner gets rich. I'm not goin' down like that. I'm my own boss, make way more money and don't sell myself out to shit like that. I'd rather die than embarrass myself like that. (case 64: Black male, 23 years old)

I gang-bang cause it gives me cash flow. You need money in this world to live well and get respect. Nobody gives poor people respect – nobody gives them their props – no matter how hard they work. My mom gets up at five in the morning every day to go clean rich peoples' toilets. I see her struggle every fuckin' day. They pay her like shit. Do you think people give her respect? Fuck no. Me – now I won't be no fool like that. No fuckin' way. I get paid, man, I get paid. (case 100: Black male, 24 years old)

Perceptions of social injustice

Through the course of our interviews, it became increasingly apparent that many of our racial minority respondents felt socially alienated and disengaged from mainstream society. These youth often expressed the belief that social injustice was widespread in Canada and that they were the victim of social inequality, racism, and economic oppression. Some felt that gangs were an outcome of structural and historical disadvantage, a cultural response to alienation and estrangement. By contrast, none of our White respondents provided this type of social critique. Contained in this largely minority world view is the depiction of gangs as expressions of protest and defiance against White oppression. This is how one 20-year-old Aboriginal man, for example, explained the apparent rise in Aboriginal gang activity in this country: 'White people have made up a society so that Native (Aboriginal) people are being set up for failure in life. Gangs is the only way they can go out and make a dollar' (case 5). The following statements further illustrate this critical perspective:

What chance has a guy like me got in the real world? A poor Black guy? Schools are shit, teachers don't think you can do the work. Nobody's gonna give me a good job. So I'll get paid and live in another way, in another world where I can get respect and nobody cares what I look like or where I came from. I know I'll probably die young or go to jail, but what other chance is there? (case 66: Black male, 22 years old)

I remember, growing up in school, they would always tell you that you could become anything you want. That's pure bullshit. When you are poor, like you got nothin'. I went to school with these rich kids – White kids and Chinese kids – who did fuckin' nothin'. But their parents gave them everything for just being fucking alive. Their parents would buy them clothes and cars and iPods and take them to travel places. They didn't realise how fuckin' lucky they are. I hated those assholes. I have no problem robbing those mother-fuckers and taking their shit. They don't deserve anything more than me. (case 99: Asian male, 22 years old)

Indeed, some of our minority respondents went so far as to denounce Canada and their position within the social hierarchy. These individuals clearly viewed their gang membership as an act of defiance against a society that had rejected and abandoned them:

This is not my country. This country does not care about me or my family. They just want people like us to clean the shit out of White people's toilets or look after their fuckin' kids. They want us to keep our place and keep the peace so they can go on with their fuckin' lives. I'm not going out like that. I'm not goin' to be some bitch. People will know who I am – I don't bow down to nobody. I won't take their fuckin' shit. (case 123: Black male, 22 years old)

Canada does not care about me. Canada does not care about my family or about Black people. This country is for rich White people. They make the rules. They run shit here. They just want us to stay quiet and know our place. They want us to take the shit jobs and not complain about racism. I'm not being no White person's bitch. I'm not working no low-paying slave job. I will sell drugs in my crew and steal shit and not bow down to White people. At least that is some power. (case 97: Black male, 21 years old).

Discussion

Canadian research suggests that certain racial minority groups are more involved in gang activity than others. This fact is highly consistent with both American and European findings that suggest that, along with sex and age, race is one of the strongest predictors of criminal behaviour (see Kennedy 1997; Tonry 1995). The challenge for many criminologists has been to find a theory that can help explain racial differences in criminal propensity.

Our previous examination of Toronto survey data (discussed above) suggests that racial differences in gang involvement are eliminated after controlling for racial differences in perceptions of racial injustice. Our in-depth interviews with known gang members from Toronto reinforce the argument that perceptions of racial injustice matter when explaining minority gang involvement. We found that respondents from all racial backgrounds cite neighbourhood and peer influences, a desire for money, respect, protection, and friendship as reasons for joining gangs and remaining involved in the gang lifestyle. However, in addition to utilitarian considerations, many of the minority youth in our sample maintain that their involvement in gangs can be directly linked to profound feelings of racial injustice and social exclusion. Indeed, many of our minority respondents expressed rather sophisticated ideas regarding racism, social inequality, social injustice, and oppression. By contrast, in explaining their gang involvement, White respondents never expressed such concerns. Thus, it appears that gang membership for some minority youth may be more than a simple quest for material goods, protection, and status. Our results suggest that gang membership can also be experienced as a profound act of pride, defiance, and rebellion. It is a means of expressing a belief that society is fundamentally unfair – of demonstrating resistance to the rules of a racist, oppressive society. It is not that these minority youths have ambitions of overthrowing 'the system' or causing a revolution. Indeed, such grand ambitions were completely absent from our interview data. Rather, many of our minority respondents seem to be expressing both anger and resignation at the fact that they reside in a racist, unjust society. Gang membership, for them, is not about social change – it is about pursuing social status and material goals while at the same time maintaining personal autonomy and pride. Indeed, many of our minority respondents stated that it was a 'dog-eat-dog' world and that they felt more self-respect and pride as a gang member than they would if they held a low-paying job within the legitimate economy.

Many of our results are consistent with standard criminological explanations. For example, the fact that our respondents often came from disadvantaged backgrounds and frequently joined gangs to attain money, respect, and protection is completely consistent with both rational-choice and strain theories of crime causation (Agnew

2004; Clarke and Felson 1993). Similarly, support for social learning theories can be drawn from the fact that most of our respondents were introduced to gangs through neighbourhood peers and frequently stayed in gangs for both companionship and social support (Akers and Silverman 2004). However, our findings with respect to perceptions of racial injustice suggest a more expressive or symbolic motivation for some gang activity. In many ways, our findings echo the arguments of Sherman's defiance theory (Brownfield 2006; Sherman 1993) and Tyler's (1990) ideas with respect to perceived legitimacy and the law. Sherman, for example, predicts that criminal sanctions will cause future offending depending on the degree to which offenders perceive sanctioning as illegitimate, have weak bonds to conventional society, deny their shame, and take pride in their rebellious orientation (Sherman 1993: 448). Clearly, our findings suggest that, among minority gang members, perceptions of racial injustice may undermine both the perceived legitimacy of the law and personal bonds to conventional society. Additionally, many of our minority gang members expressed little shame with respect to their gang involvement and often demonstrated pride in their defiance of conventional rules. However, while both Sherman and Tyler focus on the perceived legitimacy of the legal system, our results suggest that racial injustice may undermine the perceived legitimacy of an entire nation. In sum, people who perceive the very society that they live in as fundamentally biased against members of their own group may find it easier to neutralise feelings of guilt and justify criminal behaviour – including gang involvement (Sykes and Matza 1967).

Our results leave many unanswered questions. First of all, how do perceptions of racial injustice develop? Are they the result of family and peer socialisation processes, personal experiences with racism, or both? Furthermore, do some minority youth join gangs because of their pre-existing beliefs about racial injustice – or do perceptions of racial injustice develop within the gang context? Although our findings suggest that perceptions of racial injustice can help explain minority over-representation in gang activity, the vast majority of youth who perceive racial injustice do not become involved in gangs. Future research, therefore, must investigate the conditions under which perceptions of racial injustice are translated into gang activity. Finally, our findings should prove challenging to policymakers. How, for example, can we develop effective gang-prevention programmes that adequately address the perceptions of racial injustice that seem to be so prevalent among minority gang members? Importantly, can these perceptions of racial injustice be altered without first reducing racism itself? Without ultimately changing society, will disenfranchised minority youth continue to turn to gangs in order to meet practical needs, find companionship, and defy a society they often view as racially biased?

Notes

1 In this chapter, the term 'racial minority' is used to refer to people who are of 'non-White' racial background (i.e. black, East Asian, South Asian, Aboriginal, etc.).
2 The Toronto Street Gang Pilot Project was funded by a research grant from the Solicitor General of Canada through the Drug and Crime Prevention Strategies Unit.

References

Agnew, R. (2004) 'A general strain theory approach to violence', in M. Zahn, H. Brownstein and S. Jackson (eds), *Violence: From Theory to Research*. New York: Anderson Publishing, pp. 37–50.

Akers, R. and Silverman, A. (2004) 'Toward a social learning model of violence and terrorism', in M. Zahn, H. Brownstein and S. Jackson (eds), *Violence: From Theory to Research*. New York: Anderson Publishing, pp. 19–36.

Baron, S. (1997) 'Canadian male street skinheads: street gang or street terrorists?', *Canadian Review of Sociology and Anthropology*, 34(2): 125–54.

Brownfield, D. (2006) 'A defiance theory of sanctions and gang membership', *Journal of Gang Research*, 13(4): 31–43.

Chettleburgh, M. (2007) *Young Thugs: Inside the Dangerous World of Canadian Street Gangs*. Toronto: Harper-Collins.

Clarke, R. and Felson, M. (1993) *Routine Activity and Rational Choice*. New Brunswick: Transactions Publishers.

Curry, G.D. and Decker S.H. (1998) *Confronting Gangs: Crime and Community*. Los Angeles: Roxbury.

Decker, S.H. and Van Winkle, B. (1997) *Life in the Gang: Family, Friends, and Violence*. New York: Cambridge University Press.

Delbert, J. and Robinson, N. (1980) 'Chinatown's immigrant gangs: the new young warrior class', *Criminology*, 18(3): 337–45.

Esbensen, F. and Weerman, F. (2005) 'Youth gangs and troublesome youth gangs in the United States and the Netherlands: a cross-national comparison', *European Journal of Criminology*, 2(1): 5–37.

Gordon, R. (2000) 'Criminal business organizations, street gangs and "wanna-be" groups: a Vancouver perspective', *Canadian Journal of Criminology*, 42(1): 39–60.

Henry, F. and Tator, C. (2002) *Discourses of Domination: Racial Bias in the Canadian English-Language Press*. Toronto: University of Toronto Press.

Huff, C. (2002) *Gangs in America III*. Thousand Oaks, CA: Sage.

Kennedy, R. (1997) *Race, Crime and the Law*. New York: Pantheon.

Martin, F.E. and White, G. (1993) 'West Indian adolescent offenders', in T. O'Reilly-Fleming and B. Clark (eds), *Youth Injustice: Canadian Perspectives*. Toronto: Canadian Scholars' Press, pp. 429–37.

Mathews, F. (1993) *Youth Gangs on Youth Gangs*. Ottawa: Solicitor General of Canada.

Maxson, C. and Whitlock, M. (2002) 'Joining the gang: gender differences in risk factors for gang membership', in C.R. Huff (ed.), *Gangs in America III*. Thousand Oaks, CA: Sage, pp. 19–36.

Padilla, F. (1992) *The Gang as an American Enterprise*. New Brunswick, NJ: Rutgers University Press.

Sherman, L. (1993) 'Defiance, deterrence and irrelevance: a theory of criminal sanction', *Journal of Research on Crime and Delinquency*, 30(4): 123–35.

Sykes, G.M. and Matza, D. (1967) 'Techniques of neutralization: a theory of delinquency', *American Sociological Review*, 22(6): 664–70.

Tonry, M. (1995) *Malign Neglect: Race, Crime and Punishment in America*. New York: Oxford University Press.

Tyler, T. (1990) *Why People Obey the Law*. New Haven, CT: Yale University Press.

Wortley, S. (2002) 'Misrepresentation or reality: the depiction of race and crime in the Canadian print media', in B. Schissel and C. Brooks (eds), *Critical Criminology in Canada: Breaking the Links Between Marginality and Condemnation*. Halifax: Fernwood Press, pp. 87–111.

Wortley, S. and Tanner, J. (2006) 'Immigration, social disadvantage and urban youth gangs: results of a Toronto-area study', *Canadian Journal of Urban Research*, 15(2): 1–20.

Wortley, S. and Tanner, J. (2007) *Youth Gangs in Canada's Largest City: Results of the Toronto Youth Gang Pilot Project*. Ottawa: Solicitor General of Canada.

Part IV

Issues and challenges of migration and ethnicity in dealing with street gangs

Chapter 13

An interactive construction of gangs and ethnicity: the role of school segregation in France

Eric Debarbieux and Catherine Blaya

One of the key debates in criminal policy in France concerns juvenile repeat offenders and the formation of small groups, or what are referred to as 'gangs' in the sense that they are organised juvenile groups involved in crime. It is commonly held that there is an active 'core' of juvenile delinquents who hold power in certain neighbourhoods and schools. There is a widespread belief that a small group of pupils holds sway in schools, organising extortion and violence in liaison with people outside the schools (Debarbieux 2001). These opinions involve a certain number of assumptions in the field, and are even seen as being theoretically evident (Roché 2001; Wolfgang *et al.* 1972), a position which we will analyse in closer detail. This chapter will therefore challenge this representation, both in quantitative terms (do these groups always represent the same proportion of individuals?) and in terms of its social construction, looking in particular at the role of schools in this construction process. Indeed, far from considering these 'gangs' as external factors that have an impact on schools, we consider the schools as a part of the context that enables the emergence of these groups through an 'antischool', identity-building process in reaction, in particular, to the exclusion from school that primarily young, ethnic minorities experience. The ethnicised construction of gangs could, in this case, be linked with 'ethnicisation' of the school space.

This context-based analysis of the construction of gangs in France will be conducted on the basis of a field survey combining quantitative methods ($n = 3,003$) and qualitative approaches, including ethnography and interviews, in secondary schools located in deprived neighbourhoods in France. After a more detailed presentation of the issues and the methodological basis of our study, we will highlight the uneven distribution of these 'cores' between schools, and will then look for the reasons for this uneven distribution in the pedagogical context itself, before finishing with a case study to illustrate our study.

Problem and methodology

According to the offenders who responded to a self-reported delinquency survey in France (Roché 2001), the proportion of these juvenile delinquents who are repeat offenders in secondary schools is 5–7 per cent. This would appear to support the '5 per cent theory' (see Wolfgang *et al.* 1972), and these juvenile gangs are indeed estimated, generally, to represent 'an average of 5–10 per cent'. But what exactly does this average mean? Is it the same no matter what the social type of the school? Is it linked to the socio-economic difficulties experienced by the school's population or does it depend on the internal organisation of schools? These are the questions we are going to try to answer.

To do so, we will compare the responses of pupils to a survey on violence in schools and school climate. This survey (Debarbieux 1999) covered pupils between the ages of 12 and 17 in 16 urban secondary schools in severely deprived areas (northern districts of Marseille, and northern suburbs of Paris and central Paris). The sample was randomly selected among the urban schools that are identified by the Board of Education as being most at risk of violence. This was a self-administered questionnaire, conducted in whole classes without any adult from the school being present. The level of consistency is excellent for each of the separate scales used in analyses reported in this paper (Cronbach alpha = .72). This questionnaire included items on:

- victimisation suffered;
- self-reported violence, such as fights and theft with extortion (repeated theft with threat and often aggression);
- the climate of the school, especially the quality of pupil/teacher relations and relations between pupils;
- the system of punishment and the way it is accepted by pupils.

The questions concerned the school year when the questionnaire was administered. The scales are Likert-type scales in five points.

They ranged from 'hopeless' to 'brilliant'. The choice of combining studies of victimisation and school climate is one that is now clearly identified in specialised literature on violence in schools. Although research about risk factors hesitated for a long time before including variables of organisation or those linked with the schools themselves, this is no longer the case. Without neglecting the immense weight of the socio-demographic and contextual variables, particularly economic variables, many researchers have attempted to measure the role of 'school climate' in explaining the variance in the victimisation suffered by pupils and teachers, and in the feeling of safety, self-esteem, or school failure – another item that is closely correlated (e.g. Benbenishty and Astor 2005; Debarbieux 1996; Soule and Gottfredson 2003). Recent studies have also shown the extent to which school climate can predict the success of the implementation of action programmes (Payne *et al.* 2003) and this is one of the key directions in the recent review evaluating 178 action programmes (Gottfredson 2003).

Research on school climate and victimisation completed by Soule and Gottfredson (2003) with a sample of 234 schools shows that the factors that best explain increases in victimisation are high teacher turnover and lack of clarity or unfairness in the application of the rules, even though exogenous factors such as high concentrations of deprivation are also closely related. However, and as has been stressed for many years by the Gottfredson team, it is also in deprived urban areas that teacher turnover is highest. A particularly impressive quantitative study was conducted by Christine Eith of the University of Delaware (Eith *et al.* 2003). This work, based on a sample of 7,203 pupils, showed the great importance of dividing pupils into classes by ability. In this study, one of the most significant factors in explaining differences in victimisation was what American scholars call ability grouping. This risk factor was shown to be twice as important in explaining differences as, for example, coming from a single-parent family.

Like this literature, the results we now present show how certain schools contribute to creating groups of pupils outside the school order, by applying both severe internal segregation via grouping pupils into 'ethnic classes' and a system of punishment experienced as being unfair and 'racist'. We then illustrate, in a case study, how these groups can get caught up in a vicious cycle of delinquent identity formation.

Results: identification of and differences between schools

Identification of 'gangs'

The problem of method is, initially, quite similar to the practical problem: is there, in a school, a group of individuals who stand out from the others because of a totally negative attitude of outright rejection of the school and the institution, who are punished more often than other pupils, and who declare themselves to be victimisers? There is no doubt as to the response. In the schools covered by our research, we can easily distinguish[1] a group of pupils (3.7 per cent out of 3,003 respondents) who consider that everything is wrong with school and that the teachers are awful, who commit aggression more often than others, who are punished repeatedly and more frequently than the others, and who have developed a feeling of hatred and rejection of anything that represents order. In short, these are highly rebellious pupils, the aggregate figure for which provides an initial rough guide to the proportion of these 'core' pupils. These youth have been identified by means of cluster analysis of the following items: participation in extortion, frequency of sanctions, the scale of the quality of relationship with teachers and other staff, and the scale of evaluation of the overall school climate. This corresponds perfectly to all the studies that have established a direct link between rejection of school and delinquency (e.g. Gottfredson 2001). As an illustration of their attitude school, their responses to the question on the quality of relations with their teachers are particularly negative: 65 per cent of the core pupils consider these relations to be bad, against an average of 9.7 per cent of their peers. The judgements made by these rebellious pupils are very categorical. Everything is considered bad, including teachers, punishments, and relations with the school management[2] (60 per cent of these pupils, against 10 per cent of the others). The general atmosphere in the school (68 per cent against 19 per cent) and their opinion of the way 'things are learned in the school' is very negative (52.3 per cent against 6.7 per cent), which is not a widespread opinion among the other pupils, who generally continue to have great confidence in the teaching abilities of their teachers – although they do not have such a positive appreciation of their relational qualities.

Table 13.1 clearly shows the high frequency of punishment inflicted on these pupils, of whom a far greater number than their peers declare that they have been punished five times or more since the beginning of the school year.

Table 13.1 Frequency of sanction

Frequency of sanction*	Never	1–2 times	3–4 times	5+ times	Total
Involved in gangs	3.9%	19.4%	9.7%	67.0%	**100%**
Others	20.5%	42.4%	17.2%	20.0%	**100%**
Total	**19.8%**	**41.5%**	**16.9%**	**21.8%**	**100%**

Dependence is highly significant. χ^2 = 129.98, ddl = 3, $1-P$ = >99.99%.
*Responses to the question, How many times have you been punished this year at school? – schools in deprived areas in France, n = 3,003 (Debarbieux 2003).

These teenagers have thus entered into processes of institution and designation, which may not always concern criminal matters but do concern school rules. This does not mean that they constitute a 'group', or the beginnings of a gang. They could be isolated individuals, although our other results show how these young people identify with each other and join together to form a real group. If, initially, they were not considered gang members, their being on the margins of the school norms slowly leads them to identify themselves as a group, their common culture being opposition and illegal activities such as extortion. As a consequence, we shall say that these deviant youngsters are becoming gang members in the sense that they have regular group illegal activity and that, as we will show in further development, are members of groups that are street-oriented, meeting here the Eurogang definition.

Uneven distribution of pupils involved in gangs

We know from previous research completed in secondary schools across all socio-economical backgrounds (Debarbieux 1996) that youth involved in gangs amount to 2.2 per cent. But this percentage hides large variations between schools, which range from 0 to 11 per cent depending on the case. This inequality is closely correlated with social factors. These gangs appear to be twice as numerous in Priority Education Zones,[3] and there are eight times as many in sensitive zones as in privileged areas (4 per cent versus 0.5 per cent). At first sight, it would seem that our results support the hypothesis of, at least in sensitive schools, a limited number of around 4–5 per cent of pupils as being responsible for disorder and violence. Yet, if we look at the results in more depth, school by school, the conclusion we come to is quite the opposite.

In fact, we must think in terms of 'all other things being equal'. If the socio-economic factors alone were decisive in explaining the existence and proportion of these core groups, then, in each of the schools that are comparable socially, we should observe a roughly equal proportion of rebellious pupils. Being part of one of these 'core groups' would in fact be little more than the result of personal dispositions combined with social dispositions, as the very widespread criminological approach via 'risk factors' (Farrington 2000) tends to suggest. In this case, delinquency would be a more or less inherited set of 'qualities', psychological failings, and disruptive social factors. It would be a pre-existing phenomenon almost independent of any local interaction. Yet, the breakdown by 'category' of teenagers in schools that are very similar in social and demographic terms[4] shows highly significant disparities, as presented in Table 13.2.

Table 13.2 Distribution of gangs*

School code	Gangs	Others	Total
1	1.6%	98.4%	**100%**
2	3.0%	97.0%	**100%**
3	4.6%	95.4%	**100%**
4	7.1%	92.9%	**100%**
5	3.8%	96.2%	**100%**
6	3.1%	96.9%	**100%**
7	1.7%	98.3%	**100%**
8	3.1%	96.9%	**100%**
9	10.9%	89.1%	**100%**
10	5.9%	94.1%	**100%**
11	4.0%	96.0%	**100%**
12	2.6%	97.4%	**100%**
13	1.9%	98.1%	**100%**
14	1.0%	99.0%	**100%**
15	2.9%	97.1%	**100%**
16	1.9%	98.1%	**100%**
Total	**3.7%**	**96.3%**	**100%**

Dependence is highly significant. $\chi^2 = 43.04$, ddl = 15, $1–P$ = 99.99%.
*Distribution of gangs in 16 'difficult' schools in deprived areas in France ($n = 3003$) (Debarbieux 2003).

Table 13.2 is easy to read. Opposite each school, designated by an order number, stands the percentage of each category of pupils according to the automatic classification isolating a group of 'core' pupils. As all the secondary schools in this study are of the same social type, we can analyse the figures as 'all other things being equal'. Although it is true that the percentage of pupils involved in gangs is 3.7 per cent in this sample of schools, what is more remarkable is the great diversity of situations. If we take the extremes, school 14 appears to have a group of youngsters who are involved in gang activities and represent about 1 per cent of its pupils, while in school 9 the proportion appears to be around 10.9 per cent, 11 times higher, with significance rates that can leave no doubt possible.

Indeed, in analysing this uneven distribution of the gangs in schools, it is quite logical to conclude that there is a context effect, a 'school effect', that contributes to building an antischool culture. The feeling of hatred developed in relation to school is not simply the direct result of the socio-economic situation and a form of 'class hatred' that existed before the school became part of the equation. The feeling of hatred that is often openly expressed by adolescents is not something that totally precedes entry into the school world; it is something that is constructed in daily interaction, as we will describe, using a more ethnographical method[5] in further development. Of course, the issue is to know whether these disaffected and oppositional students are part of genuine gangs according to the Eurogang definition. Although our research work did not use such a definition to start with, we could retrospectively find evidence that they are long-term, street-oriented, and, by virtue of their involvement in extortion, delinquent youth that belong to a group. We could not answer the question of becoming part of a gang with our quantitative data, which had no predictive value. However, qualitative work indicates that antischool rebellion and culture can lead to gang partnership and delinquent activities as exposed below.

The daily co-production of delinquency: a case study

Let us summarise what we have said thus far. A macrosociological approach to delinquency in schools remains largely justified, and socio-economic factors, or rather the accumulation of exclusion factors, appear to be part of the explanation of the construction of an 'antischool' or 'anti-institution' culture. It is in the schools where the socio-economic background of pupils is the least favourable that their delinquency is the most frequent and the most severe. Here we have the beginnings of this delinquency 'of exclusion', a model which has been constructed, among others, by Salas (Mongin and Salas 1998). It is therefore quite obvious that schools bear the full brunt of this delinquency of exclusion, which exists, to a large extent, before the school becomes involved. But despite these macrosocial explicative factors, we could see in the previous section that schools with similar socio-economical background show very different results for delinquency. When doing quantitative research in schools, we systematically complete our work by qualitative methods: face-to-face interviews, focus groups, and observation in schools and their neighbourhood. This approach enables us to get a more in-depth view of the widely varying difficulties that schools face and that we presume to be constructed interactively. Given the number of cases observed since our observatories began research activities (a total of 116 French lower secondary schools), it seems to us that our comments can be generalised. Another ethnographic scientific survey achieved similar results and reached the same conclusion for a lower secondary school located on the outskirts of Paris (Moignard 2006).

Given the purpose of this chapter and this sample, we selected the particular case of school 9 in order to observe the strongest feeling of opposition and present a representative example of the 'high-risk school'. It is also a good choice because it is located in a neighbourhood characterised by the great importance of 'gangs' outside the school, linked with drug dealing. This community is characterised by high rates of numerous ethnic minority inhabitants and is notorious for its involvement in the drug business. As for drug dealing, youngsters under the age of 18 are 'used' as lookouts to warn the older ones of the presence of the police in the area. Some of the youth we have interviewed know the police car plate numbers by heart. The welfare agency of the neighbourhood has indicated to us who the drug dealers are and some of the researchers were introduced to them by students of the school and could interview them (Rubi 2005), following the same research methodology as for the previous research led by Debarbieux (2002). There is a gang in the district of the school, called the 'Banana Gang' after the name of a local social services building. The social workers in this part of the city indicated to us that some of its members were still in school 9 and three of them were supervised by social workers named by the juvenile justice services.

'The community is run by three young males aged 16, 18, and 25. Ahmed, the youngest, has just been permanently excluded from school 9, the second one has just been released from jail, and the oldest is the "brains"; he runs and organises the drug business.' This interview was confirmed by another one conducted with a social worker from the local welfare agency. 'There are mainly three leaders. One of them is 15. Another one, aged 18 has just been released from prison, and the third one, aged 24, is a big drug dealer and has influence on everybody around.'

We could thus be led to think that the community and the gang is intruding into the school setting. This is not entirely wrong since the gang does exist outside the school. However, its presence is not similar in all the schools of the area. As we could observe, the difficulties met in school 9 are not only the result of neighbourhood influences. Two other schools (10 and 12) with the same socio-economical features do not face the same delinquency and gang membership problems. We argue that for school number 9 there is a school effect due to a difficult school culture that contributes to the co-fabrication of a gang culture. As one of the social workers from the school sector stated, 'The youngest ones meet daily in groups. They are always the same kids and they pretty well know each other. Most of them face enormous difficulties at school.'

This secondary school with 600 students has both a much higher number of rebellious students as shown in Table 13.2, and much lower number of pupils who claim to be totally happy at school (13 per cent versus 27 per cent) than the other respondents. Most importantly, the number of extorters and the number of victims from extortion are much higher than in the other participant schools (see Tables 13.3 and 13.4).

We therefore note that, although, on average, about 10 per cent of pupils claim to be extorters, in this school it is close to 16 per cent, while the number of victims is almost twice the average for these schools, at over 15 per cent. Moreover, as the manager of the bar that is located opposite school 9 reckoned, 'It is the youth from ethnic minorities who are involved in delinquency. There is no leader, no head of the gang. They all work hand in hand. I was on the street from the age of ten and I pretty well know the business. Here, it is the young ones from the school who warn the older ones when the cops come into the neighbourhood.' Quite a few students are definitely involved in delinquency. Yet, this is not due solely to the characteristics of the pupil population, or to the neighbourhood in which the school is located (neighbouring schools of the same social type do not have such negative figures). It is also due to the way in which the staff in this school have 'organised' classes

Table 13.3 Percentage of extorters*

Extorters School code	Yes	No	Total
1	6.3%	93.7%	100%
2	12.0%	88.0%	100%
3	11.3%	88.7%	100%
4	15.4%	84.6%	100%
5	8.2%	91.8%	100%
6	11.8%	88.2%	100%
7	7.8%	92.2%	100%
8	9.2%	90.8%	100%
9	15.8%	84.2%	100%
10	8.4%	91.6%	100%
11	15.2%	84.8%	100%
12	9.4%	90.6%	100%
13	8.1%	91.9%	100%
14	5.9%	94.1%	100%
15	4.5%	95.5%	100%
16	7.1%	92.9%	100%
Total	**10.1%**	**89.9%**	**100%**

Dependence is highly significant. χ^2 = 34.97, ddl = 15, $1-P$ = 99.75%.
*Percentage of pupils who claim to be extorters in 16 difficult schools (n = 3,003).

according to ethnic criteria or ability grouping, and thereby increased tension.

In this school, tensions are high between pupils, between pupils and adults, and between adults, and these tensions focus on classes that are not referred to as 'ability groups' but as 'options'. To keep or attract middle-class children, who are becoming increasingly rare in the school, the technique is quite standard: the creation of an option in German, a European class, a special-needs class, etc. This system of options creates or widens gaps, and here it really does go too far. Certain classes are made up only of 'North Africans and Africans', and others exclusively of 'French' pupils. This policy is unofficial, but numerous quantitative works (Felouzis *et al.* 2007) and ethnographic ones (Payet 1996) have shown how French schools use subtle means, based on pedagogical arguments (academic achievement and optional assignments), to practise social selection and segregation that mainly

Table 13.4   Percentage of victims*

Extorters School code	Yes	No	Total
1	4.7%	95.3%	100%
2	7.2%	92.8%	100%
3	6.9%	93.1%	100%
4	6.9%	93.1%	100%
5	5.0%	95.0%	100%
6	9.3%	90.7%	100%
7	5.8%	94.2%	100%
8	8.1%	91.9%	100%
9	15.3%	84.7%	100%
10	14.5%	85.5%	100%
11	8.9%	91.1%	100%
12	9.1%	90.9%	100%
13	6.9%	93.1%	100%
14	3.9%	96.1%	100%
15	6.7%	93.3%	100%
16	9.2%	90.8%	100%
Total	**7.7%**	**92.3%**	**100%**

*Percentage of pupils who claim to be victims of extortion, in 16 difficult schools ($n = 3{,}003$).

affect ethnic minority children. In France, only ethnographic surveys can disclose such practices, since statistical data including questions on the ethnic background of students are illegal.

There is great demand for pupils to be socially mixed in schools, and hatred and rage are expressed strongly in this particular school. Exclusions and sanctions always hit the same classes, since all of the pupils who underachieve and misbehave are grouped together. It is this internal segregation and a strong feeling of unfair in punishment that caused this large group of rebels to form and gradually drift towards delinquency. Much more than the other pupils, they say that the places they hate most are the classrooms. And even more clearly, they state that they 'like' all the intermediate spaces, including corridors, stairs, and toilets. They effectively 'control' these spaces that are not closely watched – in accordance with the well-known tendency for the adults in schools to abandon the collective areas in favour of the classroom. Initially, a frequent presence in schoolyard fights and refusing to do schoolwork, the group gradually became more radical. At the same time, many adults also became more radical, demanding repression and exclusion, and conflicts within the team were aggravated under the effect of the suffering experienced. Extortion and bullying on 'ethnic' criteria developed, culminating in a particularly serious final episode. This was the 'ceremony of the hood', in which a child from a different ethnic background had his hood pulled down over his eyes and was hit by a group of pupils, all from the same underachieving class group, resulting in the victim being taken to hospital. The attackers were taken to court and excluded from the school, rendering matters even more difficult in the neighbourhood because, as our ethnographic work shows, this helped to widen the gap between the different ethnic groups. The social workers from the area welfare agency stressed during interviews how much most of the youth had increased their delinquent activities, and that at least two of them had become leading soft drug dealers, leaving hard drugs to the youngsters aged 18 and over. As reported by one of the agents from the urban juvenile delinquency prevention unit who supervises the youth from school 9, 'The younger ones are used as lookouts and to bring customers to the dealers. That is their way of participating in crime business. According to their age, they have different roles. The age conditions the behaviour and also peer grouping.'

Of course, it is in order that aggressors should pay the price for their assault and that it should be handled in the criminal courts. But did the school organisation not make the situation possible? Did it not produce ethnicity in the sense defined by the anthropologist Fredrik Barth? – that is to say, a process of separation in between 'us' and 'them' (Barth 1969). This construction of ethnicity gathers differences within one category: 'the Maghrebians' who are grouped in this school in the same 'sink' class. This differentiation process naturalises sociological characteristics into ethnic ones. It is based on prejudices against minority groups with different cultural practices and outlooks that distinguish them from others. In France, visible minorities are perceived as being mostly 'Maghrebians', even if the pupils we have met were not born in Maghreb and are French. As one of the policemen assigned to the school beat stressed in talking about visible ethnic minorities, 'They have learned to move in groups and recognise each other by codes which are different from our norms. That leads to extreme behaviour such as the "hood ceremony". The French kids [referring to Caucasian youngsters] explain bluntly that "when you assault a Caucasian it is safer, they are always alone, they do not have a gang or a big brother behind to give them a hand in case of need."'

We should not conclude, however, that the teachers in school 9 are racist or incapable, or that the aggressors are little angels and cannot be held responsible for their acts. This sort of black-and-white view is hardly justified. Payet (1996: 103) stresses the extent to which the phenomenon of internal segregation within the school 'must be placed in its context of competition between schools', which find themselves in a social market. In France, the percentage of ethnic minorities in a school affects house prices. In fact, middle-class families refuse to enroll their children in schools with high numbers of ethnic minority pupils and move out the area so that they can change schools (in France, there is a catchment area system for schoolchildren). According to a social worker in the neighbourhood, 'The problems of the youth who attend secondary schools such as school 9 come mainly from certain forms of ghettoisation: too many parents from the middle or upper class ask for exceptional permission to send their children outside the catchment area to other schools.' To fight against the spiral of 'ghettoisation' of schools through exemptions granted to pupils to go to schools outside their normal catchment area, and to preserve a mixed social make-up, staff in schools in socially deprived areas are trapped between two conflicting needs, in which the ethical dilemmas are great. They are likely to consider the creation of high-achieving and low-achieving classes the only way to retain children from better-off backgrounds so that the school is more socially mixed. In short, as Payet (1996: 101) put it, 'The principle can be democratic on the broader scale and discriminatory on the level of the individual school.' This does not mean, however, that these secondary schools merely manage determinisms of external origin, that they merely reflect their surroundings, or that the facts described here are unavoidable. How can we explain, in this case, that another school (school 11) close to the previous example manages to offer a standard well above the expectations? This school does not have ability groups, although ability grouping is achieved in a more subtle way by the possible choice of a rare second language, such are Russian or Chinese, or subjects such as drama or classical music. Usually, pupils who opt for such subjects are high achievers and are grouped together for timetable purposes. Its student body is exactly the same as in the other school, recruiting pupils from the same neighbourhoods and educating them in premises that are no more conducive to work. Our conclusions are in no way fatalistic – quite the contrary.

Conclusion

The much-desired elimination of the 'core pupils' that we refer to as gang members would resolve nothing, because it would not put a stop to the mechanisms that create these groups and which sometimes affect many more young people than the '5 per cent theory' would suggest. Socio-economic factors alone do not explain these situations. Violence and delinquency always have a history. They must be placed within the context of a process that is often slow, and which begins, without a doubt, in exclusion, and then develops through the interaction of perfectly avoidable microexclusions (composition of classes, sanctions perceived as unfair by pupils and repeated sanctions). As demonstrated by Vigil in his work on Chicano gang youth and the influence of schooling, educators are not well enough informed and can unconsciously foster negative behaviours and gang membership when they could play a preventive and protective role with greater information (Vigil 1999). First and foremost, it is this accumulation of symbolic violence that 'unites' these groups of individuals in a system of 'them' and 'us', 'friend' and 'foe', which is the basis of an ethnicised view of the world.

Looking beyond our survey, we should also remind readers that, according to official American sources (US Department of Education 2000), black pupils in the USA are hit by teachers at a rate that is twice the proportion they represent in the school population. Blacks make up 17 per cent of pupils, but receive 39 per cent of corporal punishment. Whites represent 62 per cent of pupils, but receive 53 per cent of corporal punishment. The well-known 'ethnic' distribution of repression in the USA makes no exception for schools: blacks are hit more often and punished more often. This 'ethnic' breakdown of punishment is not specifically American, and research in France on this issue is consistent (Debarbieux 1996; Payet 1996). The problem with this unfair 'ethnic' distribution is that it continues to produce 'gangs' along pseudo-ethnic lines, and that it results in the radicalization of small groups of pupils who increasingly become 'antistars' in their schools.

In short, it would be ridiculous to say that 'school' alone manufactures delinquency and gangs. That would be to exaggerate its role in this determinism. But certain failures of local organizations can contribute to the joint creation of this delinquency, and the case studied here is one of them. Of course, drug dealing exists in schools, and, of course, peer groups formed outside influence life inside the school. But at the same time, the working of the school widens this rejection of the institutions and plays a role in producing deviant or delinquent groups. In theory, we should also give up on the vision of an extraterritorial school that is simply 'placed in a context' and is subjected to its influence. It is a part of the context and plays a role in its surroundings in the same way the surroundings play a role in the school.

Notes

1 The so-called 'automatic classification' is particularly suitable to answer this kind of question: by taking as discriminant variables those concerning the 'school climate' (eight variables), punishment (two variables) and extortion (two variables), we can attempt such a classification.
2 They are also punished by the school management three times more often than the other pupils, a sign of their high visibility.
3 Priority Education Zones are school areas in which the student intake reflects the socio-economical difficulties of their families. Seventeen per cent of secondary schools are part of Priority Education Zones in France.
4 We use the following variables: unemployment rate of the pupils' parents, the number of foreign students, school year retention (one or more years late according to the age of the pupil). In France, the label of 'difficult schools' is an 'official' designation, by the Board of Education and is applied to schools with children from deprived social backgrounds in poor neighbourhoods in which there are large visible minorities.
5 The secondary school that is the case study that follows was surveyed by various methods: questionnaire study, face-to-face interviews with staff members and pupils, focus groups with staff and pupils, and observation work in the school and neighbourhood for several months.

References

Barth, F. (ed.) (1969) *Ethnic Groups and Boundaries: The Social Organization for Cultural Difference.* London: George Allen & Unwin, pp. 9–38.

Benbenisthy, R. and Astor, R.A. (2005) *School Violence in Context: Culture, Neighborhood, Family, School and Gender.* New York: Oxford University Press.

Debarbieux, E. (1996) *La Violence en milieu scolaire. Vol. I. Etat des lieux.* Paris: ESF.

Debarbieux, E. (1999) *La Violence en milieu scolaire. Vol. II. Le désordre des choses.* Paris: ESF.

Debarbieux, E., (2001) 'Noyaux durs?', *Les Cahiers de la Sécurité Intérieure*, janvier: 55–65.

Debarbieux, E. (2002) *L'oppression quotidienne, enquêtes sur une délinquance des mineurs*. Paris: La Documentation française.

Debarbieux, E. (2003) *Victimations et microviolences dans les écoles françaises. Enquêtes de victimation 1996–2003*. Paris, MEN.

Eith, C.A., Harrel, E.A. and Martin, S.S. (2003) 'Reading, writing and race: lessons on social bounding in the school environment', in *American Society of Criminology 55th Annual Meeting*. Denver, CO.

Farrington, D.P. (2000) 'Explaining and preventing crime: the globalization of knowledge – American Society of Criminology 1999 presidential address', *Criminology*, 38(1): 8–26.

Felouzis, G., Liot, F. and Perroton, J. (2007) *L'Apartheid scolaire: enquête sur la ségrégation ethnique dans les collèges*. Paris: Le Seuil.

Gottfredson, D.C. (2003) 'School-based crime prevention', in L.W. Sherman, D.P. Farrington, B.C. Welsh and D.L. Mackenzie (eds), *Evidence-Based Crime Prevention*. London and New York: Routledge.

Gottfredson, D.C. (2001) *Schools and Delinquency*. Cambridge: University Press.

Moignard, B. (2006) *De l'école à la rue: la construction et la structuration des conduites et des pratiques déviantes et délinquantes des adolescents dans et autour de l'école dans les quartiers populaires: une étude comparative entre la France et le Brésil*. Thèse de Sciences de l'éducation, Université Bordeaux II, 2006, à paraître en 2008. Paris: PUF–*Le Monde*, collection partage des savoirs.

Mongin, O. and Salas, D. (1998) 'Entre le tout éducatif et le tout répressif. Quelles alternatives? A propos de la justice des mineurs', *Esprit,* December: 189–210.

Payet, J.P. (1996) 'La Scolarisation des enfants et des jeunes issus de l'immigration en France', *Revue Française de Pédagogie*, (octobre–novembre–décembre): 88–116.

Payne, A.A., Gottfredson, D.D. and Gottfredson, G.D. (2003) 'School predictors of the implementation quality of school-based programs', *American Society of Criminology 55th Annual Meeting*. Denver, CO.

Roche, S. (2001) *La Délinquance des mineurs. Les 12–18 racontent leurs délits*. Paris: Le Seuil.

Rubi S. (2005) *Les Crapuleuses. Délinquance et déviance des filles de quartiers populaires*. Paris: PUF.

Soule, D.A and Gottfredson, D.C. (2003) 'When and where are our children safe? An exploratory study on juvenile victimization and delinquency', *American Society of Criminology 55th Annual Meeting*. Denver, CO.

US Department of Education, Office for Civil Rights (2000) *Elementary and Secondary School Civil Rights Compliance Report*.

Vigil, J.D. (1999) 'Streets and schools: how educators can help Chicano marginalized gang youth', *Harvard Educational Review*, 69(3): 270–88.

Wolfgang, M.E., Figlio, R.M. and Sellin, T. (1972) *Delinquency in a Birth Cohort*. Chicago: University of Chicago Press.

Chapter 14

'Nemesis' and the Achilles heel of Pakistani gangs in Norway

Inger-Lise Lien

Operation 'Nemesis'

On 9 May 2007, Norwegian and Brazilian police launched an international operation, 'Nemesis', targeting 'Pakistani' gangs in Oslo, the capital of Norway. Investigations had found that a particular branch of the B gang, the six Rasool brothers, had invested a huge amount of dollars in flats and hotels at a new holiday resort in the beautiful Natal area of Brazil. The police confiscated documents and contracts relating to flats, luxury boats, cars, and other assets. Six B gang members were detained, along with more than 20 of their affiliates in Norway and Brazil. The mother of the Rasool brothers, aged 56, was arrested at Oslo Airport as she returned from holiday in a sunny village in the Pakistani Punjab. One wife, one ex-wife, and the father, aged 63, were taken into custody in Oslo. It was an international operation, and it came as a surprise, but it was based on extensive planning and coordination between police forces in Norway and abroad.

For years, the A and the B gangs had been a thorn in the side of the authorities, and had created fear in Oslo. The Pakistani boys, who had started their criminal careers at the age of 14 and 15, had become increasingly involved in sophisticated criminal operations, including importing and trafficking drugs. Gang members have served sentences for drive-by shootings, attempted murder and murder, and other offences. In 2006, one of the A gang members, Arfan Bhatti, was arrested for planning a terrorist attack on the American Embassy and for firing several shots at a synagogue. A small group within the

227

gang has become radicalised. 'I live for Islam and hate Norwegian values,' Arfan Bhatti announced to the newspaper *VG* in 2002.[1] The A gang began operating on the streets of Oslo in the early 1980s. The oldest members are around 40 and have children, some of whom are gang members themselves. The B gang emerged in the 1990s, more than ten years ago. Some of its members are relatively old, and others are quite young. The eldest Rasool brother was 30 when he was arrested; the youngest 19.

The American police have attempted to deal with gangs by suppression tactics (Egley, Maxson *et al.* 2005; Klein 1995). The Norwegian police have until recently preferred similar tactics, operating on a case-by-case basis. Individuals were targeted, gang members were stopped, a sense of insecurity was encouraged by intercepting the gangs at their favourite hangouts, and intelligence was gathered. But very little of this seemed to work. The A and B gangs have long been fierce rivals. Several incidents involving the use of firearms made them first-page cover in the national press and news media. The reasons for the rivalry, as they themselves formulate it in both research interviews and in media presentations, are honour, dominance, and revenge.

Operation Nemesis was different in its approach and tactics than suppression. The flow of money between countries, bank accounts and business projects, was traced and analysed before action was taken on 9 May 2007. As a 'follow-the-money' tactic, it was successful in uncovering fraud, corruption, and money laundering. This type of action, it was assumed, would function as deterrence. Gang members would be expected to 'weigh the consequences of gang activity, redress the balance between cost and benefit, and withdraw from gang activity' (Klein 1995: 160). The Pakistani gangs have turned international, but so has policing. The Norwegian public responded with expressions of admiration and great satisfaction to the news about Nemesis. The police operation was lauded, and the police were obviously pleased with the result. The prime minister promised extra funding as a token of gratitude to the police. Senior Pakistani community leaders were also happy, not least because the gangs had brought suffering and fear to the community for years.

But there was one issue that upset several members of the Pakistani community immensely, and that was the arrest of the father, mother, and wives. They were charged with receiving the proceeds of crime and held in custody for several weeks. 'This has led to great disgust in the community and in the long run will be very problematic,' said the defence lawyer after the operation to *VG*.[2] One of the Rasool brothers said to journalists that he had cried a whole day over the arrest of the mother and father. 'When I heard they had arrested my father and mother I switched off the telephone, sat down in a corner and started to cry.'[3]

Shortly after the operation, I called some of my Pakistani friends in Oslo. I have done research on Pakistani migration to Norway for more than two decades, have stayed for two years in villages in Pakistan collecting data for my PhD thesis, have done gang research in Oslo for ten years, and have done research on integration, focusing particularly on the Pakistanis in Oslo. Therefore, I have built up a huge network of Pakistani informants that I could discuss this issue with. 'This is terrible,' they said, 'the police arrested the mother. It's such a shame for the whole family, and especially for the sons.' A former member of the B gang told me, 'It is fine if they take the money. But arresting the mother is the worst thing that could ever happen. It is a reason for the brothers to commit suicide. At least I would.' Another informant told me that the Rasool family had lost face in the community and would no longer be able to meet other Pakistanis with pride. Even a former member of the A gang, in a radio interview, criticised the arrest of the mother of the B gang members. 'This was too much,' he said, 'a very tough reaction that nobody could bear. How could the police act so awfully, arresting the mother?'

In this chapter we will look at the reasons behind the reactions in the community. The tactics lead to a strong shaming affect – how and why? It seems the police managed to hit the gang where it was most vulnerable – the women. I called the leader of the police operation and asked him whether the police had foreseen this. 'No,' he said, 'it came as a great surprise.' The arrest was a logical consequence of the investigation, as the mother and father had to account for valuables worth more than $100,000.

To understand the effect of the strategy, both the intended and the unintended, we will have to take a holistic perspective and look into the structure and value system of the Pakistani community in Oslo and the value system of the Pakistani gangs. Are the value systems of a special kind? Did the Nemesis operation introduce a new strategy of shaming that touched upon this value system and made the gang members vulnerable to a deterrent effect?

To answer these questions, we must look into the way morality and values are structured in some ethnic communities, and analyse the way gangs operate and build their reputation. This chapter is hermeneutic and argumentative, as it tries to uncover the meaning of certain values at stake in the Pakistani community and in Pakistani gangs.

Background and definition

Immigrants make up almost 23 per cent of Oslo's population, with the Pakistani community leading the field. Many Pakistanis live in suburbs like Furuset, Stovner, and Holmlia, which in recent years have seen a growth in violence, with robberies, fights, and shootings. According to police estimates, the two Pakistani gangs have more than 50 members each. The A gang and the B gang can be described both as organised criminal groups and as street gangs. According to the Eurogang definition, a gang is 'any durable, street-oriented youth group whose involvement in illegal activity is part of its group identity' (van Gemert and Fleisher 2005: 12). The A gang and the B gang both started out as street gangs, but have evolved and transformed themselves into organised crime groups. New members have joined, so the age span in the gangs is from 15 to 40 years, with the majority of members being in their teens and early twenties. The youngest subgroups hang around in the streets committing crime together, and they are runners for the older members. In this way, the youngest members at a lower level are part of a street-gang segment as well as connected to an organised crime group. It is therefore easy to confuse these two categories, but we have to acknowledge that in many cases there is a process of transformation from street gangs to organised crime. The process of transformation can go quick in some segments and more slowly in others. In such circumstances, the categories we use to define the groups become difficult to use. As the phenomenon we study is not clear cut, but blurred, the concepts can overlap. The group we study can at one and the same time take the form of a street gang and an organised crime group, more so at one end of the age span than on the other as in this case with the two Pakistani gangs.

Ethnicity and honour

The A and B gangs are conceived as ethnically homogeneous in the Norwegian setting, talked and written about as 'Pakistani gangs'. In this way, nationality has become an important ethnic identity marker. The gangs are, however, composed and organised on the basis of brothers from different endogamous ethnic groups. These groups are called *quom* (caste) or *biraderis* in Pakistan, but are considered ethnic groups by South Asian experts (Ansari 1960; Donnan 1988). The most common 'ethnic groups' in the A and B gangs are the Jats, the Gujrs, and the Rajas. We may argue that the gang is a minority within the Pakistani minority in Oslo, and at the microlevel they have broken down the caste barriers that exist at the community level. The ethnic *biraderi* distinction does not seem relevant at all as boundary markers in the Norwegian context, where 'Pakistani' has taken over as an imperative ethnic identity. It is coupled with a Muslim identity and a collective identity that embraces the code of honour. According to Barth (1974: 15), ethnic identity is a phenomenon related to boundary maintenance, rather than 'the cultural stuff that it encloses'. The 'cultural stuff' can be changed, but the boundary maintained. Ethnic groups, though, are culture-bearing units open to cultural change or flows over the boundaries.

The Pakistani gangs are closed and bounded groups, meaning that they have incorporated traditions from the Punjab and Islamic ideology, as well as some 'cultural stuff' of mainstream Norwegian and Western traditions.

The gang members speak Punjabi among themselves. They attend mosques run by Pakistanis during Eid, they eat Pakistani food, and they are concerned to uphold Muslim values and make sure their sisters dress in decent Pakistani clothes. They are ready to protect and avenge their women's honour. Separation of the sexes, the importance of male dominance, and sexual purity continue to be part of the value system Pakistani gang members adhere to in spite of the fact that they themselves may be promiscuous and have Norwegian girlfriends. They prefer to marry Pakistani women regarded as 'pak et zaf orat' ('clean women'). The sexual behaviour of mothers and sisters can confer or destroy the honour of both men and women, and gang members often fight for the honour of women (Lien 2002). In honour-dominated communities, girls are usually subject to very strict control, parents often paying less attention to boys, who enjoy more freedom and less social control.

Many Pakistanis and gang members use honour, together with religion, to establish a contrast to mainstream Norwegians. In this way, honour becomes part of the 'cultural stuff' by which they identify their ethnicity and separation from the society. 'Norwegians have no honour,' the former leader of the A gang argued in a television interview. Another informant said, 'We [Pakistanis] are concerned with honour and respect, while Norwegians are concerned with gender equality. Women are as promiscuous as the men. There is no honour in this country.'

This implies that some immigrants, as well as gang members, have noted that some 'foreigners' from Asian and Middle Eastern countries have a different value system. They categorise these into two separate moral codes – the 'morality of the foreigners' and the 'morality of Norwegians' (Lien 2002). The distinction follows that made by Berger *et al.* (1974), who argued that 'code of honour' and 'code of dignity' are paradigmatically different from each other, and constitute logical and structural frames within which persons define themselves, their roles, and their morals in diametrically opposite ways. Although honour relates identity to the past, to membership of families, to ethnic groups, to gender, and to position in a hierarchical society, dignity implies a true and lonely self, independent of social roles, and equal to others. 'Dignity, as against honour, always relates to the intrinsic humanity divested of all socially imposed roles and norms. It pertains to the self as such, to the individual regardless of his position in society' (Berger *et al.* 1974: 83).

This dichotomy is an abstraction. It may conceal many differences and varieties in the way honour is expressed in different places in the world. The typology can also lead to essentialism, if one is not aware of the fact that moral codes and ideologies that instruct individuals to think and act in certain ways are not necessarily followed up by passive obedience. The Cambridge philosopher Onora O'Neill (1996: 2) has argued that particularists have been wrong to claim that abstract thinking or reasoning is ethically damaging. Dichotomies can be used as tools for abstract thinking, which makes us able to create typologies and compare them, in spite of the fact that individuals in a community do not necessarily abide by the rules.

Honour is still an important concept in the USA and in Europe. When honour is formally awarded, as when a Festschrift is published to honour a distinguished career, it boosts respect for the individual. But bestowal of honour has become the task of bureaucratic institutions, while formerly it lay in the hands of members of families and clans, who fought for it in order to maintain their position in the social order when the state was weak and could not protect them. Thinking and talking about honour can expand to such a degree that it changes a people's system of logic and the way they feel about things. A tipping point may be reached, in thinking, feeling, and the way society is organised. This is a matter of qualitative and quantitative change. Historically, the change has gone from honour to dignity, from weak states to strong states, but in a globalised world it can go in both directions.

In constructing his theory of honour, Stewart (1994: 9) argues that 'honour does no longer play much part in our thinking'. In European history, in his opinion, a process of change took place, a transition from external to internal honour, leading to 'the collapse of honour in the West' (Stewart 1994: 51). But criminologists and sociologists such as Elijah Anderson (1999) and Ruth Horowitz (1983) have described gangs in marginal zones in American cities as having their own form of the moral code of honour.

In a study on Pakistan, Robert Paine (1989) has argued that there is a conflict between basic or customary laws, such as the commandments of Islam and what is conceived to be one's duty, on the one hand, and one's willpower, resistance to the rules, and readiness to break them, on the other hand. By breaking the laws, one gains a reputation for fearlessness, showing the world that one is above the rules. Paine argues that such attitudes rest on a rebound mechanism by which norm-breaking activity adds to a person's prestige and gives him a 'heightened sense of self or of being', while at the same time increasing the status of the norms. We may argue that this rule-breaking activity is essential for gang members' identity, and therefore endows them with a particular hyperhonour schema in spite of the fact that the gangs embrace both the sharia and the honour code within the community.

Ali Wardak (2000), in his work on Pakistani youth in Scotland, argues that parents are willing to overlook the criminal behaviour of their sons because they want them to submit to the idea of arranged marriage and the Islamic strictures against alcohol, pork, etc. – to submit to what is *haram*. As most gang members in the Pakistani community have been sent to Islamic schools from the age of six, they will have learned and internalised the sharia. Islam is part of their identity, and they are proud Muslims that, in several recent interviews, have expressed their willingness to fight for the honour of their religion. But at the same time, they are not necessarily willing to abide by the most important rules of *haram* in their religion. Rule breaking, therefore, is a central part of their gang-specific hyperhonour schema.

Somali, Moroccan, Pakistani, and Turkish immigrants to Norway all come from feudal villages and seem to have brought their honour concerns with them. There has been an increase in honour killing all over Europe, not least of second-generation females. Punjabi values require a woman to be pure, virtuous, and chaste. Her sexuality should be controlled, and she herself protected and provided for by men (Lien 2002). She should preferably not have a paid job. This is why Pakistani women have the lowest rate of participation in the Norwegian workforce. The honour code is a sort of ideology that gives value to both collective and personal identity. The moral code is internalised at a deep level and, for many members of the community, it continues to sway the value system even after people have migrated.

In general, members of the Pakistani community share the values to which they adhere, but the gang members seem to have developed a more brutal form of expressing their honour. According to Black-Michaud (1975), male honour has to do with abilities and power – the 'ability to defend'. The power dimension of the hyperhonour code is also mentioned by Blok (2001), who argues that for the mafia 'the ultimate vindication of honour lies in physical violence' (Blok 2001: 105). What distinguishes the honour of the Pakistani community and the hyperhonour of the gang, then, are rule-breaking activities together with the willingness to apply brutal violence in order to obtain power.

Honour, marginalisation and externalisation

Is it possible that the honour code in certain cases causes externalisation of the secular law or secular institutions? When members of a community prefer to take the law into their own hands because they are instructed by an honour code to defend themselves and their family, and not trust the institutions of society, could it lead to the withdrawal of the state institutions? Is it possible that the code of honour may work as a buffer that protects certain imported traditions, such as arranged marriages, polygamy, and female circumcision, from interference by the state? According to *Le Figaro* of 1 February 2002, Lucienne Bui Trong, a criminologist working for the French government's Renseignements Généraux (General Intelligence – a mix of FBI and secret service) in order to number the Muslim no-go zones, noted the following: 'From 106 hot points in 1991, we went to 818 sensitive areas in 1999. That's for the whole country.' The number of sensitive areas, or *zones urbaines sensibles* (ZUS), seems to have escalated in France. These are places where the state itself is worried about loss of control. Processes of externalisation of state institutions and the law, as well as marginalisation due to poverty, seem to have been going on in the neighbourhood where the Rasool brothers live. It seems to be going on in other European cities as well. A television programme, as well as interviews with the Oslo police, has indicated that the police are reluctant or afraid to enter some of the streets in the Furuset neighbourhood. Withdrawal may be a result of several processes interacting together whereby economic and social marginalisation ultimately strengthens the honour code, and this in turn leads to further marginalisation and externalisation.

Several years ago, Wacquant (1996) described the withdrawal of institutions from communities in France, both economically and socially. The riots in 2005 showed that the French authorities had few partners within the *banlieus*. The police seemed to have withdrawn 'the long arm of the law', and in some degree left the communities to themselves – that is, in some cases, in the hands of the gangs. When the honour code is very strong in a sector of a city, together with the withdrawal of state institutions, it could in fact undermine state institutions and lead to further marginalisation. Externalisation and separation may occur as the dual consequence of structural and economic factors, imported moral codes, and ideologies. In a situation of state withdrawal, there is a chance that gangs may enter the power vacuum that is thereby established. There is also a chance that the community may become isolated, autonomous, and closed as a result of the need among men of honour to deal with issues themselves in order to maintain honour, rather than seeking help from the state institutions and the police.

Why preventive strategies may fail in honour-dominated areas

Immigrant communities regard both the police and social service agencies with great suspicion. Among the young boys in the suburbs of Oslo, the child protection authorities are seen as an enemy to be avoided rather than a friend in need. 'We hate them' is an expression often used. In Norway, many programmes and actions have been taken to fight the gangs, but few seem to have worked. Most of the gang members have had a long career within the social welfare system, and have taken part in aggression replacement training, the Alternatives to Violence programme, multi-systemic therapy, or other welfare programmes (Carlsson and Decker 2005), but none of these seems to have had sufficient impact in preventing gang formation, or getting the boys out of crime.

Immigrants in general tend to prefer their own traditional ways of dealing with crime. Several senior Pakistani politicians have been involved in arbitrating between gangs in Oslo to avert the risk of hostilities. Well-known Pakistani politicians in Oslo have sat on *panchayats*, or village committees, together with local imams. Arranged marriages are used, as well, to get sons out of a criminal lifestyle, although this method often fails. Many of these sons continue their criminal careers after establishing their own family. Pakistani parents often send their sons back to the home country for rehabilitation if they are having problems at school or are in bad company. Villages in the Third World serve as backup systems for a welfare society that does not work properly. The more criminals they send back home, the more difficult it will be for their relatives in Pakistan to stop recruitment into drugs and crime or to rehabilitate children from immigrant communities in Oslo. When the police or the child protection authorities interfere too much in family affairs in Norway, sending children back is one way of avoiding the ministrations of welfare state. This, of course, undermines the efforts of the system to provide proper care, thereby estranging the community and the gangs.

Some view religion as a way out of crime, and there has been an increased effort to persuade young boys to avoid the streets and get involved in activities at the mosques. But the authorities seem hesitant about initiating partnerships with religious denominations. Imams who want to resocialise them into the traditional ways seize on children who try to escape the traditional way of life; who want to be more 'modern'. The fact that a member of the A gang was radicalised in prison and arrested in 2006 for planning a terrorist attack shows that religion does not always work to prevent crime.

Traditional practice, religion, culture, and the honour code become mainstays of the mentality of gangs. Crime prevention and rehabilitation become difficult. The community-wide scepticism about Western values and institutions may lead to withdrawal, externalisation, a retreat to the honour code, and loss of respect for the police and legal system. All of these factors make crime prevention difficult and may lead to reversion to crime in the case of immigrant youth stuck in criminal gangs.

The effects of Operation Nemesis

Nemesis had both intended and unintended consequences and sent several signals to the gang members that through the years had strengthened their position both in the Pakistani community, where ordinary persons hardly dared to speak about them, and in the society at large, as the other inhabitants of Oslo were also afraid. Following the flow of their money in Norway and abroad, examining what was spent and how they spent it, recording money as it passed between family members, and observing connections and cooperation with criminal business partners abroad broke down the walls between different spheres that were kept separate, and broke down the wall of secrecy around the gangs.

According to tax returns, the Rasool brothers in the B gang occupy a low-income bracket. As recipients of state benefits, they should not be able to invest one and a half million dollars in Brazilian property. Unless they can prove they earned the money legally, the police can confiscate it and other assets.

Pursuing affiliates of gangs and making continued connections with gangs as unpleasant as possible creates a business vacuum around the gangs, deterring erstwhile and potential partners from doing business with them. Their assets will shrink, if the strategy works, making them less attractive to other criminals.

Norway has no extradition treaty with either Brazil or Pakistan. With the police forces of several countries working together, gang members could face years in a foreign cell. Prison standards are lower than in Norway. They would be sharing a cell with brutal criminals in prisons where vermin spread disease, and violence and even murder are rife. These are the obvious lessons that the gang members have learned from the operation.

The last lesson concerns loss of honour. Having one's money confiscated is one thing, and imprisonment is not in itself the worst thing that could happen to a criminal. Gang members have been in and out of prison for years. It is a part of their life. Some say that they are proud of it and sometimes boast to their friends about time spent in prison, as it actually gains them honour and respect among friends.

What really hits the Pakistani gangs where it hurts most is having their women detained. Why? As we have seen, the honour code obliges a man to protect and provide for his women. This is his most important obligation. Loss of honour that may, but does not necessarily, go with crime is generally something that affects only men. The mother of the Rasool brothers was highly respected in the community. She used to wear jewellery on her arms, boasting to her neighbours that her sons had given her expensive presents. Who had better sons? This, however, used to irritate some of her acquaintances and made others feel inferior. But no one dared to say so openly, as her sons had weapons and were known for their brutality. So her respect in the female community was ensured and everybody knew that to slander her would be to invite trouble. The whole family honour, the women's honour in particular, was protected by a wall of fear. When they all landed in prison, however, people started to gossip as they had never dared to before.

Braithwaite (1989) argues that shaming, particularly reintegrative shaming, is important for controlling crime. According to his theory, the most effective shaming is not that by judges or police officers or shaming that stigmatises individuals, but the shaming that is created by the people that they care about most. In this case, the police have paved the way for a shaming process within the community that touches upon shared values in the honour code, the protection of women. The fact that women were arrested shamed the gang members, as it became visible to all within the Pakistani ethnic community that womenfolk had been made accomplices in crime. The gang members could protect their women neither from other men (the police) nor from the consequences of being discovered and imprisoned. Investigating the flow of money had broken down the wall between the male sphere and the women's domestic sphere and made women as guilty of crime as the men, and equally as ashamed.

Their arrest was a shock to all because it challenged cherished ideas of the virtuous and ignorant pure woman. By removing her from the protection of her male family, the police contaminated the mother, and brought shame upon her because she was suddenly dependent on other men – not her family. Suddenly, the women were forced to face their complicity in the crimes in full public view. This was achieved by the 'following-the-money' strategy and was written about in the newspapers. In this case, then, both the women and the men lost virtue, face, and standing in their own community by the actions of the police, but also, and perhaps most of all, by the fact that it was written about and made public. As the former gang member said, not being able to protect the women was reason enough to commit suicide.

This new strategy of 'following the money' allows the police not only to investigate international criminality but also to dismantle the wall between mainstream and minority communities that so far has sustained the latter's autonomy and isolation. It can affect the externalisation process by which secular law is bypassed by the honour code. It can help dismantle barriers between domestic, public, and criminal spheres insofar as conspicuous consumption can be traced. Light is shed on roles and responsibilities, on the free riders of crime such as the mothers, daughters-in-law, and business partners. Nemesis strengthens the place of secular law in the community, as secrecy can be bypassed to a certain degree by police investigations of consumption.

Nemesis is still in its early stages. The extent of its success remains to be seen. It may harden the relationship between the police and the gangs as a negative effect in the long run, resulting in stigmatising shaming. Its success depends on future strategies. The evidence collected during the operation will be used in court and may not stand scrutiny. But for the moment it seems the Greek goddess Nemesis has taken revenge on the gangs and their women. For the first time, Pakistani gangs in Oslo have been overpowered by the system, and lost their honour.

Notes

1 *VG* 26 August 2002.
2 www.vg.no/pub/vgart.hbs?artid=196471.
3 *VG*, 6 July 2007.

References

Anderson, E. (1999) *Code of the Street: Decency, Violence, and the Moral Life of the Inner City.* New York: W.W. Norton.

Ansari, G. (1960) *Muslim Caste in Uttar Pradesh.* Lucknow: Ethnographic and Folk Culture Society.

Barth, F. (1994) *Ethnic Groups and Boundaries: The Social Organization of Culture Difference.* Oslo: Universitetsforlaget.

Berger, P., Berger, B. and Kellner, H. (1974) *The Homeless Mind.* New York: Vintage Books.

Black-Michaud, J. (1975) *Cohesive Force: Feud in the Mediterranean and the Middle East.* Oxford: Blackwell.

Blok, A. (2001) *Honour and Violence.* Cambridge: Polity.

Braithwaite, J. (1989) *Crime, Shame and Reintegration.* Cambridge: Cambridge University Press.

Carlsson, Y. and Decker, S. (2005) 'Gang and youth violence prevention and intervention: contrasting the experience of the Scandinavian welfare state with the United States', in S.H. Decker and F.M. Weerman (eds), *European Street Gangs and Troublesome Youth Groups.* Lanham, MD: AltaMira Press, pp. 311–46.

Donnan, H. (1988) *Marriage Among Muslims: Preference and Choice in Northern Pakistan*. Delhi: Hindustan Publishing Corporation.

Egley, A., Maxson, C., Miller, J. and Klein, M. (eds) (2005) *The Modern Gang Reader* (3rd edn). Los Angeles, CA: Roxbury.

Gemert, F. van and Fleisher, M.S. (2005) 'In the grip of the group', in S.H. Decker and F.M. Weerman (eds), *European Street Gangs and Troublesome Youth Groups*. Lanham, MD: AltaMira Press, pp. 11–34.

Horowitz, R. (1983) *Honour and the American Dream: Culture and Identity in a Chicano Community*. New Brunswick, NJ: Rutgers University Press.

Klein, M. (1995) *The American Street Gang: Its Nature, Prevalence and Control*. New York: Oxford University Press.

Lien, I. (2002) 'The dynamics of honor in violence and cultural change. A case from an Oslo inner city district', in T. Aase (ed.), *Tournaments of Power: Honor and Revenge in the Contemporary World*. Aldershot: Ashgate.

O'Neill, O. (1996) *Towards Justice and Virtue: A Constructive Account of Practical Reasoning*. Cambridge: Cambridge University Press.

Paine, R. (1989) 'High-wire culture. Comparing two agonistic systems of self esteem', *Man*, 24: 657–72.

Stewart, F.H. (1994) *Honour*. Chicago: University of Chicago Press.

Wacquant, L.J.D. (1996) 'The rise of advanced marginality: notes on its nature and implications', *Acta Sociologica*, 39(2): 121–39.

Wardak, A. (2000) *Social Control and Deviance: A South Asian Community in Scotland*. Aldershot: Ashgate.

Chapter 15

Wolves and sheepdogs: on migration, ethnic relations and gang–police interaction in Sweden

Micael Björk

Introduction

> *One police officer to another, speaking of a police informer afforded a huge witness protection programme: 'What did he tell us? As far as I know, nothing. I think we let him disappear into oblivion all too easy. We could have threatened him with the possibility of being thrown back to the wolves – then he would have talked to us, that is for sure!'*

This chapter deals with gangs, migration, and ethnicity from the point of view of the police in Gothenburg, Sweden. Law enforcement officers speak of silence and unwillingness to inform the police, and report crime as their main problem in disadvantaged and gang-ridden housing estates. In law-abiding societies, this silence is often described with words such as *omertà* or *Cosa Nostra,* even if these terms seem far-fetched outside Italian communities (Varese 2006). From classical sociology, we can derive at least three supplementary explanations of this kind of avoidance. Fear, underclass culture, and honour based on ethnicity could all inform our understanding of conflict management in situations involving withdrawal from the police and other institutions of established law. Fear of being injured or hurt in some way, underclass culture as a type of differential association characterised by its criminal intentions, and honour as an instrument of self-help in a highly pluralistic society: if one of these notions is left out in research about what Donald Black calls 'the curtailment of interaction' (1998: 79–83), our analyses will be incomplete.

However, given the theme and scope of this book, I will make such an endeavour and cautiously discuss cultural factors and crime. More precisely, I will write about the honour dimension in street-gang activities and its links to a Scandinavian context where Muslim immigrants are segregated in underprivileged urban areas. In the eyes of the police, this is a situation where many people, including non-gang members, make their living off the record. In other words, they are engaged in a variety of black market activities. When street gangs relate to elderly people in their community, the gangs are drawn into evasive manoeuvres that seem to have strong support in honour codes that defined free men as those who obstruct common law and avoid taxation. The accounts from the police and my readings of these accounts connect with Akbar S. Ahmed's observations, especially regarding 'the notion of *asabiyyah*, group loyalty, social cohesion or solidarity' (2006: 592), which in immigration environments might craft a crucial link between gangs, crime, and ethnicity. If this is a reasonable interpretation, silence in contemporary housing estates becomes a question of loyalty to self-governed trust networks. Therefore, police have not only to combat 'ordinary' gang culture but also to deal with more established moral orders among Muslim immigrants. Hence, their understanding of the cultural factors involved in street-gang activities becomes important for a wider policing effort to restore public trust in an increasingly pluralistic society (cf. Bayley and Shearing 2001: ch. 1–5).

The immigrants with a Muslim experience I speak of come from countries in the Middle East and the Balkan region of Europe. In some cases, my study refers to people from North Africa. I adhere to the Eurogang definition of 'gang' (van Gemert and Fleisher 2005: 12; Klein *et al.* 2006), although the young people concerned could have their upbringing in more loose constellations. What the gang activities I am studying share with the gangs in the Eurogang definition is a street-oriented outlook, a strong group identity, and criminal behaviour, living in areas where the overall picture is marked by migration colonies in which the animosity towards the state is widespread (cf. Lien 2005a: 35–43). Tax avoidance, illegal firms, and unlawful trading across borders are quite common phenomena. My main subject, then, is how the criminal activities of street gangs may receive support from these semi-legal subcultures, and how the police interact with the gangs and the wider migrant communities.

This chapter is based on participatory observations of police units fighting organised crime and their recruiting of new 'soldiers' among street gangs and young adults in Sweden. The fieldwork was conducted among the metropolitan police in Gothenburg, the country's second largest city. This 'part-taking' means that my observations are, by definition, biased in that they lack interpretation from gang members and other people on specific crime acts (Lien 2005b). However, I think that the police have shown me areas of the city that bring fresh knowledge to the subject. Nevertheless, my analysis is based on police accounts and anecdotes, making sense of local gangs and their connections to wider trust or kinship networks. My choice of informants does not include Muslim experts and is not exhaustive from an explanatory point of view, yet it is reasonable because my informants are professionals with experience in specific social problems and the obstacles to gang intervention in European society. I gathered my material from the beginning of October 2004 to the end of May 2006. In sum, I carried out about 400 hours of ride-along conversations with police driving reconnaissance cars, taking individuals into custody, or investigating crimes. Fieldwork also included patrolling with police officers on foot in 'hot-spot areas' (Björk 2006; 2008).

Muslims and crime is indeed a sensitive topic (Quraishi 2006: ch. 2; Spalek 2002: 7–10). When I write about migration processes and culturally defined curtailment of interaction uniting individuals of Muslim decent, I am not speaking of Muslim 'militancy'. What I am trying to do is to reconstruct the more popular notions among Muslims regarding their perception of the state and its central powers, especially the police. I am interested in common people, or 'low' Islam, as Ernest Gellner calls these more 'rustic' – not learned, revivalist or puritan – folkways of Muslim societies (1992: 9–22; 1994: 15–29). Central to such pragmatic experiences is a righteousness based on self-sustaining practices in both religious and mundane affairs. Central to my argument is a set of metaphorical usages from the classical author Ibn Khaldun about how to solve problems without interference from state agencies like the police – and the effect of this code of honour upon street gangs in interactions with the police force. I do not say that Islamic faith is 'criminal'; that would be an absurd as well as offensive statement. But I do ask whether some honour-oriented facets of Muslim culture might support crime when there is a significant link between the minority position, certain kinship networks involved in unlawful economic activities, and street gangs. As I am approaching a controversial field of research, I will restrict my analysis to the use of sensitising concepts (Blumer 1954). Therefore, in this chapter there will be no final answers, only tentative proposals.

Free men at the outskirts of the city

To interpret the link between Muslim notions of sovereignty and gang criminality, as well as how the police interact directly with the gangs and indirectly with the migrant communities with which they are a part, I employ some metaphorical usages from Ibn Khaldun: wolves, sheepdogs, townsmen, tribes, etc. This means that my conceptual tools are transferred from one geographical context to another, from Muslim cultures to Gothenburg, Sweden. But the new Swedes have also experienced this shift in place, and it would be strange if it meant that they had entirely left their original ways of thinking behind (Hjärpe 2002). Culture elements are never static, yet some normative structures can continue to exist, and be picked up and adapted to new circumstances. It is true that some of my concepts represent some rather ancient patterns – but what if the diaspora points in such a direction, to a recapturing of old habits? Frank van Gemert (1999) has discussed this in a study on the drug trade by Moroccans in The Netherlands, and I will present some material that can substantiate such an interpretation.

What I argue for is the contemporary relevance of a traditional line of conflict in the Muslim world between centre and periphery (Arjomand 2004: 231–45; Arnason and Stauth 2004: 40–6; Zubaida 1995). What happens to the dynamic distinction between 'disciplined townsmen' and 'free tribes' in processes of migration? Will established notions of partiality in politics and government-by-networks, by and large accepted in many Muslim countries, lead to the rise of self-ruling units in the new countries of residence? Ernest Gellner, in his book *Muslim Society* (1981), has described change and the recurrence of moral orders, and the flux and reflux of a group solidarity based on self-rule among free men. In a situation where post-industrial society is shaken by 'impassable or hard-to-pass cultural cleavages' (1981: 94), such practices may be revitalised. Feelings of being scattered abroad could bolster criminality but also more avoidance behaviour with reference to central authority, that is, the Swedish government and its representatives in the police force. People in immigrant neighbourhoods may then create tribal orders, based on bloodlines or belonging to different 'houses' (Ibn Khaldun 1967: 102–14), which are in conflict with the Swedish state. If so, ethnic independence in the new environment has its equivalent in old ways of thinking. In *al-Muqaddimah*, Ibn Khaldun writes that payments of 'imposts and taxes are a sign of oppression and meekness that proud souls do not tolerate ... people whose group feeling cannot defend them against oppression certainly cannot offer any opposition or press any claims' (1967: 111). Oppression and meekness restructured in a community context 'where promise-breakers are despicable,' says one police officer with long experience of speaking about the idea of democratic policing to different groups of immigrants, 'creates a situation where many Muslim people ask me this question: "Why should we talk to you when we have our own rules?" '

Of course, Muslims living in Sweden are not a homogeneous category. Individual immigrants range from those committed to coexistence with their new countrymen to those isolated in ghetto-like surroundings. In Sweden and elsewhere in Europe, complexity and ambiguity are the rule when we are dealing with crime and religious affiliation (Macey 2002: 26–43; Spalek 2002). In addition, feelings of group solidarity may be defined outwards as well as inwards, among the ethnically based trust networks themselves. One such example of internal 'wolf packing' comes from a case of extortion involving Bandidos MC Sweden. This chapter of the world (in)famous criminal biker association has a local president with an Iranian background, together with a number of ex-street gang members and young 'hang-a-rounds' who share this Muslim experience. In Gothenburg, the president used this double involvement as a weapon in a protection racket. However, two witnesses (restaurant owners) came forward and were subsequently harassed. This retribution has included blasted cars, threatening the lives of the two witnesses' relatives, and – more unexpectedly – harassment by the local Iranian radio. One gets the impression that this last intimidation is the most difficult to bear. In a public statement, one of the witnesses said 'that the threats coming from the Iranian radio station are so terrifying that I do not dare to reproduce them in print' (Garakoei 2005). He also claims that the protection campaign is known to the whole Iranian community, but they remain silent. Members of the witness families are now relocated under assumed names.

My interpretation is not that the radio station supports Bandidos MC. Rather, they are speaking in favour of an *asabiyyah* kind of loyalty, reactivated in the urban 'desert' of Gothenburg. The broadcasters are criticising two individuals who do not know how to manage in-group problems properly. We may speak of a religiously colored culture of suspicion, evolved out of nomadic exile, directed against the central authority and its watchful sheepdogs, the metropolitan police. Or, according to the same kind of patron–client notions of appropriate Muslim conduct, 'Those who submit to state law and put their trust in it tend to lose their natural courage and vigour'

(Ibn Khaldun, cited in Arnason and Stauth 2004: 37). It is as if the two witnesses have shown themselves to lack moral fibre, and the 'house' is punishing them for their inability to engage in the proper curtailment of interaction among the wider kinship-surrogate group living in the midst of the migration colony. In other words, defending the group becomes more important than reporting crime to outside authorities. That is, 'In order to prevent any injury to honour, offences must not become public' (van Gemert 1999: 9–11).

Due to the situation at hand, there is also the possibility that the state and its sheepdogs can be used, as they should be, as an alternative power solution; that is, when illegal measures do not pay off. This is illustrated by a case in which a professional fence was held for ransom by a wholesale business firm (led by individuals with Turkish background) in the Gothenburg black-market economy. The stolen goods belonged to the firm and the fence was paying money in exchange for not losing face in the criminal 'bazaar'. However, the payments became too heavy a burden. The entrepreneur, who had been practising extortion, turned to the police, who then raided a storeroom controlled by the other illegal tradesman. The wholesale firm received some of its goods back – goods which they had already earned a huge amount of money on by way of extortion. In addition, according to the police, there were links to the Gothenburg gangland. At least one of the sons in the family behind the wholesale business firm was known to be dealing hard drugs in connection with an influential street gang called the Tigers from the northeast side of the City.

In these and comparable cases, silence among immigrants, among Muslim trust networks and members of street gangs need not to be based on fear alone. Fear is an emotion that is constructed socially and culturally. It could exist together with authority, be blended with honour codes, and evolve into local practices. My Swedish police accounts are mostly of this mixed kind. Adding the ethnic dimension, however, makes it possible to say that an important part of avoidance among Muslim immigrants can be interpreted as being motivated by loyalty to self-governing solidarity groups. Street-gang wolves would then share with adults involved in semi-legal economic activities a notion of honour, based on independence of Swedish state powers and rooted in 'low' Muslim perceptions about respect and disrespect. Ibn Khaldun again: 'Being a servant is not a natural way of making a living ... since it is weakness to rely on persons other than oneself' (1967: 300). The willingness to withdraw could then be summarised in Ernest Gellner's comment: 'The motto of a proud soul is not so much "No taxation without representation," but rather "No taxation *at all*"' (1981: 27).

Distrust as street-gang solidarity – in the face of the police

The most fundamental resource lacking in the criminal zone, on to which both ethnic networks and street gangs may border, is trust. This dilemma is not limited to constellations of migrant delinquency, although it has been a common feature in classical gang studies such as *Street Corner Society* (Foote Whyte 1943/1955) or *The Gold Coast and the Slum* (Zorbaugh 1929). In my particular case, feelings of group solidarity among Muslim inhabitants may add chains of authority to street-gang criminal activities, and these chains may in turn add cohesion in the particular crime act. Following Ibn Khaldun, we may say that guidance and leadership exist 'only through superiority, and superiority only through group feelings' (1967: 101). The most striking illustration that I have found is from a police informer, who reports that local gang members, including himself, lay their hands on the holy book, the Qu´rān, before they rob a shop, break into a house, or victimise younger boys in the neighbourhood, and promise each other cooperation through an oath of silence and non-ratting. This oath, in its social function, is comparable to the Catholic oaths binding mafia brotherhoods (Paoli 2003: ch. 2; see also Gellner 1994: 26–9). In both cases, too, the social effect is decreased communication and increased alienation in the surrounding urban realm.

What this illustrates is how criminal codes of conduct such as, 'you don't fuck people over and you don't grass' (Thompson 2004: 14), may interact with 'low' Islamic codes of conduct. According to one Swedish policeman, 'This I-will-never-be-a-snitch kind of behaviour is rapidly moving downwards in age.' If it could be confirmed by new research that such an attitude is rooted in Muslim chains of authority, the case would indeed go beyond traditional underclass culture or types of differential association (Miller 1958; Sutherland 1956). Then, we could speak of conflict management in terms of 'temporary reduction in contact' based on ethno-religious independence in the new country (Black 1998: 80–1). This is how I interpret my observations in conjunction with a limited set of police accounts. With a slightly more theoretical twist, we can say that a functional equivalent to trust may evolve, a cohesion based on distrust of the police and the polity of the Swedish government. Such a paradoxical form of unity will lead to a situation where secrecy and hostility are combined in a way that forces an individual gang member to search for new knowledge at the same time as he (or she) 'narrows down the information which he feels confident he can rely on'. The actor then becomes 'more dependent on less information', or, rather, fewer sources of information (Luhmann 1979: 72). Referring back to the Dutch case, it ought to be 'obvious that this will obstruct the work of the police' (van Gemert 1999: 11), and other agencies and actors as well. Put differently, police experiences in a highly pluralistic society may be of interest for a wider array of social work, including communities and residential areas involved in gang control programmes.

Blood-based or interpersonal in a more 'imaginary' kind of ritual kinship, criminal activities tend to be strengthened by ties of solidarity simply because of the trustworthy information which these limited gatherings provide (Eisenstadt and Roniger 1984: 259–63). But this is not always the case. One such aberration is displayed in several police accounts of one of the ringleaders in the Albanian crime syndicate in Gothenburg, a man who also has a son active in a local street gang. The problem is, for the proud father, that his son has come to be known as a coward among other recruits, especially when he is on his own. That is, he does not know how to use his fists, and he even wants to leave his new home country since a rival gang has blown up his car. In short, he has locked himself up in the family flat. According to rumours on the street, the father is disappointed. In other words, even if Islamic kinship may be beneficial in crime, it can also be counter-productive, especially if the relationship is dependent on 'low' Muslim representations of strength and manhood.

Although this Albanian father and his son have problems with their social standing, I find it plausible that a certain type of masculinity takes an active part among street gang members and their kinship networks, that is, older brothers, fathers, uncles, or cousins, including 'assertions of misdemeanour or offence on religious grounds' (Macey 1999: 50). Gellner writes about certain ways of folk Muslim thinking where 'winner-takes-all polities are largely taken for granted and accepted as inherent in the nature of things' (1994: 14). Scenes of gang–police interaction, where both inherited and transformed understandings of this kind are activated by young offenders, include posture and attitude in the interrogation room. Female police officers are particularly affected. According to one policewoman, 'The street gang associate will neither say hello nor shake my hand; it is as if he does not want to be interacting with alien women or something, I don't know.' 'And if the questioning begins in a rude way,' she continues, 'the remaining interrogation is bound to be nonsensical or full of outrage and police hatred.'

Street-gang members' aversion to the police is well known. In a volume devoted to crime and ethnicity, I think it is relevant to say that relations like these may be influenced by gendered ways of thinking (Macey 1999: 48–55; 2002: 39–43), at least when these practices are linked to a broader Muslim distrust of the police. And once again, such distrust is probably inherent in the minority status of many Islamic communities in contemporary Europe. Just as 'kinship goes ethnic' in processes of migration (Erder 2002: 128), state–society relationships may go ethnic as well. Therefore, street gangs and the wider solidarity networks with which they are connected, as in the case of the Iraqi boy whose father is head of the unauthorised taxi business in their peripheral residential area, can be interpreted as exhibiting an 'oppression psychosis', in the famous words of Louis Wirth (1961: 310). Wirth continues to describe this state of mind, due to disesteem and inferior treatment by the dominant group, by saying that if:

> a group sets itself apart from others by a distinctive culture and perpetuates itself in this isolated condition long enough, the social distances between itself and others may grow so great as to lead to the accumulation of suspicion an non-intercourse which will make it virtually impossible for members of these groups to carry on a truly collective life.

Strong words, yes. Nevertheless, when such a distinctive culture is created, if only for a short period, I propose that we ought to take into consideration symbolic action, sometimes illegal, in the name of honourable Muslim practices among free men, young and old, on the outskirts of Europe's segregated cities. Such a redescription of the old Chicago school reading confronts us with a cultural climate of self-sustaining silence, especially if blood brotherhood or kinship is involved. When this silence is criminal, it may pay dividends, indeed. The police know of cases in which parents, brothers and cousins have supported Moroccan and Algerian street gangs. More precisely, relatives have actually ordered or taken care of stolen property for their own benefit (DVD players, widescreen TVs, brand-name clothing, tobacco, expensive watches, etc.) or purchased stolen property in some local shop or market place. The police also suspect that goods have been fenced by low-price firms with ethnic ownership (cf. Bonacich 1973: 584–9; see also Zenner 1996). Therefore, approval by Muslim trust networks can make street gang criminality profitable. Lack of social control is not always the main mechanism behind youth delinquency. In the matrix of migration, ethnicity, and gangs, social control – or rather social cohesion (*asabiyyah*) – can provide its structuring principles.

Conclusion

Unwillingness among Muslim immigrants to speak to the police and report crime can depend on many things. Apart from fear and subcultural explanations, experiences of racism and ineffective policing are two such reasons. Collective histories and 'shared scripts that mythologise the distrusting state' (Goldsmith 2005: 448) are other motives for not getting involved with the police. It could also be that 'Muslim' is an explanation that is too easy for the police to use in situations of frustration. However, in this chapter, I have raised questions regarding street-gang criminality and how it may depend on processes of migration and ethnic segregation, in both the objective and subjective senses, thereby adding 'low' Islamic thinking to the curtailment of interaction and to people involved in different practices of decreased communication. If I am correct, these more or less religiously affiliated ways of conduct also affect police work, making the 'ethnic ghost' even more elusive in law enforcement efforts to counteract violence and crime among street gangs. In fact, distrust of the police shows that it is impossible for law enforcement agencies to work alone in the field of 'policing and protecting trust' (Shapiro 1987: 210), without help from other municipal authorities and, most importantly, local community organisations.

Intensified cooperation with law-abiding parts of the Muslim diaspora, which, of course, are the vast majority of people of Islamic faith in Sweden, seems to be a significant way forward. Malcolm Klein and Cheryl Maxson point to the importance of considering community processes in gang control. The participation of the police comes naturally, 'while getting neighborhoods and communities involved is very difficult' (Klein and Maxson 2006: 238). Therefore, a closer look at the emerging style of community policing, also known as reassurance policing, may be a good lead to follow (Fielding 2005; Herrington and Millie 2006). Reassurance policing calls for broad engagement in a residential area, relying on the same police officers coming back to civic associations, businessmen, and social workers in the neighbourhood over a protracted period of time. However, the main target for reassurance policing is the low level of social control in exceedingly pluralistic housing estates. Trust in the police requires trust in other people. Reassurance policing aims to strengthen mutual trust and collective goals, by building social bonds between the police and minority groups. In my interpretation, this is what the new community policing is trying to achieve: a viable homogeneity in diverse urban settlements. This is not compliance, or assimilation, but 'social efficacy', aiding the police in their dedication to public order (Sampson and Raudenbush 1999: 609–13). To misinterpret cultural factors in this job, I suppose, could lead the police and its partners off the track, setting people harshly against each other instead of reconciling differences in pluralistic societies.

I will end this short chapter by pointing out the following three areas in need of further research:

(1) *The distinction between Muslim culture and kinship in conjunction with crime.* This subject is vital for our understanding of contemporary street gangs dominated by minority groups. In addition, it may lead to the conclusion that 'Muslim' is a conception of no relevance at all in the criminal world.

(2) *The interaction between diaspora ethnicity and criminal subculture.* What are the connections, and in what circumstances can ethno-religious solidarity be permeated by 'ordinary' gangster codes? Such questions are of importance, not least for the police. This leads to a third research area.

(3) *The consequences, assessment, and practice of gang-unit policing in disadvantaged neighbourhoods (Klein 2004).* If ethno-religious codes of honour coincide with street gangs, then how should police strategies be worked out so that they do not worsen the problem while fighting it?

Research note

The nationalities and other characteristics of young and old people in the police accounts have been changed for the sake of anonymity.

Acknowledgements

I thank Abby Peterson (Gothenburg) and Elisabeth Özdalga (Istanbul); the three editors of the book, Frank van Gemert, Inger-Lise Lien and

Dana Peterson; and two anonymous reviewers for helpful comments on earlier drafts of this chapter.

References

Ahmed, A.S. (2006) 'Ibn Khaldun and anthropology', *Contemporary Sociology*, 34(6): 591–96.

Arjomand, S.A. (2004) 'Transformation of the Islamicate civilisation: a turning-point in the thirteenth century?', in J.P. Arnason and B. Wittrock (eds), *Eurasian Transformations, Tenth to Thirteenth Centuries*. Leiden and Boston: Brill.

Arnason, J.P. and Stauth, G. (2004) 'Civilization and state formation in the Islamic context: re-reading Ibn Khaldun', *Thesis Eleven*, 76(1): 29–47.

Bayley, D.H. and Shearing, C.D. (2001) *The New Structure of Policing*. Washington, DC: National Institute of Justice.

Björk, M. (2006) *Ordningsmakten i stadens periferi. En studie av polisiära gänginsatser i Göteborg, 2004–2005 'Public Order in the Urban Periphery. Gang-Unit Policing in Gothenburg, 2004–2005'*. Eslöv: Brutus Östlings Bokförlag Symposion.

Björk, M. (2008) 'Fighting cynicism: some reflections on self-motivation in police work', *Police Quarterly*, 11(1): 88–101.

Black, D. (1998) *The Social Structure of Right and Wrong* (rev. edn). London: Academic Press.

Blumer, H. (1954) 'What is wrong with social theory', *American Sociological Review*, 19(1): 3–10.

Bonacich, E. (1973) 'A theory of middleman minorities', *American Sociological Review*, 38(5): 583–94.

Eisenstadt, S.N. and Roninger, L. (1984) *Patrons, Clients and Friends: Interpersonal Relations and the Structure of Trust in Society*. Cambridge: Cambridge University Press.

Erder, S. (2002) 'Urban migration and reconstruction of the kinship networks: the case of Istanbul', in R. Liljeström and E. Özdalga (eds), *Autonomy and Dependence in the Family. Turkey and Sweden in Critical Perspective*. Swedish Research Institute in Istanbul, Transactions no. 11.

Fielding, N.G. (2005) 'Concepts and theory in community policing', *Howard Journal of Criminal Justice*, 44(5): 460–72.

Foote Whyte, W. ([1943]/1955) *Street Corner Society: The Structure of an Italian Slum*. Chicago: Chicago University Press.

Garakoei, M. (2005) 'Så har Bandidos krossat mitt liv' ('This is how Bandidos have destroyed my life'). *Expressen*, 28 December.

Gellner, E. (1981) *Muslim Society*. Cambridge: Cambridge University Press.

Gellner, E. (1992) *Postmodernism, Reason and Religion*. London: Routledge.

Gellner, E. (1994) *Conditions of Liberty: Civil Society and its Rivals*. London: Hamish Hamilton.

Gemert, F. van (1999) 'The drug trade by Moroccans in The Netherlands: weighing the cultural factor', in M. Crul *et al.* (eds), *Culture, Structure, and Beyond: Changing Identities and Social Positions of Immigrants and Their Children.* Amsterdam: Het Spinhuis.

Gemert, F. van and Fleisher, M.S. (2005) 'In the grip of the group', in S.H. Decker and F.M. Weerman (eds), *European Street Gangs and Troublesome Youth Groups.* Walnut Creek, CA: AltaMira Press.

Goldsmith, A. (2005) 'Police reform and the problem of trust', *Theoretical Criminology,* 9(4): 443–70.

Herrington, V. and Millie, A. (2006) 'Applying reassurance policing: is it "Business as usual"?' *Policing and Society,* 16(2): 146–63.

Hjärpe, J. (2002) 'Islam, Sverige och svensk Islam' ('Islam, Sweden, and Swedish Islam'), in K. Ådahl *et al.* (eds), *Sverige och den islamska världen – ett svenskt kulturarv.* Stockholm: Wahlström & Widstrand.

Ibn Khaldun (1967) *The Muqaddimah. An Introduction to History.* London: Routledge & Kegan Paul.

Klein, M.W. (2004) *Gang Cop. The Words and Ways of Officer Paco Domingo.* Walnut Creek, CA: AltaMira Press.

Klein, M.W. and Maxson, C.L. (2006) *Street Gang Patterns and Policies.* Oxford: Oxford University Press.

Klein, M.W., Weerman, F.M. and Thornberry, T.P. (2006) 'Street Gang Violence in Europe', *European Journal of Criminology,* 3(4): 413–37.

Lien, I.L. (2005a) 'Criminal gangs and their connections: metaphors, definitions and structures', in S.H. Decker and F.M. Weerman (eds), *European Street Gangs and Troublesome Youth Groups.* Walnut Creek, CA: AltaMira Press.

Lien, I.L. (2005b) 'The role of crime acts in constituting the gang's mentality', in S.H. Decker and F.M. Weerman (eds), *European Street Gangs and Troublesome Youth Groups.* Walnut Creek, CA: AltaMira Press.

Luhmann, N. (1979) *Trust and Power.* Chichester and New York: Wiley.

Macey, M. (1999) 'Religion, male violence, and the control of women', *Gender and Development,* 7(1): 48–55.

Macey, M. (2002) 'Interpreting Islam: young muslim men's involvement in criminal activity in Bradford', in B. Spalek (ed.), *Islam, Crime and Criminal Justice.* Cullompton: Willan Publishing.

Miller, W.B. (1958) 'Lower class culture as a generating milieu of gang delinquency', *Journal of Social Issues,* 24(3): 33–55.

Paoli, L. (2003) *Mafia Brotherhood: Organized Crime, Italian Style.* Oxford: Oxford University Press.

Quraishi, M. (2006) *Muslims and Crime: A Comparative Study.* Aldershot: Ashgate.

Sampson, R.J. and Raudenbush, S.W. (1999) 'Systematic social observation of public spaces: a new look at disorder in urban neighborhoods', *American Journal of Sociology,* 105(3): 603–51.

Shapiro, S.P. (1987) 'Policing Trust', in C.D. Shearing and P.C. Stenning (eds), *Private Policing.* London: Sage.

Spalek, B. (2002) 'Religious diversity, British Muslims, crime and victimization', in B. Spalek (ed.), *Islam, Crime and Criminal Justice*. Cullompton: Willan Publishing.

Sutherland, E.H. (1956) *The Sutherland Papers*. Bloomington, IN: Indiana University Press.

Thompson, T. (2004) *Gangs: A Journey into the Heart of the British Underworld*. London: Hodder and Stoughton.

Varese, F. (2006) 'How mafias migrate: the case of the 'Ndrangheta in northern Italy', *Law and Society Review*, 40(2): 411–44.

Wirth, L. ([1945]/1961) 'The problem of minority groups', in T. Parsons *et al. Theories of Society*, vol. 1. Glencoe, IL: The Free Press.

Zenner, W. (1996) 'Middleman minorities', in J. Hutchinson and A.D. Smith (eds), *Ethnicity*. Oxford: Oxford University Press.

Zorbaugh, H.W. ([1929]/1983) *The Gold Coast and the Slum. A Sociological Study of Chicago's Near North Side*. Chicago: Chicago University Press.

Zubaida, S. (1995) 'Is there a Muslim society? Ernest Gellner's sociology of Islam', *Economy and Society*, 24(2): 151–88.

Chapter 16

Concluding remarks: the roles of migration and ethnicity in street gang formation, involvement and response

Dana Peterson, Inger-Lise Lien and Frank van Gemert

Much has been written about ethnicity, migration, and crime in general (e.g. Sellin 1938; more recently, Freilich *et al.* 2002; Freilich and Newman 2007; Martinez and Valenzuela 2006; Tonry 1997; Waters 1999). What has generally been missing, with notable exceptions (see some discussion, for example, in Covey 2003 and the edited volumes by Duffy and Gillig 2004; Grennan *et al.* 2000; Hagedorn 2007; Hazlehurst and Hazlehurst 1998; Marshall 1997) in this body of knowledge is the interrelationships of ethnicity, migration, and street gang formation and involvement. Largely, this is due to lack of research on street gangs outside particular country contexts (most prominently, the USA). Acknowledgement of and attention to street gangs are growing in countries throughout the world. This text has brought together recent research conducted by members of the Eurogang Network, representing 11 countries. Various methods and samples were employed, but similar stories were told, as described in the sections below.

When we called to our Eurogang colleagues for chapters, we articulated a set of questions that would serve as a framework for the book and invited authors to submit work that addressed one or more of those questions. In this concluding chapter, we revisit those questions and the resultant chapters to draw some conclusions about what has been learned from the diverse countries, methods, and perspectives represented. We begin by returning to some sensitive issues (definitions and stigma) and then move to the framing questions, discussing them in a larger context of theoretical and empirical knowledge and implications for further research, policy, and practice.

Definitional issues

All authors in this text describe the groups under study in relation to the Eurogang definition.[1] As Klein noted in the Foreword, the intention of this common definition was to facilitate cross-national, comparative research on youth street gangs. Some may take issue with the 'narrowness' or even the 'Americanisation' of this definition, but we point out that incorporating such a definition in certain research does not preclude the study of other groups (even within the same study), nor does it presume that there are not many other varieties of 'gangs' (there are many). It simply allows valid comparisons to be made across contexts. With this in mind, there are, nonetheless, variations in the groups described in this volume. That is, groups in some studies perhaps cannot yet be defined as 'street gangs' by the Eurogang definition. While all groups appear to be durable, street-oriented, and involved in criminal activity either as individuals or groups, the definitional element of 'involvement in crime *as part of their group identity*' may be lacking in some contexts. In Barcelona, Feixa and his colleagues have suggested that youth groups are 'gangs in process', lacking this particular element, either at this time in Barcelona or at this point in their research. Similarly, in France (Debarbieux and Blaya), it is not clear that the groups are fully gangs or if they are more akin to Feixa et al.'s 'gangs in process' as a result of ethnic segregation processes in schools. On the other end of this continuum that begins with 'gangs in process', we have groups that may have transformed to resemble organised crime groups, such as the Pakistani gangs in Oslo described by Lien. Processes of the transformation from 'difference' to 'deviance' (see White's chapter, which presents an idea similar to that of Thrasher (1927) and others) may apply to transformation of groups along this continuum. Examining groups that fall under the Eurogang definition but that still represent a range of groups, either of different types or of different points along an evolutionary continuum, can provide insight into how and why groups may transform.

This underscores one of the challenges in conducting cross-national comparative research on street gangs. Despite the Eurogang Network members' agreement to use the common definition and despite the editors' efforts to ensure that all contributing scholars were employing the definition, we cannot state with certainty that all of the groups described in these chapters are truly comparable to each other. To be fair, some of the research presented in this book began prior to consensus on the Eurogang definition. Thus, the definition was applied post hoc. This does not mean that there is not value in making comparisons across the chapters and the cities or countries they represent. On the contrary, doing so reveals some interesting and valuable patterns and differences, described in later sections.

Stigmatisation or labelling

We, along with authors in this book, have already noted resistance among scholars in many European and non-European countries to focusing upon problems of gang formation, particularly in ethnic minority and immigrant communities. This is due to a (not unfounded) concern that such attention, coupled with media and government focus, would lead to stigmatisation and moral panic. This hesitancy to use the gang label has also been common in US cities (e.g. Huff 1990), and it is demonstrated in these chapters as a valid concern in other countries as well. We are in agreement, however, with anthropologist Unni Wikan (2002), who has criticised the tendency of researchers or governments to conceal knowledge that is seen as dangerous because it may lead to stigmatisation. She writes (2002: 44): 'But how do you discuss the fate of people about whom next to nothing is known and about whom you are not supposed to know much lest the facts (as it was presumed) prejudice a population susceptible to discrimination and racism?' Explicit, yet sensitive, discussion of issues regarding gangs, race or ethnicity, and immigration can illuminate stigma, prejudice, discrimination, and other negative experiences that contribute to marginalisation. As the French contributions to the book illustrate, it is only through ethnographic and other field work that marginalisation of ethnic minority youth is revealed, as, in France, ethnicity may not legally be recorded in official or quantitative form.

Obviously, we do not wish to promote the stereotype of linking migration and ethnicity with crime and gang involvement. Rather, we wish to add to the dialogues that are occurring across the world about how we as societies and individuals act and react to those perceived as 'others', and how migrants and ethnic minorities act and react in their social, political, and geographic environments. In particular, in the post-9/11 epoch, we do not wish to add to stigmatisation of Muslims, especially since several chapters in this book are focused upon Muslim youth (e.g. Moroccan boys in The Netherlands, Pakistani boys in Norway, Muslim youth in Sweden and Australia). Migration into Europe has to a large extent come from Muslim countries, putting children of these immigrants at risk, and we believe there are factors other than religion that are crucial in the processes of gang formation. Their practical situation may not be all that different from that of, say, early Irish Catholic settlers in the USA. A key difference, however, is acts of extremist terrorism that have tainted the view of Muslims in the eyes of many who cannot separate the beliefs and acts of a few from the larger population. Chapters in this text help us to better understand religious and cultural differences that can serve to further marginalise populations already disadvantaged due to minority or migrant status.

Consistent with the editors of the first Eurogang volume (Klein *et al.* 2001), we believe there is a need to provide a balanced consideration and treatment of the relationships between migration, ethnicity, and gangs, to offset targeting of specific groups by the news media, law enforcement, and public perception. It is important to keep in mind that it is not always immigrants and ethnic minorities who are gang-involved, as several chapters in this book clearly indicate. Gangs are representative of their communities, despite perceptions. The Lonsdale groups that van Gemert and Stuifbergen describe, while perhaps not always gangs, are 'native'. Aldridge *et al.* describe their difficulty in attempting to conduct broad-based research in one city where officials continually pointed them toward ethnic minority groups of young people. In fact, these authors found numerous white gangs. And Feixa *et al.* note that the term 'banda' is now used to refer only to groups of Latin American youngsters, despite the documented presence of 'native' youth gangs. This is reminiscent of early Eurogang meetings in which scholars from various countries described their local gang situations in terms of ethnicity or migration. We were to discover only later that, before the arrival of these groups and subsequent gang formation, there were groups of native youths posing difficulty for their community (see a parallel discussion by Maxson (1998) of onset of gangs in US locales). The problem was labelled a 'gang problem,' however, only after such groups were recognised among minority populations. This is a common theme, illustrated in early US writings on gangs.

With these issues regarding definition and stigma in mind, we turn now to the book's framing questions.

In what ways does migration contribute to gang formation?

One of the first questions phrased was how migration contributes to gang formation. As described briefly in the Introduction, there are multiple ways in which migration is related to gang formation and joining, and these are demonstrated in the chapters. Most commonly in the chapters, we see migration as newcomers moving in. This is due either to pull factors such as employment opportunities or other benefits, or to push factors such as war, oppression or a combination of both. Of importance is that youths are rarely decision-makers in this process and that families do not always migrate together. Another possible meaning is migration as individual gang members moving or as gangs moving. This variety is least common in the chapters, and is not specifically covered, though alluded to by Feixa and his colleagues. Here, it is as yet unclear whether gangs in Barcelona have ties to gangs outside that city or whether local youths have adopted the names of some traditional gangs. Finally, there is migration as transfer of culture in a global media age, a common theme in many of the chapters.

In terms of *migration as people moving in*, we cannot single out any particular flow and argue that there are higher risks of gang formation when migration has taken place from some countries rather than others. We do see that several theoretical perspectives (social disorganisation, strain, multiple marginality, and cultural theories) are thematic in the chapters. Neighbourhoods that migrants inhabit upon arriving in their new countries are often characterised by poverty, high rates of mobility, unfamiliarity between residents, and lack of informal social control (e.g. Feixa *et al.*, Fiori-Khayat, Kerner *et al.*, van Gemert and Decker, Vigil). As other research has shown as well, such conditions can foster the inability of parents to exercise effective management in their new, unfamiliar communities, and this may also be a part of the explanation (e.g. Lien, Feixa *et al.*, Vigil). Furthermore, limited economic opportunity structures, particularly for unskilled employment, may disproportionately affect immigrants (e.g. Vigil, White, Wortley and Tanner).

Waters' (1999) 'migration hypothesis' (status frustration among a large group of second-generation youths, in addition to assimilation pressure) is applicable to many situations described in our text. Such incidents as riots in France and group violence in Australia serve as examples akin to Mexican-American youths' experiences of the effects that multiple marginality can have when youth are alienated from social and economic, as well as cultural, spheres. Several chapters highlight the role and experiences of second-generation immigrants (particularly, Vigil, Feixa et al., Kerner *et al.*). Such youths have feelings of disconnect with both 'old country/culture' and 'new country/culture.'

Although some chapters describe interethnic conflict, an alternative explanation is asserted by Putnam (2007: 150–1). His research indicates that 'diversity does not produce "bad relations" or ethnically defined group hostility … rather, inhabitants of diverse communities tend to withdraw from collective life, to distrust their neighbors regardless of the color of their skin.' In situations such as this, cultural traditions may come into play, and these appear prominent for Latin American youth in Spain (Feixa *et al.*), for Muslim communities in Sweden (Björk), and among Pakistanis in Norway (the honour code or culture and kin networks described by Lien).

Migrant youths are more visible as well, as they tend to spend time in public space. This was described in Chapter 1 as contributing to their stigmatisation. To some extent, this is due to overcrowding in their homes. Feixa *et al.*, van Gemert and Stuifbergen, and Lien all write that migrant youths' homes in their new countries are much smaller and less hospitable than were their homes in the old country. But, there is a cultural element at work here as well: home is the domain of women, and young males thus venture into the streets to claim public space as their domain.

Migration is also related to gang formation in the *reaction of 'natives' to 'newcomers'*, at individual, group, or higher aggregate levels. The chapters by Shashkin and by van Gemert and Stuifbergen describe local, 'native' youths who band together against incoming ethnic groups. According to van Gemert and Stuifbergen, Lonsdale youth seem to describe their grouping as a result of fear and competition over typically adolescent resources such as neighbourhood space and girls. The growth of Russian skinhead gangs (see Shashkin) was in large part a racist reaction to immigrants in a time of economic and educational crisis and violence by the state. Most of these groups do not seem to have 'achieved' a high level of ideological commitment. While some groups in Russia have ties to adult white power groups, most seem to be comprised of discontented youths expressing their anger against newcomers. It should also be noted that White skinhead groups seem more common in the European setting than in the USA, although more systematic research on this is needed. Also in this category, we can consider more systemic responses to newcomers, such as the actions by schools in France (see Debarbieux and Blaya) that tend to further marginalise ethnic migrants (or even ethnic minority youth born in France), as well as the social construction of gangs by the media, as in the contributions by White and by Feixa and his colleagues.

In addition to these 'reactions to newcomers' by local youth, other residents, and societal institutions, there is tension between ethnic minority groups as well, especially in terms of who constitute the 'newcomers' (read examples of this in Asbury's 1927 discussion of groups in New York City's Five Points). Fiori-Khayat, for example, documents ethnic conflict between migrants from North Africa and from Sub-Saharan Africa, and White describes conflicts between various ethnic groups. This mirrors, among others, the current situation in Los Angeles' Hollenbeck area between African-American residents and more recently arrived Hispanic residents or even between earlier-arriving and later-arriving Chinese immigrants in San Francisco (Toy 1997).

In terms of *migration as cultural transmission*, films such as *Colors*; *Blood In, Blood Out*; *American Me*; *Boyz in the Hood*; and *Menace II Society* have done much to transport gang culture, not only within the USA (e.g. the description of girls in Jody Miller's 2001 book about the influence of *Colors* and *Panther*), but also to other countries. Frank van Gemert (2001; 2007) has described the influence of gangsta rap music on Dutch gangs that call themselves Crips and Bloods, and the opening chapter of this book includes a newspaper article from Norway about boys who have adopted gang culture and symbols from media sources. News media have also played a key role in perpetuating both gang culture and stereotypes about gangs and gang members (particularly as regards minority and immigrant youth), as portrayed by Feixa *et al*. And the Internet now serves as a key portal for migration of gang culture. Shashkin shows that skinhead gangs in Russia appear to have originated (although they evolved later, from this origin or as products of certain transformations in Russia) as a result of the transfer of Western skinhead culture through new media openness.

In Chapter 2, van Gemert and Decker pose a number of questions: 'Are new immigrant gangs simply a result of migrant families moving into neighbourhoods where gangs would exist anyway?' (suggesting neighbourhood conditions that produce gangs, as per Shaw and McKay, for example); 'To what extent does migration bring together ethnic groups and create competition that produces gangs?' (suggesting both culture conflict and competition for resources); and 'Does migration lead to a breakdown of traditional social structures that allows gangs to become alternative forms of social order?' (suggesting lack of social control, loss of culture, and marginality). All three relationships (among others) are demonstrated in the chapters, and there are interactions between them that further delineate differences in gang formation among groups. One conclusion drawn from the material presented in this book, then, is that migration can lead to an accumulation of risk factors that can particularly target second-generation immigrants living in neighbourhoods characterised by social disorganisation, as Thrasher once argued. But, this is not the only relationship of migration to gangs, and we must also account for the actions of 'natives' and the influence of the increasingly global media that transports youth and gang culture.

How does ethnicity relate to the characteristics and behaviour of gangs? Is ethnicity relevant to understanding gangs?

Just as migration situations differed, the backgrounds of groups in this book have been identified in different ways: by their country of origin (nativity), by their ethnic group tie (ethnicity), by their religious tie, or by their race. On this last method, North Americans tend to describe individuals or groups by their race, rather than ethnicity, making comparisons with other countries (and within North American countries) somewhat difficult, as it lumps together people of sometimes quite different backgrounds.[2] No matter how 'minority group' is defined, however, it seems experiences are often comparable. Current research by Winfree and his colleagues (2007) comparing five countries finds that 'nativity' is not useful in distinguishing gang members and that there are more similarities than differences between youths from the five countries. Studies in this volume that compare groups of diverse backgrounds provide additional support. Esbensen et al. show that gang membership prevalence is quite similar among Hispanic (9 per cent), African-American (8 per cent), and White (7 per cent) youths. This contrasts, though, with Wortley and Tanner's (2006) Canadian research, in which a higher prevalence rate was found among Blacks (13 per cent) and Hispanics (12 per cent) than among Whites and Asians (7 per cent).[3] Importantly, of gang members in that study (and in this volume's study), about 40 per cent were White and 70 per cent were Canadian-born. Furthermore, more minority than White respondents were Canadian-born. Clearly, gang membership is not the sole purview of racial, ethnic, or immigrant minorities.

There is some evidence that ethnicity is related to certain gang characteristics and behaviour. According to Esbensen and his colleagues, most youths reported their gangs to be mixed-sex and relatively racially or ethnically homogeneous, but contrast this with

Wortley and Tanner's findings that 60 per cent of gang members reported their gangs to be mixed race or ethnicity. In both studies, White youths were more likely to be in integrated gangs. Territoriality was more common among minority than White gangs in the USA (Esbensen *et al.*), but appeared to be common to nearly all (93 per cent) in Canada (Wortley and Tanner). Van Gemert and Decker indicate that this differs (thus far) from the European situation, where territoriality does not appear to be common.

Two other ethnic or racial differences are notable. First, of those whose groups were classified as gangs by Esbensen et al. according to the Eurogang definitional elements, 67 per cent of African-American youths considered their groups as gangs, compared to 43 per cent of Hispanic youths, and only 15 per cent of White youths. These differences, in addition to the definitional issues that are raised, are worthy of further study. It may be that White youths agree with the public perception of gangs as the purview of minorities and, thus, distance themselves and their groups by refusing to label their groups 'gangs.' Second, in terms of gang behaviour, Hispanic youth gangs in Esbensen *et al.*'s study had the highest prevalence of violent and gang-like offending, while White youth gangs had the lowest. Cultural aspects may help us to understand differences in gangs' use of violence. White's research in Australia, for example, reveals differences between ethnic groups' gangs on the basis of certain cultural aspects that influence attitudes to violence.

The chapters also show that ethnicity is relevant for understanding gangs. Youths of all backgrounds appear to join gangs for similar reasons (Wortley and Tanner; see Freng and Winfree (2004) for further evidence). A key difference, however, is that ethnic minority, but not White, youths voiced racism, discrimination, and stigmatisation (real or perceived) as motivating factors. An important finding in previous research by Wortley and Tanner (2006) is that perceptions of racism fully mediated the effect of race or ethnicity on gang membership. Other chapter authors note that such feelings and experiences might not specifically differentiate gangs, as they are related to non-gang group formation as well. But they are tied to some gang activities, particularly violence. In France, gang youths use ethnic discrimination as justification for some criminal activities (Fiori-Khayat), and in Australia, violence by gang youth is a reaction to stereotyping, exclusion, and everyday racism as well as to physical aggression against them as ethnic minorities (White).

A few chapters suggest that we need to go beyond ethnicity in understanding gangs and gang behaviour. They point out that gangs often constitute themselves on the basis of fictive kinship, as 'gang brothers', sometimes using ethnic background to communicate difference vis-à-vis others. Ethnicity can be transcended, manipulated and re-created in diverse neighbourhoods. Often, it seems that loyalty is based on belonging and identification with neighbourhood, or the street, rather than on the country of origin. While ethnicity may be an important 'first filter', for gang members in White's research, for example, class and neighbourhood are important distinguishers and criteria for membership. That is, it is not ethnicity alone that must be considered.

How are migration and ethnicity related to gang prevention and intervention efforts?

Our chapters provide a number of insights for the relationships between migration, ethnicity, and responses to gangs. Schools play a role in beginning and perpetuating the processes of 'difference to deviance'. Ethnically based 'ability groupings' or 'options' in some French schools help to create conditions, above and beyond socio-economic factors, under which youths form groups and gangs (Debarbieux and Blaya). Internal segregation (which is seen as necessary, in order to retain middle- and upper-class students) and inconsistent punishment increase group cohesion and loyalty, and opposition to school administration, teachers, and other students. In Australia, Lebanese and Samoan youth feel that teachers like and treat Asian students better than them, and this not only further alienates those youths, but also creates additional tension between the ethnic groups (see White's chapter). Such influences from prominent social institutions can impede the ability of other social institutions (e.g., law enforcement) to respond effectively to gang behaviour, if perceived legitimacy and trust are undermined. In part due to lack of trust, minority and migrant families and communities often take it upon themselves to deal with their own problems. Families, for example, often send troublesome children back to their home countries to live with relatives and get away from 'bad' influences in the new country. As Lien and others have described, however, this can exacerbate the problems, not only for those youths (who must adjust again) but also for the home country (which must deal with troublemakers) and for the new country (when troublemakers return). Mateu-Gelabert's (2002) research in New York City details the same occurrence among Dominican families.

Communities as well can be 'externalised' from the law. As Björk's chapter describes, some residents of common background live by a code of solidarity and silence derived from cultural ideas of self-reliance, kinship, and honour, allowing gangs to operate with little fear of being reported to law enforcement. In such communities, social cohesion, rather than lack of social control, is the factor that facilitates gang activity. This is an important contrast that needs to be remembered. Research has shown that close familial ties are often a protective factor against gang membership; among groups in which kinship relations are culturally valued, however, this can serve to further gang cohesion and inhibit gang intervention and suppression efforts. Traditions of honour, sovereignty, and kin and gender relations create distance between citizens and societal agents, making it difficult for law enforcement officers to do their jobs effectively. Björk has suggested that reassurance policing approaches may work better, by bridging the cultural gap between the state and citizens and creating mutual trust and coexistence rather than coerced compliance and assimilation. This approach contrasts with the Norwegian police response, which capitalises on culturally based traditions to hit gangs hard not only financially but culturally. In Norway, Operation Nemesis targeted the financial operations of Pakistani gangs, but appeared to be effective through an unforeseen and indirect cultural impact: damaging the honour of the individuals and group through shaming associated women (mothers, wives of gang members). This latter approach might result in creating greater distance if citizens (as well as gang members) find law enforcement to be insensitive to important cultural values such as honour. Furthermore, such an approach would be 'effective' only with ethnic groups that hold such values and for gangs that engage in profit-making activity. Additional research can shed light on whether tactics such as Operation Nemesis are accepted or rejected by the immigrant groups whose members are targeted.

Conclusion: into the global future

In this closing section, we wish to highlight similarities in the relationships of migration, ethnicity, and gangs as well as potential differences that deserve more research and practical attention. These latter include further attention to and exploration of differences within groups and differences between groups in similar migrant situations; the roles of cultural and religious traditions; the actions and reactions of 'natives', especially as they relate to the formation of racist gangs;

the roles of the media and global youth cultures; and the actions of countries as they affect other countries.

The three traditions summarised by Bankston (1998) appear to apply in the contexts described in this book. Opportunity structures (economic and social), cultural traditions (ethnic culture, youth culture), and social disorganisation (weakened social institutions, generation gaps) all play a part in understanding relationships between migration, ethnicity, and gangs across groups and contexts. These ideas are not new to gang research, having been described by such authors as Asbury (1927) and Thrasher (1927), among others. This does not mean these chapters are not important, however. One key point to be made is that these patterns, common in the USA, are now emerging elsewhere, as migration and ethnic diversity increase and as street gangs are recognised and acknowledged.[4] Given the long history of failure in the USA to address gang problems adequately in most communities, other countries are perhaps better poised to have more success if lessons learned are applied swiftly as such issues emerge. Although groups may differ in their origins, reasons for migrating, and current country contexts, there is similarity of experience, feelings, and frustrations with common results. But, given the differences in migration situations and ethnic groupings, as well as the rise in the global media and diffusion of youth and gang cultures, potential differences should be explored in future gang research.

Despite this book's replication of knowledge, and building of new knowledge, the age-old criminological question still challenges us: if all migrants and ethnic minorities commonly confront such experiences as marginalisation, why are not all or more of them gang members? These chapters collectively address and help explain differences *between* groups, but they fail to provide much insight into differences *within* specific groups, as Wortley and Tanner point out. In his chapter, Vigil notes that only 10–20 per cent of young Mexican-Americans become gang-involved, and Esbensen *et al.* report rates of 7–9 per cent among three race or ethnic groups. Similarly, only about 5 per cent of Latin American immigrants are documented as gang members by law enforcement in Barcelona (Feixa *et al.*). Extant research does offer some suggestions, and these should be further explored in future research. Feixa and his colleagues provide some insight in their descriptions of situational differences of Latin American migrant youth. While they do not go so far as to analyse how these may produce differences in gang involvement, such factors as reasons for and processes of migration, age at migration, living situation, and

266

legal status are important for inclusion in additional research. Just as there are interactions that produce differences between groups, there are interactions that produce within-group differences. Although such meso- and microlevel interactional processes are not specifically described by the authors in this book, this is a fruitful avenue for future research. Guerra and Smith's (2005) edited text follows these lines by describing common risk factors among ethnic groups and then exploring contextual factors that increase or decrease risk of violence engagement across and within groups. Such an exploration would be useful in determining the particular factors that interact to produce gang membership among certain youths and not others in a population.

Do the chapters in this book indicate that ethnic minority or immigrant youth are *more likely* to form or join gangs than are other youths? We cannot say that definitively. In most cases, the samples and data preclude comparisons across groups (that is, they are not representative, but see Esbensen *et al.*, even though a purposive sample). To answer that question, there is need to compare across groups, and not just across groups of immigrants or ethnic minorities. Furthermore, there is need to assess why some groups (or individuals) are *not* susceptible to gang formation and joining (e.g. van Gemert and Decker note the differences between Moroccan and Turkish immigrants in The Netherlands). What cultural, economic, or other situational aspects produce lower rates? Answering this question again requires more representative samples.

What else do these chapters indicate in terms of directions for research and practice? For the Eurogang Programme and other research, we have several suggestions in addition to those posed throughout this chapter. With few exceptions (Esbensen and Weerman 2005; Huizinga and Schumann 2001; Weerman and Esbensen 2005; Winfree *et al.* 2007), true cross-national comparative research has not yet been undertaken by Eurogang Network members. Although we are able, post hoc, to compare across countries described in the current chapters and draw some conclusions, a more scientifically sound and valuable approach would be to engage in collaborative implementation of Eurogang definitions and instruments at the outset. Klein, in his Foreword, describes this as a next key step for the Eurogang Programme, and it is one that is in the works. As van Gemert and Stuifbergen (this volume) note, 'simply adopting an existing American frame will not work.' We must incorporate the century of learning from USA research while also developing new perspectives and explanations, if necessary, to describe and explain street gangs outside the USA context. This requires comparative research, to determine similarities and differences in form and function, to come to new models and appropriate approaches.

For policymakers, youth workers, and the like, these chapters also offer some suggestions. As has been written previously, it is important not to label and thus stigmatise migrant groups, even those among whom gangs have formed, as doing so may contribute to their further marginalisation. Instead, the conditions that produce marginalisation and gangs should be ameliorated. Different national assimilation or acculturation strategies (coupled with different social programmes and interacting with public views of immigrants and ethnic minorities) appear to produce different results (Vigil). Integration policies in Spain (Feixa *et al.*) and the USA (Vigil), for example, are found to be inadequate, either in plan or in implementation. Thus, assimilation per se may not be the answer, but assistance in adjustment would be useful. Educational institutions are key players that can help or hinder (Debarbieux and Blaya, Vigil, White), and these are being overwhelmed by different cultures and languages. It is important for each receiving community to address the question posed by Vigil: 'What barriers and obstacles exist, especially culture conflict ones, that prevent access, exposure, and identification with the dominant culture?' Providing support to educational institutions is but one means of removing barriers. In Barcelona, providing official recognition to gangs as legitimate cultural groups may prove to be another. Research by Feixa and his colleagues will reveal whether their efforts will be more successful than were similar efforts in the USA in the 1950s and 1960s.

It is also crucial to determine how to deal with cultural or religious traditions that isolate groups from the established legal system. Here, we can question, for example, whether it is easier for ethnic groups arriving from feudal, tribal areas to establish gang-like structures in modern cities? Is it easier to establish underground structures if one is accustomed to life in settings where the state is weak or almost non-existent? And, what is the role of religion? In what ways, for example, are Muslim boys in gangs vulnerable to recruitment for terrorist acts? This is a growing fear in Europe, whether founded or unfounded. There are a few boys in the Pakistani gang in Norway who have been radicalised and accused of taking part in a plan of violence against the American Embassy. There is a potential risk here. But, it is also the case that, most often, the boys who have been recruited to take part in terrorist acts have been law-abiding, educated, employed, and not gang members (e.g. the London bombings). Similar fears have also been voiced in the USA; for example, in the case of Chicago former gang member Jose Padilla, accused of collaborating with al-Qaeda. The news media have speculated as to whether terrorist groups will enlist street gangs in domestic terrorism. We do not wish to perpetuate this fear, but only raise these issues as potential lines of enquiry that will provide an empirically sound base of evidence to support or refute these concerns.

The news media and the Internet have grown in scope and influence, and their portrayal of gangs shapes public opinion and promotes stereotypes as well as exports gang culture. Even as we write this chapter, a new series has begun on the History Channel; *Gangland* is a look at American street gangs and organised crime, but despite its documentary-like approach, it has sensationalised aspects. Shashkin's work underscores the interaction of media with specific structural characteristics. That is, it was the interaction of Western ideas of skinhead culture and the social, economic, and political situation of young people in Russia, coupled with increased migration, that led to skinhead gang formation. In this regard, we see that not all young people exposed to gangsta images and cultures will adopt those cultures. In addition to structural factors, individual characteristics also play a role in who is susceptible. It is unrealistic to suggest that measures be taken to curtail these industries. Therefore, we should focus our efforts instead on ensuring that youth (all youth) have the resources, resiliency, voice and contributing role in society that can help them make good and informed choices about their behaviours and to navigate the intersections of global youth culture, current country dominant culture, and (where applicable) 'old country' culture. Determining how best to do this is the challenge of policymakers, practitioners, and researchers. It requires acknowledging the situation, taking considered steps to address it, and effectively evaluating those steps, preferably in a comparative manner that allows communities to learn from one another and to work with one another as members of a larger world community whose actions affect one another. But one example is the action of the US government in deporting Salvadoran youths. Borrow and Walker (2004) are among the authors who describe a rise in gangs and gang activity (in this case, in Honduras) as a result of US policies and actions. Further research to determine to just what extent gangs 'migrate' and the source or processes of such migration are also needed. It is increasingly common to hear of gangs 'franchising', but this claim needs empirical examination.

In closing this chapter and book, we wish to reiterate the following: gangs are found in non-immigrant neighbourhoods, among non-ethnic minorities, and in non-urban areas. These 'native' gangs should not be overlooked, and they should be kept in mind so as not unfairly to locate the 'gang problem' solely among migrant or ethnic minority groups. It may indeed be the case that gang formation and rates of gang membership are higher among minority groups, but this is a reason for focused assistance, not labelling and suppression.

Notes

1 A street gang is defined by the Eurogang Network as 'any durable, street-oriented youth group whose involvement in illegal activity is part of their group identity'.
2 For example, 'Hispanic/Latino' can include persons of Puerto Rican, Mexican, El Salvadoran or many other backgrounds, and 'African-American' or 'Black' can include persons from many different African nations, as well as, for example, Jamaica.
3 It is worth noting that in a different study using a different sample, Esbensen and Winfree (1998) found prevalence rates nearly identical to that of Wortley and Tanner (2006): 12 per cent of African-Americans, 14 per cent of Hispanics, 6 per cent of Whites, and 8 per cent of Asians.
4 The fact that these are occurring simultaneously deserves two related comments: first, it is difficult to disentangle the relationships because, second, perhaps the gang problems have been acknowledged *as* 'others' arrive.

References

Asbury, H. (1927) *Gangs of New York: An Informal History of the Underworld.* New York: Alfred A. Knopf.

Bankston, C.L., III (1998) 'Youth gangs and the new second generation: a review essay', *Aggression and Violent Behavior*, 3(1), 35–45.

Borrow, A. and Walker, J. (2004) 'Honduras', in M.P. Duffy and S.E. Gillig (eds), *Teen Gangs: A Global View.* Westport, CT: Greenwood Publishing Group, pp. 59–75.

Covey, H.C. (2003) *Street Gangs Throughout the World.* Springfield, IL: Charles C. Thomas.

Decker, S.H. and Weerman, F.M. (eds) *European Street Gangs and Troublesome Youth Groups.* Walnut Creek, CA: AltaMira Press.

Duffy, M.P. and Gillig, S.E. (eds) (2004) *Teen Gangs: A Global View.* Westport, CT: Greenwood Publishing Group.

Esbensen, F.-A. and Weerman, F.M. (2005) 'Youth gangs and troublesome youth groups in the United States and The Netherlands: a cross-national comparison', *European Journal of Criminology*, 2, 5–37.

Esbensen, F.-A. and Winfree, L.T., Jr. (1998) 'Race and gender differences between gang and nongang youths: results from a multi-site study', *Justice Quarterly*, 15, 505–25.

Freilich, J.D., Newman, G., Shoham, S.G. and Addad, M. (eds) (2002) *Migration, Culture Conflict, and Crime*. Burlington, VT: Ashgate.

Freilich, J.D. and Newman, G.R. (eds) (2007) *Crime and Immigration*. Burlington, VT: Ashgate.

Freng, A. and Winfree, L.T., Jr. (2004) 'Exploring race and ethnic differences in a sample of middle school gang members', in F.-A. Esbensen, L. Gaines and S.G. Tibbetts (eds), *American Youth Gangs at the Millennium*. Prospect Heights, IL: Waveland Press, pp. 142–62.

Grennan, S., Britz, M.T., Rush, J. and Barker, T. (eds) (2000) *Gangs: An International Approach*. Upper Saddle River, NJ: Prentice-Hall.

Guerra, N.G. and Smith, E.P. (eds) (2005) *Preventing Youth Violence in a Multicultural Society*. Washington, DC: American Psychological Association.

Hagedorn, J.M. (ed) (2007) *Gangs in the Global City: Alternatives to Traditional Criminology*. Chicago: University of Illinois Press.

Hazlehurst, K.M. and Hazlehurst, C. (eds) (1998) *Gangs and Youth Subcultures: International Explorations*. New Brunswick, NJ: Transaction.

Huff, C.R. (1990) 'Denial, overreaction, and misidentification: a postscript on public policy', in C. Ronald Huff (ed.), *Gangs in America*. Thousand Oaks, CA: Sage, pp. 310–17.

Huizinga, D. and Schumann, K.F. (2001) 'Gang membership in Bremen and Denver: comparative longitudinal data', in M.W. Klein, H.-J. Kerner, C.L. Maxson, and E.G.M. Weitekamp (eds), *The Eurogang Paradox: Street Gangs and Youth Groups in the U.S. and Europe*. Amsterdam: Kluwer Press, 231–46.

Klein, M.W., Kerner, H.-J., Maxson, C.L., and Weitekamp, E.G.M. (eds) (2001) *The Eurogang Paradox: Street Gangs and Youth Groups in the U.S. and Europe*. Amsterdam: Kluwer.

Marshall, I.H. (ed) (1997) *Minorities, Migrants, and Crime: Diversity and Similarity Across Europe and the United States*. Thousand Oaks, CA: Sage.

Martinez, R., Jr. and Valenzuela, A., Jr. (eds) (2006) *Immigration and Crime: Race, Ethnicity, and Violence*. New York: New York University Press.

Mateu-Gelabert, P. (2002) *Dreams, Gangs, and Guns: The Interplay Between Adolescent Violence and Immigration in a New York City Neighborhood*. New York: Vera Institute of Justice.

Maxson, C.L. (1998) 'Gang members on the move', *Juvenile Justice Bulletin*, October, Washington, DC: US Department of Justice, Office of Justice Programs, Office of Juvenile Justice and Delinquency Prevention.

Putnam, R.D. (2007) 'E pluribus unum: diversity and community in the twenty-first century. The Johan Skytte Prize Lecture', *Scandinavian Political Studies*, 30(2), 137–74.

Sellin, T. (1938) *Culture Conflict and Crime*. New York: Social Science Research Council.

Tonry, M.H. (ed) (1997) *Ethnicity, Crime, and Immigration: Comparative and Cross-national Perspectives*. Chicago: University of Chicago Press.

Toy, C. (1997) 'A short history of Asian gangs in San Francisco', in G. Larry Mays (ed), *Gangs and Gang Behavior*. Chicago: Nelson-Hall, pp. 228–45.

van Gemert, F. (2001) 'Crips in orange: gangs and groups in The Netherlands', in M.W. Klein, H.-J. Kerner, C.L. Maxson and E.G.M. Weitekamp (eds), *The Eurogang Paradox: Street Gangs and Youth Groups in the U.S. and Europe*. Amsterdam: Kluwer, pp. 145–52.

van Gemert, F. (2007) 'Bloods in Amsterdam', Paper presented at the European Society of Criminology annual meeting, September (Bologna, Italy).

Vigil, D. (1988) *Barrio Gangs*. Austin, TX: University of Texas Press.

Waters, T. (1999) *Crime and Immigrant Youth*. Thousand Oaks, CA: Sage.

Weerman, F.M. and Esbensen, F.-A. (2005) 'A cross-national comparison of youth gangs: the United States and The Netherlands', in S.H. Decker and F.M. Weerman (eds), *European Street Gangs and Troublesome Youth Groups*. Walnut Creek, CA: AltaMira Press, pp. 219–55.

Wikan, U. (2002) *Generous Betrayal: Politics of Culture in the New Europe*. Chicago, IL: University of Chicago Press.

Winfree, L.T., Jr., Maljevic, A., Weitekamp, E.G.M., Kerner, H.-J., Reich, K., Bott, K., Weerman, F., Medina-Ariza, J.J. and Aldridge, J. (2007) 'The confluence of race and youth gangs: a comparative look at youth in five nations', Paper presented at the European Society of Criminology annual meeting, September (Bologna, Italy).

Wortley, S. and Tanner, J. (2006) 'Immigration, social disadvantage and urban youth gangs: results of a Toronto-area study', *Canadian Journal of Urban Research*, 15(2), 1–20.

Index

Added to a page number 'f' denotes a figure and 't' denotes a table.